The Indigenous People of the Caribbean

The Ripley P. Bullen Series

The Indigenous People of the Caribbean

Edited by

Samuel M. Wilson

Organized by the Virgin Islands Humanities Council

University Press of Florida

Gainesville Tallahassee Tampa Boca Raton

Pensacola Orlando Miami Jacksonville

Copyright 1997 by the Board of Regents of the State of Florida
Printed in the United States of America on acid-free paper
All rights reserved

03 02 01 00 99 98 C 6 5 4 3 2

03 02 01 00 99 98 P 6 5 4 3 2 1

First paperback printing, 1999

Library of Congress Cataloging-in-Publication Data
The indigenous people of the Caribbean / edited by Samuel M.
Wilson.
    p. cm.—(The Ripley P. Bullen series)
"Organized by the Virgin Islands Humanities Council."
Includes bibliographical references and index.
ISBN 0-8130-1531-6 (cl.:alk.paper)
ISBN 0-8130-1692-4 (pbk.:alk.paper)
1. Indians of the West Indies. 2. Indians of the West Indies—
Antiquities. 3. Caribbean Area—Antiquities. 4. West Indies—
Antiquities. I. Wilson, Samuel M. II. Virgin Islands Humanities
Council. III. Series.
F1619.I53 1997
972.9'01—dc21 97-20170

The University Press of Florida is the scholarly publishing agency
for the State University System of Florida, comprised of Florida
A & M University, Florida Atlantic University, Florida Interna-
tional University, Florida State University, University of Central
Florida, University of Florida, University of North Florida,
University of South Florida, and University of West Florida.

University Press of Florida
15 Northwest 15th Street
Gainesville, FL 32611
http://nersp.nerdc.ufl.edu/~ufp

For the people of the Caribbean

Contents

Figures and Tables

Tables

Foreword

The Florida Museum of Natural History is very pleased to sponsor publication of *The Indigenous People of the Caribbean*, edited by Samuel M. Wilson. This collection of articles by a distinguished group of cultural anthropologists, archaeologists, linguists, and historians provides an excellent detailed introduction to the native societies who have lived in the Caribbean archipelago. As Wilson and his authors point out, the modern descendants of some of that region's pre-Columbian peoples still live there today. They, too, receive attention in this important volume.

Research regarding the native peoples of the Caribbean is flourishing. Many of the scholars actively involved in that research are contributors to this volume, making this a valuable resource for students and the general public.

Archaeological investigations are especially well represented here. That is because all but the last five centuries of Caribbean history predate the period of written documents. To learn about most of the past we must study the material remains left by the pre-Columbian cultures.

Ripley P. Bullen, former curator at the Florida Museum of Natural History and the person for whom this publication series is named, was a major contributor to Caribbean archaeology. As an undergraduate student assistant at the museum in 1966, I washed potsherds that Ripley and his wife, Adelaide K. Bullen, had excavated from archaeological sites in the Lesser Antilles.

Bullen, who died in 1976, began his Caribbean work in the Virgin Islands in 1959. Later he would investigate sites in Honduras and a host of locations in the Caribbean, including Grenada, Barbados, St. Vincent, the Grenadines, St. Lucia, St. Croix, Martinique, Marie Galante, Guadeloupe, St. Martin, Trinidad, Tobago, Curacao, Aruba, Guyana, Surinam, Puerto Rico, Dominican Republic, and Jamaica. Ripley infused new life into the

International Congress for the Study of Pre-Columbian Cultures of the Lesser Antilles and edited five of the conference's *Proceedings*. His contributions to that international conference were recognized when its members elected him "chairman for life."

Bullen's legacy is still strong. At the Florida Museum of Natural History my colleagues Kathleen Deagan and William Keegan and their students continue archaeological investigations in the Caribbean, examining a variety of topics. And, as noted above, this volume is evidence that many other institutions and individuals are actively engaged in Caribbean research as well.

Sam Wilson and his collaborators have summarized what we know, and they point out problems for future research. As we come to the end of one millennium and embark on the twenty-first century I hope we see the launching of similar publishing projects for other regions of the Americas. Out of scholarly syntheses comes new knowledge.

Jerald T. Milanich
General Editor, Bullen Series

Preface

People lived in the Caribbean for hundreds of generations before Europeans arrived. With great difficulty, their descendants have survived the five hundred years since Columbus landed and still live in the islands and surrounding mainland.

This book is designed to introduce readers to what is known about the indigenous people of the Caribbean. We have tried both to provide a broad overview and to examine many specific topics in some detail. The long prehistory of the Caribbean, going back nearly six thousand years, is dealt with at length. We also discuss the period of European conquest, the subsequent history, and the importance of the indigenous people in the Caribbean today.

This volume came about through the efforts of the Virgin Islands Humanities Council. As the Virgin Islands observed the passage of five hundred years since the second voyage of Columbus brought him to St. Croix, the Humanities Council focused its attention on the people who were living in the Caribbean at the time of Columbus's arrival. The council brought together an international group of scholars who were experts in various aspects of Caribbean history, culture, and environment. At an exciting series of public lectures, this group discussed and debated aspects of Caribbean society and history and attempted to fit all the separate pieces of information and evidence into as complete as possible a picture of the indigenous people of the Caribbean. We are trying to do the same thing with this volume.

The editor and authors extend profound thanks to the Virgin Islands Humanities Council and its executive director, Magda G-Smith, for making this project possible. The conference was funded by an exemplary award grant from the National Endowment for the Humanities and supported by the Conference Planning Committee, including Humanities Council members Vincent O. Cooper, Lorraine Joseph, William A. Taylor, Barbara Gilliard-Payne, and Wallace William. In shaping the conference agenda, the council received valuable suggestions from Ricardo Alegría, Miguel Rodríguez, Ignacio Olazagasti, and David R. Watters. We also express our thanks to Tad Tuleja, who helped to edit these essays into a consistent and readable style, and Harry Iceland, who translated passages from the Spanish chronicles in Ignacio Olazagasti's paper.

1

Introduction to the Study of the Indigenous People of the Caribbean

Samuel M. Wilson

The Caribbean islands were the first places in the Americas to be conquered by the Europeans, and the region's indigenous people bore the brunt of the first wave of colonial conquest. Most of the indigenous groups in the Greater Antilles did not survive this first period of conquest. Five hundred years later we have come to know about them through those descendants that did survive, through the historical documents left behind by people like Father Bartolomé de Las Casas, and through the archaeological remains of these peoples' villages and ceremonial areas.

Very soon after the conquest, European writers began to speculate on the long history of the native peoples of the Americas. Las Casas, who would later be called the "protector of the Indians," conducted what was probably the first archaeological research done by Europeans in the New World and made the following observations:

> I have seen in these mines of Cibao [on Hispaniola], one or two yards deep in the virgin earth, in the plains at the foot of some hills, burned wood and ashes as if a few days past a fire had been made there. And for the same reason we have to conclude that in other times the river came near there, and such a place they made a fire, and afterwards the river moved farther away. Soil accumulated there, as the rains brought it down from the hills, and covered the site. And because this could not happen except by the passage of many years and most ancient time, there is therefore a strong argument that the people of these islands and the mainland are very ancient.

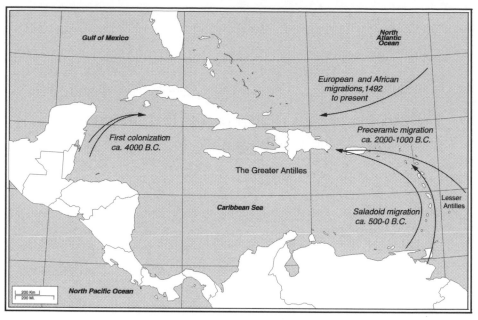

Figure 1.1. Map of the Caribbean showing major migrations.

It has turned out that Las Casas was right. Archaeologists have determined that people have been living in the Caribbean islands for nearly 6,000 years. They moved into the islands from a number of places on the surrounding mainlands over several millennia, and through the centuries, there was probably a good deal of coming and going, with new migrations and continuing interaction with mainland people even after European contact. However, the first Caribbean colonizers and their successors made a number of important changes in the way they lived: first, they made the transition from mainland to island living, which involved major adjustments in how they got food; second, in time, they adopted (or the new people brought with them) a way of life based on agriculture, growing the crops their ancestors had grown in the lowland river basins of South America; finally, in the centuries before Columbus arrived, they developed large, complex political systems.

This book is about the indigenous people of the Caribbean, from the earliest immigrants to their modern descendants. We have tried to cover this vast topic comprehensively while also giving detailed insights into aspects of Caribbean prehistory and culture that we find to be of particular interest. This is a large undertaking, since the Caribbean archipelago consists of hundreds of islands spanning over 2,000 miles (3,200 km) and the time period involved stretches from 4000 B.C. to the present (figure 1.1). We have not, of course, been able to cover every aspect of Caribbean prehistory and history. The millennia-long "Archaic" period in the Caribbean, when people made a living by fishing and collecting wild foods in the islands, is not given the attention it deserves. And although it is discussed in the chapters in part 6 of this book, the rich history of how indigenous people survived from the conquest to present is not laid out in detail.

Not surprisingly, therefore, one realization that has emerged from this project is that there is still a great deal that is unknown about the indigenous people of the Caribbean. Archaeologists, historians, linguists, and ethnographers have begun to understand the overall picture of the region's human history, and that aggregate is what is featured in this volume. But there is still a great deal for us and for future generations to discover, and this fact presents some difficulties to those who are putting together such a study. Since we do not have all the answers, we must present what we feel are the most reasonable scenarios. Yet what seems reasonable to one scholar may seem ridiculous to another. With more than twenty authors participating in this volume, it has been impossible to reach consensus on everything. We have nevertheless tried to provide good general introductions to our range of topics, stressing what is agreed upon over what is in dispute.

Overview of the Volume

This book came about through the efforts of the Virgin Islands Humanities Council. In 1993, commemorating the five-hundred-year anniversary of the arrival of Europeans in the Virgin Islands, the Humanities Council organized a symposium titled "The People Who Encountered Columbus: Tainos and Island Caribs of the Lesser Antilles." Magda G-Smith, executive director of the Virgin Islands Humanities Council, organized the conference, which was supported in part by a grant from the National Endowment for the Humanities and which focused attention not on European issues but on the indigenous people. The speakers at the conference were—and are—among the foremost specialists in their fields. The essays in this volume are adapted from their talks.

Like the Caribbean itself, the conference was diverse. The participants came from nine countries and included residents of seven islands. The international character of the conference was to be expected because any attempt to understand the indigenous people of the Caribbean involves looking at the Caribbean region as a whole. And to do this, one must take into account information from islands where the dominant languages include Spanish, French, Creole, Dutch, and English. The cultural diversity of the researchers who are interested in the indigenous peoples of the Caribbean is part of what makes the whole field so rich and interesting.

Although a little more than half of the essays in this volume discuss Caribbean prehistory and ethnohistory, the preconquest period is not considered to be more important than the later periods; several essays address themes of indigenous resistance and survival, bringing the discussion up to the present day. The essays that do deal with Caribbean prehistory focus on specific time periods or on fairly specialized aspects of particular cultures. The following overview of Caribbean prehistory is provided so that readers may put these chapters into a larger context.

PREHISTORY OF THE CARIBBEAN

The Caribbean islands were colonized about 6,000 years ago and since then have experienced several large migrations of people from the surrounding mainlands. There has also been considerable movement and interaction among peoples within the archipelago.

The earliest evidence of human colonization of the Caribbean is found in Cuba, Haiti, and the Dominican Republic, where sites have been dated to around 3500–4000 B.C. The flaked-stone tools at these early sites are similar to those from sites on the Yucatán peninsula, which suggests that the earliest migrants may have come from the west across the Yucatán Channel or via other routes from Central America. These people hunted, fished, and gathered the wild plants and animals of the sea and island interiors. As far as is known, they did not cultivate food crops.

People moving from the mainland to the Antilles had to make substantial changes in their ways of getting food. As in most island settings, these islands' plants and animals were different from those of the mainland. In particular, there were fewer large land mammals. To survive in the new environments, each group of immigrants who came into the Antilles had to adapt their economy to the island ecosystems.

By around 2000 B.C. a number of regional archaeological variants—distinguished by their different kinds of stone tools and other artifacts—had developed in Cuba and Hispaniola, a process that also occurred later in Puerto Rico. The economy of these descendants of the earliest immigrants was still based on hunting, fishing, and collecting wild resources. The elaborate ground-stone artifacts they made included decorated bowls, pendants, axes, and other objects.

Another group of nonhorticultural migrants moved into the Caribbean sometime before 2000 B.C., this time from the northeast coast of South America. They moved through the Lesser Antilles, occupying many of the islands, and into Puerto Rico; traces of their small settlements are scattered today throughout many of the Lesser Antilles. Some of the raw material they used in making their articles, such as chert or flint, are distributed widely in the Caribbean, a fact demonstrating that these islanders were competent ocean travelers. The population size of these preceramic migrants was never very large, but they may have persisted until the Lesser Antilles were colonized anew by migrants from South America.

All of the nonagricultural people lived in the Antilles for thousands of years—much longer, in fact, than the village-dwelling farmers who arrived later or the African, Asian, and European people who succeeded them. Unfortunately the attention they receive in this volume is not proportional to their long history of living in the Caribbean. For further information on the preagricultural people of the Caribbean, see Davis 1993; Lundberg 1989; Pantel 1988; Rouse 1992, Veloz Maggiolo and Ortega 1976; Veloz Maggiolo and Vega 1982.

Between 500 and 250 B.C. people who made ceramics and grew food crops moved into the Lesser Antilles and Puerto Rico. They came from the Orinoco drainage and the river systems of South America's northeast coast. This migration probably involved more than one mainland group and place of origin, but within a few centuries a relatively homogenous Caribbean culture had emerged. Their beautiful ceramics, decorated with white and red painting, and the distinctive kind of ceramic adornment known as zone-incised cross-hatching are both called Saladoid, after the Venezuelan site of Saladero.

The Saladoid people are, in part at least, the ancestors of the Taino Indians who were living in the Greater Antilles when Columbus arrived. Some of their characteristic artifacts, like the carved stone and shell objects called *zemis,* were important symbols in their religion. Very similar objects, in more and more elaborated forms, were still in use when the Europeans arrived. When they moved into the islands from South America, the Saladoid people brought dogs and the agouti with them, as well as a number of mainland domesticated plants including the very important root crop manioc (yuca, cassava). They also collected the wild foods on the islands, gradually shifting their focus from terrestrial resources like land crabs to marine species from the deep reef and open sea.

The Saladoid people settled extensively on the large and rich island of Puerto Rico, choosing sites near the coast and on the major rivers. They also crossed over to the eastern end of Hispaniola, where they lived in contact with the descendants of the first migrants from Central America, who had been living there for thousands of years. Judging from the few Saladoid sites that have been extensively excavated, Saladoid villages typically had several large houses (over ten meters or thirty-two feet diameter) built of poles and thatch, similar to those used by the indigenous people of lowland South America. The houses surrounded a central plaza, and most sites have substantial midden deposits. The history and ways of life of the Saladoid people are discussed in the essays by Haviser, Righter, Rodríguez, and Watters.

Between A.D. 500 and 1000 a series of changes took place in the Caribbean. Archaeologists in the Lesser Antilles and Puerto Rico have seen changes in settlement organization, economy, and pottery manufacture, as well as evidence of population growth. Settlements became more numerous in the Lesser Antilles, and the descendants of the Saladoid people colonized the rugged interior of Puerto Rico. They also moved beyond the small Saladoid foothold on Hispaniola, colonizing the island and moving beyond into Cuba and Jamaica. The hunting and gathering people who already lived in many of these areas were apparently incorporated into the newly emerging society, for there are some similarities in style between artifacts of the hunter-gatherers and those of the new migrants (whose ceramics are called Ostionoid). People also began colonizing the Bahamas about this time.

As the ceramics-using, horticultural people began moving into Hispaniola, Jamaica, and Cuba, their population grew rapidly. There is also evidence of the development of larger political units than had ever existed in the Caribbean before. In earlier times every village had been autonomous, but by A.D. 1000 chiefdoms had emerged—political systems in which many villages were united under the leadership of a single person or family. A more complex form of social hierarchy, marked by a distinction between commoner and elite, may also have developed about this time.

In the Greater Antilles a number of regional ceramic traditions developed after A.D. 800. Between A.D. 1000 and 1492, there is evidence of the further development of social hierarchies and political complexity. The famous stone-lined ball courts and ceremonial plazas were built, and artists developed flamboyant traditions of ceramic production, wood carving, and stonework. The Taino people and their culture are discussed in the essays by Keegan, Petersen, Olazagasti, Oliver, and Highfield.

At the time of the Spanish conquest the Taino were organized into a series of complex chiefdoms, polities encompassing as many as one hundred villages and tens of thousands of people. Villages of two to three thousand people are described by Spanish chroniclers. They grew their food using intensive agriculture and divided up the work of producing food into many individual specialties, such as fishing and cultivating cassava. In Taino society there was a clear social hierarchy, with elites, commoners, captives, and slaves, and other special categories such as religious specialists and healers. Elites or rulers from the different chiefdoms interacted with one another through trade, warfare, intermarriage, and the ball game. Ocean-going canoes carrying as many as one hundred people conveyed these rulers and their people among the islands of the Greater Antilles, northern Lesser Antilles, and Bahamas.

POSTCONQUEST HISTORY

When Europeans arrived, they found the Caribbean to be densely inhabited by diverse indigenous groups. Noticing differences between the people of the Greater and Lesser Antilles, the Europeans joined these observations with half-understood stories the Taino told them about other islanders. What emerged was a view of the Caribbean as having two kinds of people—Caribs and Tainos (Arawaks). What now seems more likely is that in 1492 the Caribbean contained many different ethnic groups, spread out through the Lesser Antilles, Greater Antilles, and Bahamas. Nearly all of these people were speakers of Arawakan languages, probably mutually unintelligible, and nearly all of them were descendants of the Saladoid immigrants. Centuries of living apart from one another had contributed to the Caribbean peoples' diversity, even though there was probably continuous trade and interaction among the islands and with the mainland. Aspects of Island Carib societies are discussed in the essays by Allaire, Petitjean Roget, Gonzalez, Wilson, and Joseph.

For more than a century, European efforts at colonization were focused on the Spanish settlements in the Greater Antilles. In the early decades of the conquest the indigenous population of the Greater Antilles was decimated by warfare, forced labor, and especially disease. The indigenous people of the Lesser Antilles were also hard hit during the period from 1492 to 1620. Their islands were raided by European slave traders, and their contact with Europeans led to the introduction of devastating diseases such as smallpox, influenza, yellow fever, and measles.

After 1620 the French, Dutch, English, and other European groups began to colonize the Lesser Antilles. At times there was relative peace with the indigenous people, but such periods did not usually last long. Between 1620 and 1660 this wave of conquest reduced indigenous control in the Lesser Antilles from the entire archipelago to parts of the islands of Dominica and St. Vincent (where, as Garnette Joseph discusses, Island Carib people still live today). Later, as Gonzalez shows, some indigenous Caribbean groups were forced to move to the Central American mainland.

SUMMARY

The authors of this volume have combined their efforts to provide an introduction to what is known about the indigenous people of the Caribbean. We know that we have barely touched upon some topics, but hope that the reader can use this study as a starting point in a search for information about Caribbean peoples.

The prehistory and history of the Caribbean islanders is a fascinating and critical part of the story of human cultures in the Americas. In the beautiful and relatively isolated Caribbean archipelago emerged complex societies like those of the Taino and Island Caribs. And while these people were related to mainland societies, they were clearly distinct—and uniquely Caribbean.

What we find worthy of celebration is that, despite the ravages of five centuries of European conquest, the indigenous people of the Caribbean have survived. The role they have played in the formation of modern Caribbean culture is immense, and the voice of their descendants is growing ever stronger in the modern Caribbean.

Part 1: Background to the Archaeology and Ethnohistory of the Caribbean

All of the essays in this volume rely to some extent on information from three sources: the archaeology of the Caribbean; the accounts made by Europeans of indigenous people and the history of their interactions; and the Caribbean islanders themselves, through written and oral tradition, and other records. The third source of information is dealt with in part 6, "Indigenous Resistance and Survival." The other two sources of information require some additional discussion in part 1.

Ricardo Alegría provides an overview of the critical European documents dealing with the early contact period in the Caribbean. The context or background of these documents—why they were written and for whom, with what biases, and so on—is essential to an understanding of them. Although there is a considerable body of historical material on the Taino, a handful of critical sources form the basis for most of our interpretations. As Alegría notes, these texts, and the archaeological evidence, embody "multiple ways of knowing"—differing perspectives concerning the indigenous people.

The archaeological evidence from the Caribbean is complex and, as discussed in the introduction to this volume, sometimes subject to differing interpretations. Louis Allaire provides a discussion of the prehistory of the islands of the Lesser Antilles. He also offers a view of the history of how archaeologists have tried to piece together and understand the past.

2

The Study of Aboriginal Peoples: Multiple Ways of Knowing

Ricardo Alegría

The Antilles, having been the first center of Spanish colonization in the New World, felt the impact of the European conquest more keenly than any other area in America. So devastating was this impact that fifty years after the encounter, the aboriginal population of the Greater Antilles had almost entirely disappeared (Alegría 1969b). For the Spanish too, although in an entirely different way, the first years of the colonization of America were full of confusion and insecurity. For almost two decades after Columbus's first voyage, the status of the newly discovered lands and their relation to the Crown was in controversy, since the policy to be followed in regard to the Indians had not been clearly defined. Even the question of whether the natives were to be treated as human beings was a matter for debate.

Columbus sold into slavery a number of the Indians he had brought back from the first expedition. With Isabella's repudiation of that practice in 1509, the Crown redefined the aborigines of the discovered territories as chattel and proclaimed them to be subject to the protection of the state. That protection came at a price, however, for as subjects the Indians were required to pay tributes to the king—not directly to the Crown but to the colonizers, whom the king had granted the privilege of collecting these tributes as a reward for their work in establishing a settlement and in extending the Christian religion. According to official policy, the Indians were to be placed in the care of the colonizers so that the latter might protect them and teach them the Christian religion. The Indians, in exchange for this supposed benefit, were expected to work for their protectors, or *encomenderos* (Sauer 1966).

The colonizers, in their eagerness to impose their religion and to obtain the greatest possible profits, were far from scrupulous in their treatment of the natives. Indeed, their cruelty hastened the disintegration of the native culture and its eventual annihilation. By 1510 the Indian population of the islands was almost totally extinct, and colonizers had to import natives from South America to work in the Antillean gold mines. At present the remains of the Antillean aborigines' culture includes only a few traditions in the folklore of their mestizo descendants; the greater part of the scholarly nomenclature for the naming of native plants and animals; and several items of material culture such as gourd maracas, hammocks, baskets, fish traps, and strainers used in the processing of foods like cassava.

To reconstruct the aboriginal culture, we must rely chiefly on writings about the Antillean peoples produced by men who lived with them and observed their culture before these people underwent the great changes. These writers of the sixteenth century were principally explorers, missionaries, and colonizers, and they were hardly trained in ethnographic observation. But before we judge their lack of ethnographic skill too harshly, we should remember that, to them, ethnography was purely secondary to the central purposes of narrating the feats of the conquistadors and condemning the heresy of the natives. We should also keep in mind that they lived in a period of superstition and religious prejudice and that for the past five centuries their country had been engaged in a religious war against the Moors. If we pay close attention to the historical context and the situation prevailing in Spain during this period, we can interpret their writings more accurately.

We find an outstanding example of the operation of this type of background bias in the way that the Spaniards judged the social structure of the Indians in Spanish terms: it was because of the hierarchical structure of Spanish society that writers of this period always characterized the social structure of the Indians as aristocratic. Sven Lovén (1935) grasped this point very well in describing how the Spanish came into constant conflict with the Indians over tribute negotiation. Whenever they saw an Indian who seemed even slightly more important than the mass of common people, they concluded that he must be a "nobleman."

In spite of this error about aristocracy, our sources nevertheless offer us an extraordinary amount of information, especially about the caciques of the West Indies. They had frequent contact with the Spaniards who represented their people in negotiations with them. They were used as informants and signatories of treaties. In their descriptions of these people, whom the early writers called the "Native Nobility," we have more valuable data for the history of chiefs and chiefdoms than of any other social institutions of the aborigines.

For the historical period, especially for the Greater Antilles, the record begins with Columbus, who wrote two letters to the Catholic monarchs as well as navigational logs, or diaries, of his first two voyages (Dunn and Kelley 1989). The original diaries unfortunately are lost, but Bartolomé de Las Casas was able to do an adequate synthesis of the first diary and also a shorter synthesis of the second. But a copybook of Columbus's that was discovered in Spain only three years ago contains a letter in which he describes his second trip—the trip during which the Lesser Antilles and Puerto Rico were discovered. That document is of great importance because it calls into question or supersedes many earlier points of view.

Until the discovery of this letter, we had to use other, admittedly important, sources such as Diego Alvarez Chanca's description of Columbus's second trip (Chanca 1949). Chanca's letter is usually used as the principal source for understanding the events of Columbus's second voyage, although historians have also referred to Columbus's crewmen Michele de Cuneo, Nicolò de Syllacio, and Juan Coma, who also wrote letters describing the voyage (Columbus 1988). Now these other sources will be of less importance because we have in this letter a chronicle of Columbus's own, and it is of great interest indeed. For example, he describes in detail a village near his landfall on Puerto Rico, and some of these details are obviously taken from notes he had made at the time.

Some people say that Columbus had great racial prejudice because he attributed such importance to the skin color of the Indians. They forget that Columbus wanted to make clear the fact that the Indians were not black—because if they were black, it meant that he was actually in Africa, and Africa, according to the treaties with the Vatican, belonged to Portugal. Thus the alleged racial prejudice of his descriptions was really a way of proving that he was not in Africa but indeed had reached the "Indies" he had set out for.

Another very important source for us is the book written by Columbus's younger son, Fernando Colón, the *Historia del Almirante* (History of the admiral). Even before Columbus died in 1506, people were questioning his importance, and some, like the chronicler Oviedo, were even saying that the New World had always been under Spain's dominion, even before Columbus sailed. Fernando wrote his book in part to defend his father's achievement, using a document of his father's to present the family point of view. It also included a lot of information on the Indian populations of the Greater Antilles.

But the most important aspect of Fernando Colón's book is that it includes a small contribution by a linguistically accomplished friar, Ramón Pané, on the Indians' religion. Columbus was very much interested in knowing about the religion of the Indians. In his original letter to the queen he expressed the opinion that the Indians had no religion whatsoever; this was clearly an attempt to persuade Isabella that it would be easy to convert them to Christianity. Nevertheless he ordered Pané to make a study of the religion of the Indians of northern Hispaniola, and the friar, quickly acquiring the native language, produced the volume whose title could be translated as *Legends and Beliefs of the Indians of the Antilles* (Pané 1972; Arrom 1974).

In this work, Ramón Pané recorded not only the Indians' religious beliefs but also some of their myths. Because these narratives have an artistic, literary quality, we can call Pané's work the beginning of American literature. Indeed, from both the literary and the historical standpoint, it is a very important work—a supreme source for our understanding of the indigenous people of the Caribbean. Unfortunately the original Spanish manuscript was lost, and we have only an Italian version that includes many errors of transliteration—Indian words written as if they were Italian. José Arrom (see Pané 1974), however, has done a very good translation of it.

Another very important source is Pietro Martire d'Anghiera, or Peter Martyr, an Italian scholar who came to the Spanish court as a teacher of the royal princes and the children of the nobility. Isabella encouraged a Renaissance style in the royal court and insisted that Latin and Greek be taught to noble children. Peter Martyr was an important man both in Spain and in Italy, friendly with popes and cardinals and in the beginning with Columbus. Since they were both Italian, he received direct information from Columbus and also from the other conquistadors and expedition members. After the discovery, he started sending letters to his important friends in Italy and Spain, and the letters finally were collected into a small booklet, *Decadas Oceanica,* and later in *De Orbe Novo* (Of the New World).

This booklet, first published without Peter Martyr's permission in 1504 and republished in various editions over the next quarter century, gave the author a significant place in the history of the Americas. He was probably, quite literally the first person to notice the importance of the discovery of

America and, as the title of his later volume indicates, he was also probably the first to use the term the "New World." Martyr was able to see that Columbus was wrong in thinking that he had found the East Indies. Instead, Martyr recognized that Columbus had happened upon a region that was completely unknown in Europe.

Some people say that Peter Martyr was never in America and that he was a liar and an inventor of tales. The Spaniards especially disliked him because he reported the gossip of the Spanish court to his Italian friends. But his writings are all very interesting. I have learned more about the history of Spain during that period from reading the letters of Peter Martyr than from studying more "reliable" histories of Spain. Peter Martyr was there for many years, he was very close to Queen Isabella, and he stayed with King Ferdinand until the moment of the king's death, after almost everyone else in Spain had abandoned him.

I also consider Peter Martyr to be important because he is the man responsible for giving to the other European languages some of the words of the Indians of the West Indies, including the first published vocabulary of Indian words, a list of 100 words that appeared in 1516. Columbus himself had used some Taino words in his letters—for example, *canoa* meaning "canoe," a term that was quickly incorporated into the early Spanish dictionaries. But Europeans learned about the language of the Taino mostly from Peter Martyr.

The two main sources for information about the Indians of the Greater Antilles, however, are Bartolomé de Las Casas and Gonzalo de Oviedo. As is well known, Father Las Casas came to the West Indies as a colonizer in 1502, and at first he used Indian labor and treated the Taino Indians in the same way that all the other colonizers did. But very soon he had a change of heart. Realizing how badly these native people were being mistreated, he decided to dedicate his life to improving their condition.

In his defense of the Indians, he had to present an elaborate case supporting the contention that they were human beings and that some of the same cultural practices that Europeans considered objectionable in them had also been common among the Europeans' own ancestors. Using examples from Greek and Roman mythology, he tried to demonstrate that the thinking of these aboriginal peoples was not so different from that of Europe's own early pagans. Using European analogies, he even tried to explain the practice of cannibalism.

Of the many books that Las Casas wrote to protect the Indians, three are most important. The first one, *Brevíssima Relación de la Destrucción de las Indias* (An account of the destruction of the Indians) was published in 1542 and became a principal source for the "Black Legend" about the cruelty of the Spanish conquest. This legend became widely known because it was used by anti-Spanish Protestant writers to attack Catholic Spain, which was their countries' powerful political rival. They went to great lengths to illustrate the Black Legend dramatically, publishing Las Casas's book in French, German, Latin, and English.

In Spain itself, Las Casas was largely rejected, and the Spanish authorities prevented publication of his other books, not only because the *Brevíssima Relación* helped Spain's enemies but also because, in his defense of the Indians, Las Casas tended to exaggerate. For example, he inflated the number of Indians that were in the Caribbean to show how many Indians had been killed by the Spaniards. According to him, at the time of the discovery there were 600,000 Indians in Puerto Rico. That number is impossibly high.

But the *Brevíssima Relación* is a less important book than Las Casas's more detailed *Historia de las Indias* (History of the Indies). Although he never finished this book, it is a very rich and useful source for our purposes, with a great deal of information about the customs of the Indians. Las Casas himself asked that the book not be published until fifty years after his death because in it he was brutally honest about everyone. But some people used the book even before those fifty years were up, and though it was not published until 1883, historians had access to it for centuries before that. And now we have a new annotated edition.

In a third book, *Apologética Historia Sumaria,* Las Casas tries to impress the reader with amusing analyses of other books in order to support his thesis that all the customs of the Indians that seemed so strange were no more unusual than the customs of earlier Europeans, especially those in the Mediterranean. The *Historia Apologética* nonetheless contains some very important information that we should use in our studies on the Indians of the Caribbean.

Father Las Casas was always the defender of the Indians and did bring about some improvement in their treatment, but ultimately he was unsuccessful. It is important to remember that he was not opposed to Spain's colonization of the Americas but only to the manner in which it was being done. In fact he submitted a plan to colonize the Paria area in South America himself, proposing that the colony be established without the customary mistreatment of the Indians. But the Indians, in revenge for something that had happened before, killed two of his colonizing friars. Thus abandoning the idea of a more benign form of colonization, Las Casas became a bishop in Mexico, where he continued to write on the general theme of protecting the Indians.

As important as he is for understanding the aboriginal peoples, Father Las Casas had a rival: Gonzalo Fernández de Oviedo y Valdés. A nobleman who had been raised in the court and was very close to the Spanish kings (first Ferdinand and later Charles V), Oviedo came to America in 1514 as a government official. It should be kept in mind that when he arrived, some of the aboriginal populations had already disappeared and their remaining societies were already disintegrating. Nonetheless Oviedo's work is extremely valuable. Indeed his *Historia Natural y General de las Indias* is one of the most important of all books on the West Indies. We in Puerto Rico are especially glad that a chapter of the *Historia* is devoted to our island. Before he wrote the *Historia*, Oviedo authored the *Sumario de la natural historia de las Indias*, a prefatory summary of what would become the larger work. Irritated by inaccuracies in this work, and especially by the disparagement of Indians, Father Las Casas responded to Oviedo in his own later books.

Also extant are certain government documents that contain valuable information for us in our effort to reconstruct the story of the Indians. We have, for example, the letters of a number of conquistadors who were fighting in court to obtain the labor of Indians and who wrote seeking the king's favor in that regard—letters that contain details of the conquistadors' experiences in America and a great many particulars about the Indians and their way of life.

Nevertheless we need to know more about the Indians who were here before the Spaniards arrived, and we must find out about them through archaeology. It was the middle of the nineteenth century before archaeologists were writing in Europe and in America, and even that early, some people were doing something like archaeological work in the West Indies. In Cuba, Miguel Rodríguez Ferrer was doing excavations as early as 1850, and over the next thirty years, many others followed his lead. Rodríguez Ferrer's *Naturaleza y Civilización de la Gradiosa Isla de Cuba* was published in 1876. But ultimately the work of these early archaeologists is not very important. Most of them were amateurs who tended to interpret the materials they found according to the ideas of the Old World, looking for traces of the Old World cultures in America.

At the beginning of the twentieth century, professional archaeologists started to come from the United States to the West Indies. The first one,

Jesse Walter Fewkes, wrote *The Aborigines of Puerto Rico and the Neighboring Islands*—a book that appeared in 1907 and is still a classic. Fewkes dedicated himself to buying artifact collections from all over Puerto Rico and some of the Lesser Antilles and to carrying out field research in the islands. His books and articles are what I consider the first true archaeology done in the West Indies.

In the next few decades some archaeological work was begun on some of the Caribbean islands, but our understanding of Caribbean prehistory did not really change until the 1930s and 1940s. One important effort was the scientific survey of Puerto Rico and the Virgin Islands conducted by the New York Academy of Sciences. The New York Academy supported a great deal of archaeological work and brought Irving Rouse and Froelich Rainey to the West Indies; as we know, their work and publications are very important.

People from the islands themselves also developed an interest in archaeology, and scholars from Puerto Rico, from Hispaniola, and from Cuba began to study anthropology. Over the decades since the 1940s, various Caribbean research institutions have developed, such as Puerto Rico's Center for Archaeological Research, the Fundación de Historia y Arqueología, and the Center of Advanced Studies of the Caribbean and Puerto Rico; the Dominican Republic's Museum of the Dominican Man, or Museo del Hombre Dominicano; and the Virgin Islands' Archaeological Society. These institutions have sponsored many archaeological research projects that have helped to clarify questions about the aboriginal populations.

So, although we know a great deal about the aboriginal people of the West Indies, we still have many archaeological problems to solve (see Alegría 1988). We hope that some of the younger archaeologists who are beginning to work in the West Indies, in both the Lesser Antilles and Greater Antilles, will be able to solve some of these problems and thus to clarify the situation of the native populations.

We have to know more, for example, about the early migrations from South America. We are not certain if the first Indians came from South, North, or possibly Central America. Nor do we know yet if there was more than one migration of the later Indians from South America, the Arawaks. Rouse claimed that there was indeed only one (Rouse 1986)—a migration that evolved from the Saladoid to the Taino. But others have contended that there were different waves of people coming from South America.

We don't know for certain if the Caribs ever reached the Greater Antilles. We have a description of the Ciguayos from Hispaniola that reminds us of the Caribs because it mentions long hair, powerful bows and arrows, and other traits, but the Caribs remain a problem in West Indian archaeology. We don't really know, for example, if the evolution that Rouse described, from the Saladoid to the Taino, passed by way of the Ostionoid people or if, instead, the Ostionoid people represented a different migration from South America that was responsible for the disappearance of the Saladoid.

It is clear from this example and from other issues I have raised that a great many interesting questions in West Indian archeology still exist. I especially hope the new generation of archaeologists will be able to resolve some of them.

3

The Lesser Antilles before Columbus

Louis Allaire

Undoubtedly the archaeologist's greatest satisfaction is that he may claim to be the only scholar whose profession is capable of providing answers to basic questions about the distant past of a particular area. How long has the area been inhabited? What is the origin of its earliest populations? What was their culture like? What happened in the course of time before the coming of Europeans? What major changes are known to have taken place? What other peoples, if any, interfered with these developments through indirect influence, invasions, or migrations? With whom did these people interact? Did they trade? Did they invent anything? Did they leave any artistic achievements?

Such questions are at the center of the prehistory of the Lesser Antilles—that is, the period from the earliest peopling of these small islands to the coming of the Europeans and the first written accounts. Certainly these answers can only reflect the current state of archaeological knowledge; they are based on a few pieces in a puzzle where most pieces are missing and where not all of the pieces that are eventually found will even fit.

THE EARLIEST INHABITANTS

The first question that logically comes to mind concerns the origins of the earliest human population in a particular region. To answer this question for the Lesser Antilles, we must first look back at the West Indies as a whole and, indeed, at adjacent parts of the mainland. Several plausible answers have been proposed. It is reasonably certain that human groups were living in the Caribbean islands, including the Leeward Islands of the

Lesser Antilles, by 2000 B.C.—that is, about 4,000 years ago (Rouse 1992; Rouse and Allaire 1978). Our assessment of an earlier occupation must be based on a few radiocarbon dates, the earliest of which is 3600 B.C. from Haiti (Vignier site); that date was obtained from surface scatters of sea shells, perhaps not the most reliable context. The date is nonetheless consistent with a date of ca. 3100 B.C. (Levisa site) for Cuba. These dates are suggestive, but we need more of them. Although they are sufficient to suggest a 4000 B.C. date for the earliest entry of human groups into the Caribbean islands, most radiocarbon dates still belong to the period after 2500 B.C. For instance, the earliest date for the Leeward Islands is also around 2000 B.C. and seems to suggest that the island of Antigua was among to first to be inhabited there (Allaire 1990; Rouse 1992).

The earliest remains in Cuba and Hispaniola consist of stone tools such as large blades and cores (known as the Casimiroid series) without any other evidence of stone grinding or shell and bone artifacts. The inhabitants took advantage of the large supplies of flint materials on these islands, which may have been used as quarries well into later prehistoric times. Where these Archaic people came from is a question that still remains unanswered. Possible homelands may be either the coast of Belize or the coast of Colombia and Venezuela (Veloz Maggiolo and Ortega 1976).

Stone-ground axes and pestles, as well as tools made of shell and bone, appear after 2000 B.C.; they are associated with the earliest sites both in the Leeward Islands and the Virgin Islands (Rouse 1992). It has been suggested that this new technology was derived from Trinidad, where similar tools were known at least as early as 4000 B.C. More than the lack of a similar complex and the great diversity in these early preceramic sites, a major argument against a Trinidadian origin is the lack of preceramic sites in the Windward Islands, that is, all the islands from Guadeloupe to Grenada. Two possible early preceramic sites, however, have been found in the interior hills of Martinique, which contain edge grinders (pebbles with a smooth edge) and crude flakes. The dates of these sites has not been established, and their closest relationship could just as well be with Trinidad as with similar sites on Puerto Rico.

Whether a second migration, known as the Ortoiroid (named after the Ortoire site on Trinidad), took place is not clear. These changes may have simply taken place locally in the Greater Antilles, although sporadic or more regular contacts with the mainland and Trinidad may also have been the case. Interestingly, the majority of preceramic sites are in the Virgin

Islands and the Leeward Islands, closer to the Greater Antilles, and especially on Antigua. We would have expected more evidence for the Windwards to support early contacts with South America.

THE AGRICULTURAL COLONISTS

In contrast with the lifeways of these initial settlers, the next major event in the prehistory of the Lesser Antilles is the beginnings of pottery making and agriculture, brought about through a substantial population movement from South America, which must have been well under way by 200 B.C. (Siegel 1989). This is at the basis of all later developments in the small islands until Carib times and European contacts. Here we are on better ground: the origins of the agro-ceramic occupation is definitely toward the mainland of the Orinoco basin and areas adjacent to Trinidad and the nearby Guianas. The mother culture is one known today as Saladoid (after the Saladero site in Venezuela), having developed in the lower Orinoco before spreading not only to the islands but also to the eastern coast of Venezuela.

Essential to that culture is its pottery, which is everywhere characterized by a distinctive bell-shaped vessel decorated with modeled incised designs, especially on the heads, lugs, and handles (known as *adornos*), as well as the diagnostic fine zone-incised cross-hatching. The original Saladoid pottery also included well-made vessels painted with white-on-red painting. This is the case of early Saladoid styles on Trinidad (especially the Cedros site), hence its classification as Cedrosan Saladoid. This painted tradition style is also found in the islands but was not present or adopted everywhere. We have to contend with the Huecan phenomenon (named after the La Hueca site on Vieques, just east of Puerto Rico), where sites lack white-on-red painted decoration. Why this complex painted style was lost or never used by the Huecan people of eastern Puerto Rico and Vieques, and perhaps some Leeward Islands as far south as Guadeloupe, still baffles archaeologists.

Early radiocarbon dates suggest that these may be the earliest Saladoid sites in the islands, beginning perhaps as early as 400 B.C. or perhaps, more cautiously, around 200 B.C. This date in a way is not unexpected; after 500 B.C., the mainland was experiencing major demographic increases and associated population movements, in a period known to archaeologists as "Regional Developmental." The time was ripe for an expansion toward the islands. This original migration may well have happened deliberately through previous knowledge and contacts with preceramic populations in the more distant Lesser Antilles. It may also have happened accidentally when a canoe or boatload was carried out to sea by strong currents or bad weather while attempting to cross between the Guira peninsula of Venezuela and Trinidad. From Grenada, with all other islands visible from each other, exploration and colonization must have progressed rapidly.

What is certain, and we tend to forget it, is that the typical Cedrosan Saladoid, once established, continued to share strong similarities with many sites of the east coast of Venezuela well into the first centuries A.D. This is especially true of the quite complex, white-on-red painted designs. It has been said, for instance, that we may be able to connect one sherd from Venezuela directly to another from Martinique (Allaire 1977).

The rapidity of the expansion of the ceramic style itself is amazing. Within less than two hundred years, it is found relatively abundantly everywhere from Trinidad all to way to eastern Hispaniola, and very often with strong similarities throughout. Archaeologists have yet to sort out the demographic realities behind this distribution. The situation would call for a greater population base on the coast of South America than seems warranted for that time. An alternative explanation would consider the great and extensive mobility of these seafaring island peoples. This explanation would interpret the site distributions as that of a small and highly mobile population constantly resettling in the many unoccupied and fertile islands of the Lesser Antilles.

As revealed by abundant remains of clay griddles, the subsistence of this early Saladoid population was everywhere dependent on manioc cultivation and on the making of cassava bread. Fishing and extensive shellfish collecting contributed to the subsistence as well as the hunting or capture of the few other small mammals or reptiles available in the islands: the agouti, rice rat, iguana, and sea turtle. Almost everywhere, early sites are also associated with dense layers of crab claws, in sharp contrast to later periods. Crab must have been a major nutritional complement to populations perhaps still accustomed to relying on the impoverished fauna of these islands (Petersen, this volume).

Much research remains to be done on many aspects of early Saladoid culture, and Saladoid society is almost entirely unknown. The early colonists seem to have belonged to egalitarian groups; no evidence of chiefdom or complex society, where a hereditary chief would rule over several villages, is suggested by their remains. We cannot deny, however, that the artistic qualities of their ceramic decoration, the major expression of their skills, is remarkable and almost rivals the arts of some South American chiefdom-level societies. Not only is their pottery technologically fine, delicate, and graceful, but the painted decoration in white and red—and later with polychrome elements such as purple, black, yellow and orange—follows rigid and complex rules of composition and symmetry that must have required a difficult apprenticeship. Likewise, the modeled *adornos* represented in imaginative and conventional manners a variety of zoomorphic or anthropomorphic beings that may reflect Saladoid mythology and religious beliefs and may prefigure the Taino zemi cult. Indeed, many elements of later Taino religion seem to have been introduced by the early Saladoids; this is the case, for example, with the three pointed stones that will become one of the most distinctive art objects among the Tainos.

Other Saladoid ceremonial artifacts include their distinctive and often elaborate incense burners—apparently an island invention, although some are known from coastal Venezuela. The Saladoids must have had a rich spiritual life, a conclusion that is in sharp contrast with the evidence for later periods. The La Hueca remains, for instance, are especially associated with a remarkable inventory of small ornaments and jewelry in semi-precious stones such as greenstone, mother-of-pearl, and shell, which must have been destined for inter-island trade (Chanlatte Baik and Narganas Storde 1984). Greenstone pendants in crude frog shapes are, however, known to have originated as far away as the Amazonian basin of South America (Boomert 1987, Cody 1991).

What seems to be certain is that the Huecan type of Saladoid is not represented in the Windward Islands. There, between Guadeloupe and Grenada, decoration develops along a different set of designs. The more typical Cedrosan in the Windward Islands displays instead developed white-on-red painted vessels, some of which were probably used for ceremonial purposes, others very likely for beer making. The Cedrosan Saladoid eventually replaces the Huecan variety everywhere and remains in the Lesser Antilles until the next major cultural changes begin to appear.

BARRANCOID EXPOSURES

New trends begin to appear soon after A.D. 350, and the new manifestations will reach their full climax around A.D. 500, but they will be thereafter short-lived. These new manifestations are marked by a further development of the earlier Cedrosan style of ceramic decoration toward more elaborately decorated, more sculptural types of vessels. The period has often been characterized as the "baroque" phase of Saladoid stylistic evolution, and it is nowhere better represented than in its modeled incised decoration found especially on handles, *adornos,* and incense burners. There is no doubt that this period, which in many ways represents a form of "Developed Saladoid," is still one of the most poorly understood phenomena in Caribbean archaeology, despite the considerable number of sites and local museum collections. Although it is still unclear exactly what it means, it is one of the best represented periods in the Lesser Antilles.

What caused these innovations is not fully understood, and a definitive solution must await more detailed research. However, it is clear that many elements represent unmistakable influences from the Barrancoid ceramics of the mainland as well as from Trinidad. The expression "Saladoid with Barrancoid influences" has been used in reference to the phenomenon, but one may wonder whether we are not instead dealing with "Barrancoid of Saladoid tradition."

The Barrancoid peoples (named after the site of Barrancas on the Lower Orinoco in Venezuela) were then among the most dynamic population in eastern Venezuela and adjacent areas and would eventually take over Trinidad around A.D. 500. Their influence may therefore have been more direct than is usually assumed, and it may also have reached well into Vieques, such as at the Sorce site, and have also included the Virgin Islands. Population movement may also have been involved to a greater extent than has been generally assumed, and indeed the first peopling of Barbados dates to the beginnings of this period. Linguistic influences may also be in evidence, as reflected in the spread of later Arawakan languages such as Maipuran—to which the language of the Island Caribs belonged. One wonders whether in fact this Barrancoid wave did not prefigure the later Carib expansion in the Lesser Antilles but to a much greater extent and with even greater consequences for the islands' development.

THE LAST NATIVE CENTURIES

It is not surprising that the next major changes reflected archaeologically after the sixth century A.D. are still affected by this Barrancoid element. The marked decrease in pottery quality and the simplification of decoration beginning with the eighth-century Troumassoid cultures display many stylistic similarities shared by later Barrancoid styles of coastal Venezuela. Obviously the role of the mainland had never been entirely interrupted, and if indeed stylistic similarities in early Saladoid times were so strongly oriented toward eastern Venezuela, there is no reason to believe that the physical potential for maintaining contacts with the continent had not at all times been present.

This period is, however, also the beginning of late prehistoric times for the Lesser Antilles. In a way it is also the beginning of the end. First of all, the Leeward Islands and the Virgin Islands go in different directions from the Windwards. The Troumassoid cultures in the Leewards and Guadeloupe (the latter an island still relatively unstudied) evolve locally into the Mamorean cultures well represented in Antigua and other Leewards. The Virgin Islands follow a similar line into the Magens Bay culture, which displays obviously closer similarities with the Greater Antilles and especially Puerto Rico, at the end of the first millennium A.D., where the Ostionoid cultures are beginning to emerge. The archaeology of this late period is still poorly known, though the remains show none of the sophistication of previous ceramic styles.

Farther south, however, in the Windward Islands, from Martinique to Grenada, the Troumassoid is more diversified. It includes red painted, linear painted, and modeled incised decoration. A technologically interesting innovation that appears during this period, probably in the Leeward Islands, is the footed griddle that may now be set directly over the fire to bake the cassava bread. This seemingly more efficient cooking instrument never spreads to either the Greater Antilles or the continent. It is curiously not found on Grenada, and it was not used by the historic Island Caribs either (Allaire 1977).

Following the year A.D. 1000, Troumassoid cultures in the southern Leeward Islands eventually yield to the Suazoid (named after the Savanne Suazey site on Grenada; Bullen 1964) manifestation, which becomes well-established by the thirteenth century. Suazey pottery is the climax of ceramic decline, with its simple and bulky plain vessels sometimes decorated with finger indentations along the rim. Finer red painted or incised vessels were also produced, probably for ceremonial purposes, while a flat human-head adorno with flaring, pierced ears is typical of the style. Site distribution appears to have emphasized arid regions and shellfish-rich mangrove areas near coral reefs. The massive footed griddles nevertheless testify to the cultivation of bitter manioc as a staple food in infertile areas. Overall, Suazey ceramics in style appear at first glance highly original with few obvious exterior relationships. At closer examination, however, a substantial stylistic influence from Taino art and pottery decoration of the Greater Antilles permeates the finer ceramic and other small artifacts, which are probably linked to religious or ceremonial activities. This is hardly unexpected because of the greater developments of the contemporaneous societies located in these islands and the recent discovery of actual Taino outposts in the Leeward Islands, well represented by the Kelby Ridge site on Saba, dated to around A.D. 1300 (Hofman and Hoogland 1991).

Likewise, but in an even more subdued manner, one may recognize the distant influence of contemporaneous cultures of the mainland, especially from coastal Venezuela, then dominated by the "Macro-Dabajuroid" group of cultures, which seem to have manifested the same population dynamics as their Barrancoid predecessors (Oliver 1989). We must always bear in mind that there were never any physical or technological barriers to communication between the Lesser Antilles and the mainland; it is in this context that the role of mainland culture must be understood. These new mainland influences, hinted at in many aspects of ceramic shape and decoration, seem to have affected more strongly the southernmost islands from Martinique to Barbados (Allaire 1987).

The Suazey culture is by all accounts the last truly prehistoric assemblage yet identified in the Lesser Antilles. No Suazey site has yielded reliable evidence dating it to the historical, that is, post-1500 period. Because their culture differed radically from that of the Island Caribs, the Suazey must have undergone a late prehistoric depopulation prior to the Island Carib expansion. But small island environments are prone to unpredictable depopulation, simply because their inhabitants are highly mobile. Such hiatus situations between prehistoy and history are not unique to Caribbean archaeology. An analogous example is the mysterious disappearance of the Laurentian Iroquois population from the lower St. Lawrence River between the time of Jacques Cartier's visit in the 1530s and Champlain's voyages seventy-five years later. The process has been dubbed an "ethnic revolution."

Instead, more recent research has revealed a "Cayo" style of pottery unique to St. Vincent that clearly dates to historical periods because of its association with glass and metal artifacts. These Cayo ceramics may be the pottery of the historic Caribs. Similarities with pottery of the Guyanas also reinforces this interpretation (Boomert 1985).

The prehistory of the Lesser Antilles reveals today a greater diversity of cultural manifestations than seems to be suggested by the historic Island Carib pattern. Whereas the classic manifestations of Cedrosan Saladoid were remarkably uniform in their distribution throughout the islands, Troumassoid cultures experienced more regionalization, especially in the Leeward Islands and Guadeloupe, where the situation awaits much further research. The fate of the Virgin Islands reflects their intermediate position, yet it has always been tied to that of the Greater Antilles. The Windward Islands, in contrast, offered an environment that would have sustained a more substantial population. But here again, major islands like Dominica and Guadeloupe are still poorly known. The region from Martinique to Grenada, including Barbados, demonstrates considerable cultural inventiveness and creativity.

Part 2: The Encounter

When looked at from a fairly long view, the meeting between the Spanish and the indigenous people of the Caribbean was an "encounter" of peoples the way a train wreck is an encounter. The results were catastrophic for the islanders. This section looks at the "contact period" (a span of time that in many ways continues right up to the present) in several ways. Richard Cunningham's essay, "Biological Impact of 1492," takes the longest view, looking at what happened to Caribbean species and ecosystems in the centuries after the European arrival. Drawing examples from texts, illustrations, and plays, Alissandra Cummins looks at the diverse ways in which Europeans conceptualized the indigenous people of the Americas. Birgit Faber Morse's essay creates a bridge between the complex contact-period history of St. Croix and that island's archaeology. In a sense these essays give a first impression of the processes going on during the period of initial contact in the Caribbean.

Many of the other chapters in this volume, because they utilize descriptions of events and observations made in the early years by European chroniclers, offer further testimony on the years following the arrival of the Europeans. Morse's essay also addresses a complex issue, one that reappears throughout this book: who were the Island Caribs? In the Europeans' first approximations, the Caribbean was seen as the domain of two groups, Tainos (or Arawaks) and Caribs. Morse's essay shows clearly that the ball-court site at Salt River was related to the development of complex chiefdoms on Puerto Rico and the rest of the Greater Antilles. In its pottery and architecture it seems to be an extension of the Greater Antilles. One might assume that St.

Croix was part of the Taino world in 1492. But in the early records of Spanish contact, the people of St. Croix are described as "Caribs." Is this evidence of confusion on the part of European observers or evidence of earlier conquests in the islands? The political situation in the northern Lesser Antilles was certainly unsettled when Columbus and other Europeans came onto the scene. There seem to have been several different groups involved, and the extent to which they are related to each other is unclear (Wilson 1993). The ethnic identity of the people on St. Croix remains a matter of debate.

4

The Biological Impacts of 1492

Richard L. Cunningham

On October 7, 1492, Christopher Columbus, observing southbound migratory birds, changed his course from west to west-southwest. Five days
later he made landfall in the Bahamas. Thus the biology of the New World
affected the Old World's course of history even before the Old World forever
affected the biology of the New.

Columbus's log is replete with superlative descriptions of the natural
beauty that was encountered on that first voyage. Huge trees (canoes) capable of holding about 150 men, flocks of parrots and other birds so dense
as to blot out the sun, and fragrant and beautiful flowers were among the
subjects of these descriptions (Fuson 1987). Five hundred years later, there
is still much beauty to be seen in the West Indies, a fact that helps to make
tourism central to the islands' economy. But centuries of environmental
change have had disastrous biological impact on the Caribbean. Within
two decades of their initial contact with the Spanish, the Taino Indians had
disappeared from the Bahamas in what was probably the New World's
first vertebrate extinction caused by contact with the Old World (Watts
1987). That extinction was followed by many others.

The process of extinction, it should be remembered, had not been introduced by the encounter. As early as the late Pleistocene, as glaciers were
retreating, climate change and the rise of sea levels were contributing to
the loss of West Indian land mammals. Of the seventy-six recognized species
of West Indian terrestrial mammals, sixty-seven (about 90 percent) became
extinct in the last twenty thousand years. This is an extinction rate of one
species every 299 years. When humans arrived in the islands about 4,500
years ago, their use of the fauna as food accelerated the depletion, increasing
the extinction rate to about one species every 122 years. The remains of

several extinct mammalian species have been found in the island's archaeological sites (Watts 1987; Gill 1978; Sauer 1966).

After 1492, however, the New World extinction process worsened, and the West Indies were hit particularly hard. The first post-encounter mammalian extinction—that of the hutia—can be traced to 1550, only fifty-seven years after the colonization of Hispaniola. Between 1600 and 1973, six species of birds, thirty-four of mammals, and ten of reptiles disappeared from the West Indies: a total of fifty species. By contrast, during this same period North America lost only eight species of vertebrate animals (Day 1981; Nilsson 1983; Woods 1989). Of the thirty-nine species of Western hemisphere mammals that have become extinct since 1600, thirty-four once flourished in the West Indies.

LOSS OF WEST INDIAN FAUNA

Of the fifty species that disappeared from the islands in the wake of the encounter, I will mention only a few examples as representative.

Hutias

A hutia native to Hispaniola had become extinct by 1550, making it probably the first of New World mammals to have been eliminated by the arrival of the Spanish. Another species of hutia, native to Puerto Rico and also now extinct, was perhaps transported to other islands by the Tainos. Such transporting was not uncommon, an act similar to the Spanish practice of dropping off pigs on uninhabited islands as a future food source.

Other Rodents

Neither Puerto Rico nor any of the Lesser Antilles have any surviving native non-flying mammal species. Hispaniola contains one species each of the insectivore Solenodon and a capromyid rodent. Cuba has the greatest surviving diversity of native mammals of any West Indian island. From four to nine species of capromyid rodents and a single species of Solenodon (which is near extinction) still survive on this largest island of the Caribbean (Morgan and Woods 1986a and b).

Aquatic Mammals

The Caribbean monk seal was the first large New World mammal discovered by Columbus. On his second voyage in 1494, his men killed eight of them on a small island near Hispaniola. The seals became a food item for the European colonizers, and they were also hunted into the nineteenth century for their fur and oil. The species is now apparently extinct, with the last reliable sighting in 1952 near Jamaica. The West Indian manatee, which has undergone a less severe but still major decline, is now uncommon to rare in the Caribbean and is possibly extinct in the Lesser Antilles.

Bats

The flying mammals have fared better than their terrestrial counterparts, having suffered the fewest extinctions of any West Indian mammal group. Of the fifty-nine bat species known from the West Indies, eight of them, or 14 percent, are now extinct.

Parrots

Parrots have suffered dramatically throughout the Caribbean. The Cuban red macaw, which was endemic to that island, is now extinct; the last specimen was shot in the Zapata Swamp in 1864. Several West Indian islands may have had other species of macaws that have vanished since European colonization. At present the Caribbean contains eight species of endemic Amazonian parrots. Six are currently endangered, including the imperial parrot of Dominica, which is nearing extinction.

THE IMPACT OF INTRODUCED ANIMALS

Humans generally cause extinctions by exploiting species for food and by encroaching on their habitats. In the West Indies a significant third cause was the increase in natural competition that occurred with the introduction of certain Old World mammals. Rodents of the genus Rattus, mongooses, dogs, and cats were among the accidental or intentional post-Columbian introductions that put a devastating pressure on native species.

Particularly damaging in this regard were the large attack dogs the Spanish imported to intimidate the Caribbean people. In 1493, on Columbus's second voyage, twenty purebred mastiffs and greyhound attack dogs were introduced into Hispaniola. They proved to be a major military factor in the conquest and eventual extermination of native peoples. In addition, dogs escaped their masters to roam freely in the wild throughout the islands. Their population increasing because there were no other large native mammalian predators in the West Indies, dogs became a significant ecological factor. They apparently had a devastating impact on the native fauna, especially the smaller endemic mammals (Varner and Varner 1983).

Other domesticated animals also had an impact. In addition to dogs, Columbus's second voyage brought in horses, cattle, pigs, sheep, goats, and chickens. The cattle and pigs had an immediate ecological effect. Pigs adapted extremely well and soon thousands were roaming wild in Hispaniola, Puerto Rico, Cuba, and eventually Jamaica. By the 1520s there were hundreds of cattle roaming Hispaniola.

The least welcome of the Old World animal immigrants were an accidental introduction: black rats. The rats spread throughout the Indies, feeding on native plants and preying on native wildlife. They fed on domesticated crops, a situation leading to the eventual introduction of the mongoose to keep their numbers down. Rats spread disease that affected the entire human population: the native Indians, the Europeans, and their African slaves.

PLANTS: THE TWO-WAY FLOW

Columbus's voyages began the process of "Europeanizing" the New World. On his second voyage, he introduced oranges, citrons, lemons, pomegranates, figs, and bananas as well as seeds and cuttings of wheat, melons, onions, chickpeas, radishes, grape vines, fruit stones for fruit trees and—most significantly—sugarcane. The sugarcane brought to Hispaniola in 1493 was the precursor of the crop that was to change the environmental face of the West Indies. By the 1530s there were thirty-four sugar mills on Hispaniola. Forced to work in these mills, the native Indian population was replaced by black African slaves as their numbers gradually declined.

But the movement of food plants was not a one-way flow of Old World to New World. Though the immediate treasures sought by the Spanish were gold and silver, eventually the greatest riches the Old World acquired were not mineral but vegetable. Five New World crops were to become principal sources of food in human communities the world over: maize (corn), potatoes, sweet potatoes, beans, and manioc. Among the other New World plants that have also had major international impact were tomatoes, green peppers, chili peppers, pineapple, papaya, avocado, squashes, pumpkin, peanuts, cocoa, guava, and tobacco (Crosby 1972; Watts 1987).

THE CASE OF HAITI

About the size of the state of Maryland, Haiti contains 10,714 square miles; two-thirds of the country is mountainous and the rest is semi-arid. Haiti's population is about 6.3 million, or about 1 million more than that of Maryland. There are about 588 people per square mile, and the annual growth rate is 2.3 percent. About one-third of the land is used for agriculture, with coffee, sugarcane, corn, rice, and sorghum being the principal crops.

Haiti is the poorest nation in the Western Hemisphere. In 1983 its per capita income was $333. In 1987 the unemployment rate was about 50 percent, and almost 40 percent of the people suffered from malnutrition. Not only does Haiti face serious economic and social problems; it is also one of the most environmentally degraded countries in the world, providing a supreme example of what happens when people abuse the environmental heritage of their country. Today only 2 percent of its land remains forested. With the lowland forests long gone, poverty is now forcing people up the steep mountain slopes to plant crops and cut wood for fuel. Wood cutting for charcoal production has become a major contributor to deforestation. About one-third of the land is now seriously eroded due to forest clearing (Kurlansky 1988; Paryski, Woods, and Sergile 1989).

Haiti was once one of the most biologically diverse countries in the West Indies, and some of that diversity still exists. The island of Hispaniola contains many endemic plants and animals, some of which—like the gray-crowned palm tanager—occur only in Haiti. About 36 percent of Haiti's plants are endemic, and the flora includes about five thousand species, including three hundred species of orchids. Yet human mismanagement has definitely taken a toll. Of the twenty-eight species of terrestrial mammals that once lived in Haiti, only two survive, and both are threatened; over 90 percent of Haiti's non-flying mammals have become extinct since the Pleistocene.

There is some hope in Haiti for environmental protection. For example, two national parks have been established. Their public support depends, however, upon tourist dollars and the understanding of the economic values for protecting watersheds contained in the parks.

SUMMARY

The history of the New World has been one of changes brought on initially by the clash between Old World and New World cultures. Current environmental change throughout the Americas is due basically to increasing population and urbanization, economic incentives, greed, new technology, and environmental ignorance and apathy. Among the most significant factors threatening the biological heritage of the West Indies are tropical deforestation, air and water pollution, soil erosion, waste disposal, overpopulation, poverty, urbanization and overdevelopment, tourism, and the effects of alien plants and animals. The continuing legacy of the Columbus encounter is not just historical and cultural; it is and always will be biological.

5

The Salt River Site, St. Croix, at the Time of the Encounter

Birgit Faber Morse

The Salt River site is located in the center of St. Croix's northern shore at the base of Salt River Point, which is a small prominent brush-covered peninsula stretching east towards the mouth of Salt River inlet. It seems to have been the largest coastal settlement on the island at the time of the encounter and the only one with continuous habitation throughout the pre-Columbian Ceramic Age, which in the northern Lesser Antilles began shortly before the time of Christ and lasted into the historic period. We know this from two large and well-documented excavations, the results of which have been analyzed and compared with current research findings in St. Croix and nearby islands. The two principal excavators were Danish anthropologist Gudmund Hatt and Virgin Islands archaeologist Gary Vescelius. My aim in this chapter is to identify and reconstruct from the archaeological evidence the culture at the Salt River site during the latter part of the fifteenth century and to determine its affiliations.

CHRONOLOGY OF ARCHAEOLOGICAL WORK

St. Croix seems to have been ignored by the Spanish for some time after Columbus's initial visit in 1493. In 1587 John White, on his way from England to Virginia, stopped for a couple of days at Salt River Bay. His men reported seeing some natives and also discovered pottery fragments near their landing. Vescelius (1952) labeled this sighting the first archaeological and last ethnographical account of St. Croix. Over a century elapsed until the first Dutch and English settlers arrived in the early part of the seventeenth century and started the construction of a fort on Salt River

Point. By this time the aboriginal community was extinct, probably the victim of Spanish raids from Puerto Rico in the early 1500s. Later in the 1600s the French occupied the island and expanded the fort, incorporating prehistoric archaeological material in the construction.

Around the turn of this century Capt. H. U. Ramsing of the Royal Danish Engineers carried out the earliest recorded fieldwork on St. Croix in the vicinity of Salt River, presenting his findings to the Danish National Museum (Hatt 1924). After the United States acquired the Danish West Indies in 1917, Theodoor de Booy conducted the first systematic archaeological survey of the island for the Museum of the American Indian in New York, where his finds are now stored. At Salt River he excavated deposits of food debris and pottery fragments called *middens* that he had found in a semicircle around a small hill on the western side of the bay (De Booy 1919). The provenicnces for the artifacts he found are good, but his excavations lack detailed recording of the stratigraphic layers in which the artifacts were found. A more careful field-worker was Gudmund Hatt, whose finds from the Virgin Islands are housed in the Danish National Museum in Copenhagen. Hatt's attention to the details of provenience and stratigraphy are excellent, and his field notes, although not easy to read, illuminate his excavation at Salt River, where in 1923 he found evidence of the islands' only known ball and dance court (at position "A" in Hatt's map, figure 5.1).

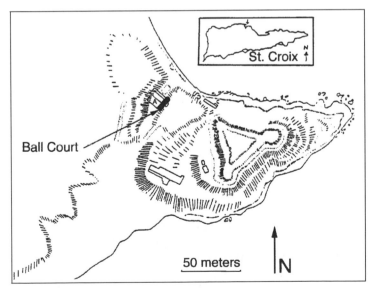

Figure 5.1. Gudmund Hatt's map of the Salt River site, showing the location of the ball court.

During the seventy years since Hatt dug at Salt River, many excavators have come and gone. In the 1930s, Folmer Andersen, an avid local archaeologist, collected artifacts from many Cruzan sites that now form the nucleus of the collection at the National Park Service Museum in Christiansted; it includes many pieces from Salt River. In 1937 Herbert Krieger of the Smithsonian Institution in Washington conducted a survey and an excavation on St. Croix that included Salt River. His excavation techniques were below standard for his time, but his conclusions agreed with Hatt's (Krieger 1938).

Vescelius's comprehensive survey of the island in 1951 was carried out under the auspices of the St. Croix Museum Commission and the Yale Peabody Museum, where his finds and some of his field notes are now housed. He and his team surface collected at thirty-five sites and excavated at about a dozen, most extensively at the Salt River site. His attention to stratigraphy and his care in recording the detailed proveniences of the artifacts makes his the best research collection of them all (Morse 1989). During the late 1970s, when Vescelius was territorial archaeologist for the Virgin Islands, he and Bruce Tilden did an extensive survey and an excavation at Salt River, but nothing has yet been published about them.

DANCE AND BALL COURT

The early Spanish chroniclers—especially Gonzalo de Oviedo in *Historia General y Natural de las Indias* (1535) and Bartolomé de Las Casas in *Historia de las Indias* (first published in 1883)—described the "bateys" or ball and dance courts and the way the ball game was played among the Classic Tainos in Hispaniola and Puerto Rico (Alegría 1983). No ethnohistorical sources have yet been found that mention courts and the ball game in the Virgin Islands. Our knowledge here stems solely from the archaeological evidence, beginning with Hatt's discoveries in 1923.

During his excavation at Salt River, Hatt found within the prehistoric site an open, flat area almost devoid of artifacts, located near the northwest corner of the colonial fort (Hatt 1924). This area, measuring slightly more than 30 by 25 m, was surrounded on the north and west side by a ridge composed of midden material. When a cut was made through the ridge, a low wall of flat grey sandstone slabs was discovered at its foot, facing the open area (figure 5.2). The length of the stone row was about 8 m running northeast to southwest, and the height of the slabs varied between 29 and 42 cm (Hatt 1941).

The wall was broken in two places by the removal of stones, but nine of

Figure 5.2. Carved stone slabs lining the ball court at Salt River.

them remained in place; several had crude carvings or petroglyphs engraved on them. In Hatt's photograph the wall is seen clearly from the southwest, along with several of the ceramic vessels and a triangular head of coral stone that was found behind it during the excavation. In the midden northwest of the court, Hatt discovered three other fragments of similarly carved stones, with pits and grooves forming simple anthropomorphic figures. These could have been part of a second stone row on the other side of the court that was destroyed by earlier excavations.

The first and southernmost slab of the stone wall is of particular interest since it has two figures in a horizontal position, one enclosed within the other. Hatt, interpreting them as a representation of a pregnant woman, suggested that they may specifically represent "the mother of the sky god," who was also the goddess of fertility. A smaller stone, one of the three fragments found behind the wall, shows an unusually well-executed carving of a frog with a human face. This was a popular motif in precolumbian St. Croix; frog figures carved in stone and shell have been found in several excavations and are often associated with fertility and rain. They are first found in the earliest horizon of the Ceramic Age that has been documented (see Morse 1989, 1990) and thus probably represent a succession of iconographic styles for over a thousand years.

The second stone in the wall has a rather complicated figure, the outline of which cannot easily be detected. It consists of a face in a horizontal position with deep pit eyes and a second face to its right. On the interior surface of this slab is a vague outline of still another face. On a third wall slab it is possible to discern a face consisting of two eye pits and a mouth groove.

The last slab at the northeastern end of the stone row also bears a face, vaguely represented by pit eyes and a mouth, with five vertical incised lines above it. The stone is partly broken, but even in this state it is the tallest of the slabs, measuring 42 cm in height and 52 cm width. Of special interest is a circular depression about 10 cm in diameter in the right corner below the figure. Three drilled holes were found within this depression. Two were quite shallow, but the third was narrow, only slightly more than 1 mm wide, and it passed right through the stone.

Hatt felt that the funnel-shaped hole served some ritual or magical purpose. He notes that this kind of device was not foreign to native medicine men in Hispaniola, who used certain tricks in connection with the worship of their *zemis*, or idols. He mentions the case of a famous "talking" idol discovered there by some of Columbus's men, who related that a pipe led from the image to a dark corner in the cacique's house, where a concealed man spoke into the pipe so that it sounded as if the words came from the idol (Hatt 1924). Hatt surmised that this curious perforated stone might have been used in a similar way.

It was also possible to pour water into the funnel from behind, letting it ooze through and thus wetting the front of the stone. Hatt recalls Father Ramón Pané's story of the rain-producing zemis in a cave in Hispaniola looking as if they were perspiring, which is a natural appearance for a stalagmite and suggests that rain zemis preferably should be wet (Hatt 1941). The identification of weeping figures representing the rain deity has been expanded upon by José Arrom in *Mitología y Artes Prehispánicas de las Antillas*.

BURIALS

During Hatt's excavation at Salt River, numerous human bones were discovered scattered in the ridge behind the stone wall. Only four skeletons showed evidence of deliberate burial. Two of these were found behind the southwestern end of the stone row, lying in a stratum of clayey soil at a slightly lower level. The ridge consisted of a kitchen midden resting on the clayey stratum. Here two more skeletons were found mixed in with ashes, seashells, and the bones of fish and manatees. It was evident that refuse from past meals had repeatedly been thrown out from an area just behind the stone row toward the northwest, where the village site was bordered by an old lagoon that has now dried out. A fifth burial was found just northeast of the court area; it was a skeleton of an infant contained in a beautiful incised bowl together with some shell material (figure 5.3; Hatt 1924).

Hatt originally thought that the area in front of the stone slabs had been used for playing the ball game and that the area behind them had been kind of a sanctuary, where zemis were worshipped and cannibalism might have been practiced. He felt that the native Cruzan encountered by Columbus were of Tainan background but had adopted certain Carib traits from their aggressive eastern neighbors in order to defend themselves. Later, though, Hatt (1941) seems to have discounted the idea of cannibalism and writes that the zemi cult was a kind of ancestor worship associated with the bones of the dead and the skull in particular. The use of bones of the departed as zemis is often mentioned in the early chronicles. Human bones were sometimes enclosed in wooden figures that were treated as fetishes and called by the name of the person whose bones they contained (Las Casas 1951a). Both Fewkes (1907) and Lovén (1935) mention that the

Figure 5.3. Ceramic vessel from Salt River.

Spaniards observed this habit among the Tainos and that it may have led them to distorted stories of cannibalism, which they could use politically against the native population.

Associated Artifacts

Hatt was the first archaeologist to study the stratigraphy of Virgin Islands sites and the first to use this study to draw systematic conclusions about chronology. He excavated at about thirty sites on St. Croix, St. Thomas, and St. John in 1922–23 and assigned them to a sequence of three cultures: Krum Bay, which is preceramic; Coral Bay–Longford, which is characterized by white-on-red pottery; and Magens Bay–Salt River, which has modeled incised pottery. The names are derived from the various localities in the three Virgin Islands where Hatt found archaeological evidence. He also came to the conclusion that the earliest ceramics originated in the Lesser Antilles to the south, whereas the later ceramics derived from the Greater Antilles to the west. He reached this decision by comparing his finds with the ceramic styles and other material from excavations in the neighboring islands (Hatt 1924).

Vescelius (1952) originally applied the eastern Puerto Rican sequence of cultures to St. Croix but later recognized the need to set up a separate sequence for the Virgin Islands. After his excavation there in 1979, he inserted Prosperity as the initial ceramic culture, preceding Coral Bay–Longford.

Later, Irving Rouse divided Magens Bay–Salt River into two cultures: culture 1, which yielded plainer artifacts; and culture 2, which had more decorated ones. He also assigned these cultures and Hatt's earlier ones to the system of general periods numbered from 1 to 4 that he had previously set up for the Greater Antilles (Rouse 1982).

The stone walls that made up Hatt's ball court were found in the top excavation level. They corresponded to period 4 in Rouse's general chronology, dating from A.D. 1200–1500. Among the artifacts that Hatt found in close association with the stone slabs was a column, forty-two centimeters long, that may have served as a pedestal for a large triangular head found nearby—both are made of cut coral. The head has a roughly carved face on both sides and probably served as a zemi, as could a number of smaller coral heads found in the same excavation. Numerous potsherds were found exhibiting zoomorphic appliqué and modeling with incision and punctation used to fill out details. Shell, bone, and stone ornaments, especially perforated shell disks used as pendants, were also discovered. All are characteristic of period 4.

Simple three-pointed figures mostly made from the tip of the conch shell (*Strombus gigas*) were very common throughout the site. Hatt found more than seventy there, and they were particularly numerous in the ridge behind the stone row. He felt that they must have played a special role and have had some religious or magical use for the natives of St. Croix (Hatt 1941). Two large three-pointers made of stone with faces carved on their ends were donated to the Danish National Museum in the middle of the last century (figure 5.4). They supposedly came from the Salt River area.

Also typical of the Classic Taínan culture are the ball collars or belts, so called because they probably were worn around the waist (Ekholm 1961). Hatt recovered almost twenty stone fragments of these and several small

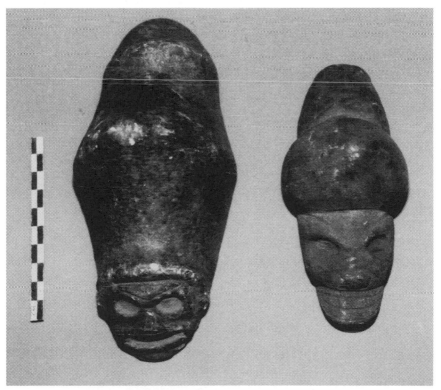

Figure 5.4. Carved stone three-pointed figures (also called *trigonolitos* and *zemis*).

stone balls in the highest excavation level in and around the court area. No whole specimen was found, but the National Museum in Denmark possesses two ball belts that came from the area before Hatt's time. A broken one with a large decorated panel belongs to the heavier type; the less decorated one is more slender. The belts and fragments are all made from greenish grey stone, which is indigenous to St. Croix.

COMPARISON

After finishing his excavations on the three U.S. Virgin Islands, Hatt concluded that their ceramics and associated artifacts were so similar that he could organize them into a single seriation. He did not, however, find any signs of ball courts and their ceremonial paraphernalia on the other two islands. Neither did Bullen (1962) or Sleight (1962) during their survey of St. Thomas and St. John in the late 1950s. These islands are located some sixty kilometers north of St. Croix. At the same distance to the northwest is Vieques, where a ball court was excavated at El Destino in the high central part of the island during the late 1970s by Rodríquez and Rivera (1981).

Farther west on the larger island of Puerto Rico is the richest occurrence of ball courts in the Caribbean area. Several sites there contained evidence of more than one; Caquana (Capa) in Utuado has, besides a large square plaza and a small oval one, nine rectangular courts (Alegría 1983). In Puerto Rico the rectangular ones are in the majority and are often marked on their longer sides by rows of upright slabs, many of which bear petroglyphs. During Hatt's fieldwork in Hispaniola he saw several courts and they were mostly rectangular and surrounded on two sides with low earth mounds (Hatt 1932).

Ceramic sherds in the Puerto Rican courts indicate that their earliest appearance was in period 3, but their greatest use was during period 4. It seems to have been a pattern for the earliest known ball courts in Puerto Rico to also serve as burial repositories (Siegel 1989). Burials from later periods have been found in cemeteries and mounds close to but outside the courts—which is the case at Salt River.

CONCLUSIONS

Gudmund Hatt was the first to recognize the stratigraphy and seriation of Virgin Islands ceramics and his findings established the foundation for modern Caribbean archaeology. It was his preference as a theoretically oriented anthropologist to search for cultural centers and the means of cultural transmission. He realized that the Tainan influence from Puerto Rico and Hispaniola was strong at Salt River toward the end of the pre-Columbian era. He saw it in the simple stone carvings as well as in the more advanced sculptures that were closely tied up with the worship of zemis (Hatt 1941). He did not, however, discover any late prehistoric remains like those in the Windward Islands from where the Caribs would have come.

The Tainan ball court phenomenon seems to have developed in Puerto Rico during period 3, when the Classic Taino there were organizing themselves into settlements hierarchies and cultural authority structures, and from there it spread west and east during period 4. The Salt River site, containing the easternmost established Tainan ball court, was an outpost of the Classic Taino interaction sphere. Further information is needed, particularly radiocarbon dates, to establish temporal links between the Taino settlements in St. Croix and those in eastern Puerto Rico and the Eastern Taino occupation of the northern Lesser Antilles. The recent discovery of Tainan culture on the island of Saba, the first of the Leeward Islands east of St. Croix, suggests an ongoing process of Taino expansion. The Salt River area, with its ideally located and protected harbor, could have been a gateway community at the time of the encounter for people with cultural affinities and ties to both Puerto Rico and the Lesser Antilles.

6

European Views of the Aboriginal Population

Alissandra Cummins

The fifteenth-century meeting between Amerindians and Europeans was decisive for both in completely different ways. For the Amerindians it meant devastating changes in their cultural, political, and economic landscapes—few of the native societies survived the upheaval. For the Europeans the meeting gave impetus to the drive for capitalist and imperial goals—an expansion of their nation states to the Western Hemisphere. In that expansion, early impressions of the native peoples who would soon suffer by it set a pattern for European observation and evaluation. In this chapter I discuss four of those early impressions, chosen chiefly because of their reflection of European opinion. The originators of these widely known works were Christopher Columbus, Francis Drake, Theodor de Bry, and William Shakespeare.

COLUMBUS: THE BASEL LETTER

One of the chief characteristics of the native Arawaks that was noted by Columbus was their generosity in sharing knowledge and resources. He first admires this in a four-page letter initially published at Barcelona and later published in Latin at Rome and at Basel as *De Insulis Inventis Epistola* (Letter on the discovered islands). In this 1493 document, after remarking on the Tainos' nakedness, "handsome bodies," and "very good faces," Columbus goes on to say in awed tones that "when they have been reassured, and lost their fear, they are ingenuous and liberal with all their possessions. . . . If one asks for anything they never say no. On the contrary they offer a share to anyone with demonstrations of heartfelt affection and they are immediately content with any small thing, valuable or valueless, that is given them" (Major 1972). This letter was published nine times in 1493 alone, and there were nearly twenty versions by 1500. Though it had an enormous impact, the generous admiration of native peoples that it reflected soon disappeared.

Part of the reason was that the potentiality of settlement in this newly discovered world required the displacement of its "handsome" and "ingenuous" inhabitants. Whether or not he was aware of the ethical contradictions here, Columbus's writings certainly indicate that they existed. He marvels that "I have not been able to find out if they have any private property. As far as I could see, whatever a man had was shared among all the rest; and this particularly applies to food." He notes further that they were "very gentle, and do not know what it is to be wicked, or to kill others, or to steal." Fearing the less gentle tendencies of his own crew, he orders them "to be careful not to offend any one in anyway, and to take nothing from them against their will." Columbus did not approve of the vast amount of gold that some sailors received in payment for their trinkets and rubbish, and later forbade such transactions, instead giving the Indians personally gifts of "a thousand pretty things that I had brought." This last action is indicative of the contradictory nature of Columbus's rapport with and admiration for the Indians, for while he may have disapproved of his crew's greed, he was surely not personally blind to the attractions of gold, and his "pretty things" were surely a means of securing its owners' trust.

Not that he is entirely honest about this, even with himself. He notes earnestly, for example, that he made them these gifts "in order to gain their love and to incline them to become Christians." Therein lies the heart of the situation. One could not really call it a dilemma because Columbus had no doubts at all about the appropriateness of his strategies for winning over the Indians, and those strategies were designed in the service of both God *and* gold.

The religious aspect of it was clear to the admiral. An extremely pious man, he set up a large cross wherever he landed, named harbors and islands for the saints, and noted the time in his logbook by the hour of terce and vespers. Here in the Caribbean he found a unique opportunity: the conversion of a people who evidently did not have any religious creed but believed simply "that power and goodness dwell in the sky." They were, moreover, he writes, "firmly convinced that I have come from the sky with these ships and people."

He further notes that this was not because they were stupid; indeed he found the Amerindians to be "men of great intelligence." Nor were they themselves lacking in piety. Each village maintained an "image house," a house of worship containing "wooden images carved in relief and called by them zemies." But the funerary rites and other ceremonies he observed seemed to him of significance only as a way of keeping everyone obedient to the chief. Other than this, their worship of stones in groups of three and other religious observances were merely "superstitious belief." They were thus prime candidates for conversion.

Believing that what was needed in the Indies were devout religious persons capable of training the Amerindians to be tractable servants to serve the needs of the colony, and thus those of the king and queen of Spain, Columbus emphasized the importance of allowing only "Catholic Christians . . . allowed in the Indies." His assumption that the Indians should be made to serve the greater glory of God first, and then of Spain, was inevitable to a man of his religious sensibility, but it also reflected the uneven relationship that had been established between the two races from the beginning.

The most visible evidence of that inequality was slavery, and Columbus, feeling that all Indians were "fitted to be ruled and to be set to work to cultivate the land," in effect had no difficulty with the inevitability of their slavery. This view caused Bartolomé de Las Casas some discomfort later on in his editing of the admiral's logbook.

Columbus's naive vision of the New World natives in a state of primordial innocence awaiting the privilege of being exploited by the "men from heaven," as they called the Spaniards, did not endure beyond the second voyage and his discovery of the annihilation of La Navidad—evidence that the Amerindians, having realized that the invaders were only too human, had started to exact reprisals. The subsequent hostile reception to the Spaniards at Jamaica (May 1494) and the battle in Hispaniola (March 1495) served to confirm his view that "the conquest of these people [was] the work of His will and His mighty hand" and to reaffirm "the civilization and nobility of all Christians." By the time of his death in 1506, the "Indians" at whom Columbus had marveled in 1493 were referred to (in his last will and testament) as "cannibals." This name was to prove a tenacious legacy that branded the Amerindians forever afterward.

THE DRAKE MANUSCRIPT

While Columbus's *Epistola* had been printed for a public—although admittedly somewhat limited—audience, the French *Histoire Naturelle des Indes,* often called the Drake Manuscript, was probably produced simply as a personal record or diary of events. Francis Drake's pilot Nuño da Silva, captured during his circumnavigation of 1577–80, later testified that "Francis Drake kept a book in which he . . . delineated birds, trees and sea lions. He is an adept in painting" (Drake 1963). Francisco de Zarate, a Spanish nobleman captured by Drake in 1579, confirms this view and also notes that Drake "carries painters who paint for him" (Drake 1963). The Drake manuscript, which contains almost two hundred captioned images of West Indian plants, animals and Amerindian life (figure 6.1), therefore appears to be the work of at least two and possibly more artists. Some of the images are almost naive in style; others have been more professionally, almost scientifically, rendered; still others are wildly exuberant fantasies. None of the artists has been positively identified.

Understanding the different personalities involved in the manuscript's production, and the primary purpose behind its creation, is therefore vitally important in an analysis of this document. Whatever else he was, Drake

Figure 6.1. Illustration from the manuscript of Sir Francis Drake, *Histoire Naturelle des Indes,* fol. 113. Courtesy of the Pierpont Morgan Library, MA 3900.

was a pirate and an adventurer. He had come to the Caribbean to find gold as much as to create problems for the Spanish crown. With a deep antipathy for the Catholic religion, he had no qualms about exploiting enemy territory and resources. At the same time an opportunist like Drake, seeking legitimacy for his questionable activities, was not above deliberate exaggeration where he felt it might glorify his cause. The fact that the cause was not simply one of queen and country but largely one of self plays a large part in how the manuscript developed and therefore how it should be read.

The illustrations in the Drake manuscript have been carefully organized according to subject. For example, botanical drawings and zoological images abound. However, special attention is paid to the ingenuity and practicality of Amerindian husbandry and the cruelly exploitative system of Spanish mining and metalworking. The end result is an incisive depiction of the Spanish territories of the New World from the perspective of a trespasser hungry for the opportunity of exploitation. His view of the Amerindian may therefore be considered as less sympathetic and ennobling—or indeed more denigrating—than others of the period.

De Bry: *Historiae Americanae*

Theodor de Bry, an engraver who was born at Liège and worked at Frankfurt, was the first to illustrate the literature of American travel with any sort of consistency. His great series of printed books, with their large number of beautifully executed copperplate engravings, brought to a broad European public the first popular visualization of the exotic world opening up across the Atlantic (figure 6.2). In effect his *Historiae Americanae,* published in fourteen volumes beginning in 1590, was the first picture book of the New World. With the Renaissance of European science and learning running at full speed, accompanied by the development of highly efficient printing and engraving techniques, De Bry seized the opportunity to make widely accessible material that had until then been largely restricted to a small segment of the population.

Here once again we must examine the question of who De Bry was and what his sources and his intentions were. His aim, by and large, was not complicated. The successful engraver and publisher was one of a new breed of businessmen who saw the profit to be made from fueling and feeding the curiosity of the European public. His motto, *nul sans souci,* or "nothing without effort," tells part of the story; De Bry spared no expense and no effort to acquire the best materials and to spend "diligent pains in engraving the pictures on copper plates, to render them clearer" (De Bry 1976).

Figure 6.2. De Bry's illustration of an indigenous leader from Parin preparing for a ceremony.

De Bry selected his sources very carefully. The French Huguenot Jacques le Moyne de Morgues, who was attached as an artist to the disastrous French settlement in Florida, produced a series of exquisite watercolors in the 1560s, most of which unfortunately no longer exist. John White, one of the pioneer settlers in Virginia in 1585, produced a comprehensive set of paintings of birds, insects, fishes, and Indians—the latter being treated like the animals as a kind of exotic wildlife. De Bry's third source was the sensational story of Hans Staden, who spent nine months in the 1550s as a prisoner of the Tupinamba, cannibal Indians of Brazil. His account was illustrated with crude woodcuts that aroused the prurient curiosity of the European public, and these images became the standard iconography of all American Indians without anyone's seriously questioning their relevance to the Amerindian lifestyle of the West Indies.

Not only in the De Bry book but in many lesser volumes depictions of Caribbean native peoples were often the end product of an artist's interpretation of a little-known reality, which in turn was reinterpreted by the engraver's hand. To some of the artists, trained in the European studio tradition, representing the figures and shapes of the Amerindians seem to have presented considerable difficulty. The French artist Jean de Lery, for example, confessed to having problems with the anatomy of the Brazilian

Indian because, he complained, "Although I diligently perused and marked those barbarian people, for a whole year together, wherein I lived amongst them, so as I might conceive in my mind a certain proportion of them, yet I say, by reason of their diverse gestures and behaviors, utterly different from ours, it is a very difficult matter to express their true proportion."

The engravers added further interpretations, some of them the result simply of the formulaic views that they already had in stock. The prints that accompanied the Basel letter, for example, were among the first European representations of the indigenous Amerindians and their historic encounter with Columbus. Yet while they purported to represent a true image of this meeting, in fact they were little different from the norms of the period and could have represented any landscape, ship, or non-European peoples. In fact they may have been produced from existing woodcuts in the printer's shop, with little direct relevance to Columbus's experience apart from the nakedness of the unknown tribe (figure 6.3).

Figure 6.3. An early stylized illustration reflecting European artistic conventions and little about the indigenous people of the Americas.

As a result, European public imagery of Amerindians was imbued twice over with European attitudes and expectations of the New World. We the viewers finally bring a third perspective into play as a result of our Westernized education and upbringing. It may well take another five hundred years to erase and reformulate our own ideology and create a more accurate iconography of the Amerindian.

THE TEMPEST

In 1611 Shakespeare's last complete play, *The Tempest,* was performed before the Court at Whitehall. Despite its ostensible setting in the Mediterranean, *The Tempest* actually demonstrates on the theatrical stage the struggle for power that had been going on for more than a century on the real stage of the Caribbean. In this provocative, disturbing picture of a "brave new world" Caliban (an anagram of "canibal"), deprived of his territory, is presented as the incubus of Sycorax, a "foul witch," while Prospero deprived of his dukedom becomes the island's sole "human" inhabitant. Thus is established the balance of power enacted on a global scale. Prospero as a human equals civilization and thus automatically earns the right to take control from the disproportioned, misshapen, "inhuman" orphan Caliban.

In a poetic sense the play recapitulates the tragic history of the previous century. At first the exiled Prospero, being of superior mentality and spirit, is indulgent to the inferior Caliban. Prospero boasts that

> I have used thee,
> Filth as thou art, with human care, and lodged thee
> In mine own cell. . . .

Indeed Caliban confirms this:

> When thou camest first,
> Thou strokedst me and madest much of me, wouldst give me
> Water with berries in't, and teach me how
> To name the bigger light, and how the less,
> That burn by day and night: and then I loved thee
> And show'd thee all the qualities o' the isle,
> The fresh springs, brine-pits, barren place and fertile. . . .

We see here a reflection of that all-too-brief period of the first encounter, when Columbus and the natives exchanged "free" gifts. Prospero's daughter, Miranda, also gives a gift to the non-European, noncivilized being in teaching him how to speak English:

I pitied thee,
Took pains to make thee speak, taught thee each hour
One thing or another: when thou didst not, savage,
Know thine own meaning, but wouldst gabble like
A thing most brutish, I endow'd thy purposes
With words that made them known.

But when the period of wonder and harmony ends, the native Caliban is enslaved much like Columbus's Arawaks, as Prospero banishes him to a hard rock. Miranda, utilizing a conveniently self-serving form of memory, recalls that it was Caliban's foul nature that led to his punishment:

thy vile race,
Though thou didst learn, had that in't which good natures
Could not abide to be with; therefore wast thou
Deservedly confined into this rock,
Who hadst deserved more than a prison.

Caliban, thus stripped of his possessions and his freedom, not surprisingly is bitter about his contact with civilization:

You taught me language; and my profit on't
Is, I know how to curse. The red plague rid you
For learning me your language!

We understand that this is not merely the language of words but the language of civilization, which has been transformed into the language of oppression and hate. For the European, for Prospero, this transformation is reflected in the transmutation of slave Caliban into

A devil, a born devil, on whose nature
Nurture can never stick; on whom my pains,
Humanely taken, all, all lost, quite lost;
And as with age his body uglier grows,
So his mind cankers.

This is an English text of the seventeenth century, but the sentiments recall the attitude of Columbus's contemporaries who felt that the Amerindians were "devilishly" inhuman.

Thus, from the Hispaniola beach to the London stage, the uneven relationship between the "civilized" and the "savage" remained a dominant theme of European discourse; it was a principal lens through which the expanding West viewed aborigines. And the discourse repeated itself again and again: Prospero and Caliban, John Smith and Pocahontas, Robinson Crusoe and Friday, Inkle and Yarico. Each of these is simply a different version of the "instinctive," primordial New World versus "rational" Europe. All of these stories must be situated within the colonial paradigm whose broad outlines were established in 1492, when Columbus first envisioned the Indians as separate and unequal.

Part 3: The First Migration of Village Farmers, 500 B.C. to A.D. 800

There have been several major migrations of people into the Caribbean, from the first colonization almost six thousand years ago to the one undertaken by Europeans and Africans beginning five hundred years ago. In his book *The Taínos* (1992), Irving Rouse calls all of these migrations but the first "repeoplings." Part 3 of the present volume deals with one of the most dramatic of these human movements, one that played the most important role in shaping the indigenous cultures of the Caribbean.

The people who moved into the Caribbean in the last centuries B.C. have come to be called Saladoid, after an archaeological site in Venezuela at which their characteristic pottery was found. The Saladoid migration has been the focus of a great deal of attention by archaeologists over the last thirty years. Several basic questions have been addressed. When did they move into the islands? Where did they come from? Was there only one migration or several? Did they move gradually up the chain of the Lesser Antilles, or did they move rapidly? Archaeologists do not have all of the answers to these questions, and often they have several answers to each of them. But as the following essays show, a clearer picture of the Saladoid colonization is emerging.

Jay Haviser, whose essay addresses questions of the timing and nature of the migration, illustrates his discussion with a table of radiocarbon dates for early Saladoid sites; this gives a good example of the "raw data" that archaeologists use to figure out what sites were occupied when. Elizabeth Righter's essay gives a good illustration of what kinds of archaeological remains the Saladoid people left behind. David Watters shows that the sea did not isolate the Saladoid people from one another but rather linked them to other islands and the South American mainland. The essays by Miguel Rodríguez and Henry Petitjean Roget point to deeper understandings of the religion, ideology, and worldview of the Saladoid people.

As is discussed in the introduction, in this volume we have placed considerable emphasis on the Saladoid people and their descendants, the Island Caribs and the Taino. In looking at the archaeology and ethnohistory of the Saladoid and later Caribbean peoples, however, it is important to recognize the importance of the aceramic (nonceramics using) people who lived in the Caribbean for thousands of years before the arrival of the Saladoid people. Their presence influenced where the Saladoid migrants colonized, perhaps limiting their expansion to the eastern tip of the Dominican Republic. The way they lived and utilized the seas surrounding the islands probably provided a model for the development of the Saladoid economy. Most importantly, it appears quite likely that the aceramic people of the Greater Antilles interacted with the descendants of the Saladoid people and that from this interaction emerged the Taino people. In other words, the Taino were descended from both the Saladoid people and the Archaic populations of the Greater Antilles (Wilson 1996). Clearly the Taino were different from lowland South American groups to which they were distantly related, and some of these differences can be attributed to the Tainos' legacy from their Archaic forebears.

7

Settlement Strategies in the Early Ceramic Age

Jay B. Haviser

Most archaeologists agree that the first horticultural peoples to move into the Caribbean came from the northeastern coasts of Venezuela and the Guianas, primarily from the interior Orinoco River region, and that they migrated downstream to the seacoast and then out into the Antilles (Rouse 1986). In the fourth or fifth century B.C. these people began to move into the Lesser Antilles. The ceramic decoration that represents these earliest immigrants is called Saladoid by some, Huecoid by others, and Early Ceramic by others (for a general discussion, see Siegel 1989).

Recent studies of the earliest ceramics in the Antilles have begun to identify different distinctive styles, and there are now three basic views to explain these differences. One group of archaeologists suggests that zoned-incised cross-hatching is separate from white-on-red painting in the early ceramics and represents a pre-Saladoid or parallel Saladoid migration of different peoples from north-central Venezuela (Chanlatte 1986). They call this group Huecoid (from studies at the La Hueca/Sorce site, Vieques,) or Guapoid (from the Rio Guapo site, Venezuela).

A second proposal is that the early nonpainting styles, particularly zoned-punctation, represent a very ancient horticultural group probably from the Guianas, who had older origins than the Saladoid and were at a stage of development transitional between the Archaic and Ceramic levels. This culture group has been called the Early Ceramic (see Haviser 1991).

The third view is that the difference in styles of the early Saladoid simply reflects plurality within the Saladoid culture group itself, possibly different family lineages or subgroups. In accordance with this theory, the Saladoid has been divided into the Huecan-Saladoid, more associated with zoned-incised-crosshatching, and the Cedrosan-Saladoid, more associated with white-on-red painting decoration (Rouse 1989).

Despite these differing approaches to taxonomy, however, archaeologists are in general agreement about recognizing a shift in styles from the early to the later periods of the Saladoid era. They are also in general agreement about how to date finds, because few dispute the validity of the radiometric dating technique for excavated remains anywhere in the region. Where radiometric dates are not available, archaeologists typically rely on artifact comparisons to establish relative dating. Table 7.1 lists uncalibrated radiometric dates associated with the early Ceramic Age (ca. 500 B.C. to A.D. 500), from Trinidad to eastern Puerto Rico. For this study, sites of the period ca. 500 B.C. to A.D. 500 will be arbitrarily separated into two groups. The first group (to be called here "early period") will consist of sites identified to ca. 500–0 B.C. The second group (to be called here "late period") will consist of sites identified to ca. A.D. 0–500. Table 7.2 lists the sites used in this study and their time periods.

Table 7.1. Uncalibrated radiometric dates from early Ceramic Age sites

Island	Sample no.	Site	Years B.P.[a]	Median Date
Trinidad	IVIC-642	Cedros	2140±70	190 B.C.
Trinidad	IVIC-638	Palo Seco	2130±80	180 B.C.
Trinidad	IVIC-641	Palo Seco	2060±80	110 B.C.
Trinidad	IVIC-640	Palo Seco	1995±70	49 B.C.
Trinidad	IVIC-643	Cedros	1850±80	A.D. 100
Trinidad	Beta-4902	Atagual	1805±90	A.D. 145[b]
Trinidad	IVIC-639	Palo Seco	1480±70	A.D. 470
Grenada	U. Georgia	Pearls	1914±51	A.D. 36
Grenada	U. Georgia	Pearls	1725±54	A.D. 225
Grenada	U. Georgia	Pearls	1711±74	A.D. 238
Grenadines	RL-70	Chatham Bay	1470±100	A.D. 480
St. Vincent	RL-28	Kingston PO	1790±100	A.D. 160
St. Vincent	RL-73	Buccament West	1670±160	A.D. 285[b]
St. Vincent	RL-75	Arnos Vale	1540±110	A.D. 410[b]
Barbados	I-2486	Chancery Lane	1570±95	A.D. 380

Table 7.1 (continued)

Island	Sample no.	Site	Years B.P.[a]	Median Date
St.Lucia	Y-1115	Grande Anse	1460±80	A.D. 490
Martinique	Nancy	Fond Brulé	2480±140	530 B.C.
Martinique	Nancy	Fond Brulé	2215±115	265 B.C.
Martinique	Ly-2197	Fond Brulé	2100±210	150 B.C.
Martinique	BDX-156	Fond Brulé	2010±300	60 B.C.
Martinique	BDX-161	Fond Brulé	1865±300	A.D. 85
Martinique	Y-1116	La Salle	1770±100	A.D. 180
Martinique	RL-156	Vivé	1730±110	A.D. 220
Martinique	S-85	Vivé	1655+150	A.D. 295
Martinique	Ny-478	Fond Brulé	1650±260	A.D. 300
Martinique	Ly-2196	Fond Brulé	1630±210	A.D. 320
Martinique	Uga-113	Vivé	1530±75	A.D. 420
Martinique	Y-1762	Diamant	1490±60	A.D. 460
Marie Galante	Ny-500	Taliseronde	1515±85	A.D. 435
Guadeloupe	GrN-20166	Morel	1910±30	A.D. 50
Guadeloupe	Y-1137	Morel	1730±70	A.D. 220
Guadeloupe	Y-1138	Morel	1710±100	A.D. 240
Guadeloupe	GrN-20165	Morel	1720±35	A.D. 240
Guadeloupe	GrN-20163	Morel	1635±30	A.D. 325
Guadeloupe	Y-2245	Morel	1400±80	A.D. 550
Guadeloupe	Y-1136	Morel	1380±100	A.D. 570
Montserrat	Beta-44828	Trant's	2430±80	480 B.C.
Montserrat	Beta-41682	Trant's	2390±90	440 B.C.
Montserrat	Beta-18491	Radio Antilles	2390±60	440 B.C.
Montserrat	Beta-18490	Radio Antilles	2210±70	260 B.C.
Montserrat	Beta-18489	Trant's	2140±80	190 B.C.
Montserrat	Beta-18581	Radio Antilles	2120±60	170 B.C.
Montserrat	Beta-41680	Trant's	1960±90	10 B.C.
Montserrat	Beta-41678	Trant's	1890±70	A.D. 60
Montserrat	Beta-41679	Trant's	1750±80	A.D. 200
Montserrat	Beta-41681	Trant's	1740±90	A.D. 210
Montserrat	Beta-18582	Trant's	1620±90	A.D. 330

Table 7.1 (continued)

Island	Sample no.	Site	Years B.P.[a]	Median Date
Antigua	I-7980	Indian Creek	1915±80	A.D. 35
Antigua	I-7981	Indian Creek	1855±80	A.D. 95
Antigua	I-7979	Indian Creek	1790±85	A.D. 160
Antigua	I-7855	Indian Creek	1765±80	A.D. 185
Antigua	I-7838	Indian Creek	1750±80	A.D. 200
Antigua	I-7837	Indian Creek	1715±80	A.D. 235
Antigua	I-7854	Indian Creek	1670±80	A.D. 280
Antigua	I-7355	Indian Creek	1505±85	A.D. 445
Antigua	I-7356	Mill Reef	1505±85	A.D. 445
Antigua	I-7352	Indian Creek	1440±85	A.D. 510
St. Eustatius	GrN-11512	Golden Rock	1755±20	A.D. 248[b]
St. Eustatius	GrN-11513	Golden Rock	1635±20	A.D. 352[b]
St. Eustatius	GrN-11510	Golden Rock	1545±35	A.D. 388[b]
St. Eustatius	GrN-11509	Golden Rock	1415±30	A.D. 520[b]
St. Eustatius	GrN-11514	Golden Rock	1350±60	A.D. 570[b]
St. Eustatius	GrN-17074	Golden Rock	1325±30	A.D. 610[b]
Saba	GrN-18558	Spring Bay	1640±35	A.D. 352[b]
Saba	GrN-16026	Spring Bay	1560±60	A.D. 386[b]
Saba	GrN-16030	The Bottom	1490±60	A.D. 460[b]
St. Martin	PITT-0450	Hope Estate	2510±40	560 B.C.
St. Martin	PITT-0449	Hope Estate	2300±55	350 B.C.
St. Martin	PITT-0219	Hope Estate	2275±60	325 B.C.
St. Martin	PITT-0220	Hope Estate	2250±45	300 B.C.
St. Martin	PITT-0446	Hope Estate	2225±40	275 B.C.
St. Martin	PITT-0448	Hope Estate	2050±45	100 B.C.
St. Martin	PITT-0451	Hope Estate	1515±35	A.D. 435
St. Martin	PITT-0445	Hope Estate	1490±35	A.D. 460
St. Martin	GrN-20168	Hope Estate	1530±35	A.D. 430[b]
St. Martin	GrN-20169	Hope Estate	1520±35	A.D. 440[b]
St. Thomas	Gx-12845	Main Street	1770±235	A.D. 180
St. Thomas	Beta-50066	Tutu	1610±70	A.D. 340
Culebra	Beta-52607	Lower Camp	1410±70	A.D. 505[b]

Table 7.1 (continued)

Island	Sample no.	Site	Years B.P.[a]	Median Date
Vieques	I-13425	Sorcé	2110±80	160 B.C.
Vieques	I-11319	Sorcé	1915±80	35 B.C.
Vieques	I-11322	Sorcé	1945±80	A.D. 5
Vieques	I-13428	Sorcé	1930±80	A.D. 20
Vieques	I-12859	Sorcé	1880±80	A.D. 70
Vieques	I-11321	Sorcé	1845±80	A.D. 105
Vieques	I-11685	Sorcé	1740±75	A.D. 210
Vieques	I-11687	Sorcé	1565±75	A.D. 385
Puerto Rico	I-13856	Tecla	2380±80	430 B.C.
Puerto Rico	I-14979	Pta. Candelero	2120±80	170 B.C.
Puerto Rico	I-11296	Convento	2100±80	160 B.C.
Puerto Rico	Beta-14380	Maisabel	2060±60	110 B.C.
Puerto Rico	I-13867	Tecla	2050±80	100 B.C.
Puerto Rico	I-14978	Pta. Candelero	2020±80	70 B.C.
Puerto Rico	I-13921	Tecla	2020±80	70 B.C.
Puerto Rico	I-11297	Convento	1995±80	45 B.C.
Puerto Rico	Beta-14381	Maisabel	1960±90	10 B.C.
Puerto Rico	I-13820	Tecla	1950±80	0 B.C.
Puerto Rico	I-13929	Tecla	1920±80	A.D. 30
Puerto Rico	I-13866	Tecla	1900±80	A.D. 50
Puerto Rico	I-11266	Convento	1865±80	A.D. 85
Puerto Rico	I-13868	Tecla	1850±80	A.D. 100
Puerto Rico	Beta-9972	Hacienda Grande	1840±50	A.D. 110
Puerto Rico	Y-1233	Hacienda Grande	1830±80	A.D. 120
Puerto Rico	Beta14997	Maisabel	1810±70	A.D. 140
Puerto Rico	I-1091	Tecla	1780±85	A.D. 170
Puerto Rico	I-10916	Tecla	1720±80	A.D. 230
Puerto Rico	I-10921	Tecla	1705±85	A.D. 245
Puerto Rico	Beta-14992	Maisabel	1660±100	A.D. 290
Puerto Rico	Y-1232	Hacienda Grande	1580±80	A.D. 370
Puerto Rico	Beta-14994	Maisabel	1520±50	A.D. 430

[a]Uncorrected C-14 determinations.

[b]Originally published as calibrated dates, presented here as medians of C-14 determinations.

Table 7.2. Early Ceramic Age dates in the Lesser Antilles

	Radiometric dates	Artifact comparisons
Early period	Cedros, Trinidad	Pearls, Grenada
	Palo Seco, Trinidad	Black Point Grenada
	Fond Brulé, Martinique	Morel, Guadeloupe
	Trant's, Montserrat	Vielle Case, Dominica
	Radio Antilles, Montserrat	Indian Creek, Antigua
	Hope Estate, St. Martin	Cayon, St. Kitts
	Sorcé, Vieques	Sugar Factory, St. Kitts
	Tecla, Puerto Rico	Friars Bay, St. Martin
	Pta. Candelero, Puerto Rico	Prosperity, St. Croix
	Convento, Puerto Rico	St. Georges, St. Croix
	Maisabel, Puerto Rico	
Late period	Atagual, Trinidad	Vielle Case, Dominica
	Pearls, Grenada	Sugar Factory, St. Kitts
	Chatham Bay, Union Is.	Hichman's, Nevis
	Kingston PO, St. Vincent	Godet, St. Eustatius
	Buccament W, St. Vincent	Sufferers, Barbuda
	Arnos Vale, St. Vincent	Rondevous, Anguilla
	Chancery Lane, Barbados	Coral Bay, St. John
	Grand Anse, St. Lucia	Prosperity, St. Croix
	La Salle, Martinique	Salt River, St. Croix
	Vivé, Martinique	Longford, St. Croix
	Diamant, Martinique	Richmond, St. Croix
	Taliseronde, M. Galante	Monserrat, Puerto Rico
	Morel, Guadeloupe	Friars Bay, St. Martin
	Mill Reef, Antigua	
	Indian Creek, Antigua	
	Golden Rock, St. Eustatius	
	Spring Bay, Saba	
	Hope Estate, St. Martin	
	Main Street, St. Thomas	
	Tutu, St. Thomas	
	Lower Camp, Culebra Is.	
	Hacienda Grande, Puerto Rico	

SETTLEMENT STRATEGY THEORIES

Settlement distribution-pattern studies are always hampered by the limitations and variation of available data about sites, and the Caribbean is no exception in this regard. For this study, a comprehensive database was compiled from a wide range of publications that identify early Ceramic Age sites in the Lesser Antilles. Figures 7.1 and 7.2 present this database of sites

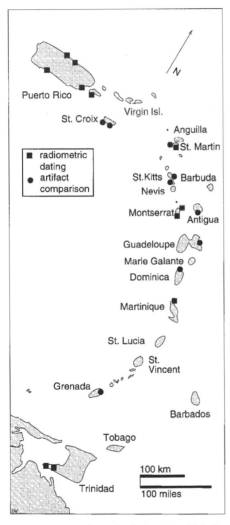

Figure 7.1. Early-period sites (ca. 500–0 B.C.) in the Lesser Antilles. Sites with squares are by radiometric dates; those with circles by artifact comparisons.

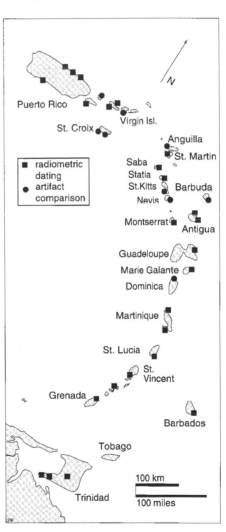

Figure 7.2. Late-period sites (ca. A.D. 0–500) in the Lesser Antilles. Sites with squares are by radiometric dates; those with circles by artifact comparisons.

(listed in table 7.2) as they are distributed in the Lesser Antilles for the early period (figure 7.1) and for the late period (figure 7.2).

Before an interpretation of the data analyzed in this study, it is important to present an overview of the various perspectives in current archaeology regarding early Ceramic Age settlement patterns in the region. On the most basic level of settlement analysis, the individual site, few intensive studies have been done in the Lesser Antilles. This fact has, of course, resulted in minimal theoretical debate about intrasite settlement patterns. The most outstanding intrasite settlement pattern work done to date has been at the Golden Rock site, St. Eustatius. Although this site dates to the late period (ca. A.D. 300–700), two different forms of intrasite patterning were noted. The earliest settlement consisted of various small, circular, pole-construction huts, with adjoining wind screens, scattered over the site area. The later settlement consisted of very large, circular houses (*malocas*), centrally located within the site. Until other sites in the Antilles are excavated in similar large-scale, detailed techniques, the Golden Rock site will serve as the model for early Ceramic Age intrasite settlement patterns (Versteeg and Schinkel 1992).

On a second level of settlement analysis, the individual islands, considerably more work has been done, although the database is still quite limited. Various archaeologists during the last decades have alluded to intra-island settlement patterns. However, all have been constrained by small databases— a circumstance allowing them to produce only site lists and map locations, with limited interpretation of patterning. Nonetheless, in recent years there has been a growing number of more focused, intensive, intra-island settlement-pattern studies done in the region. From these, most archaeologists have concluded that early Ceramic Age sites tend to be most often associated with fertile soils and abundant, often flowing, fresh-water sources. Another settlement characteristic, which has drawn a bit more debate, is the association of these early sites with inland, coastal plain, or coastal strand locations. I return to this issue later in this chapter.

As an extension of the intra-island view of settlement patterns, archaeologists have also conducted inter-island cluster comparisons based on intra-island data. From these studies have evolved two basic perspectives of inter-island regional settlement patterns. According to what might be called the "conservative" perspective, these early pioneers maintained the mainland preference for inland settlement, making riverine adaptations and terrestrial subsistence the core of early Ceramic Age Caribbean settlement. According to the "opportunistic" perspective, on the other hand, the colonizers were highly flexible in their adaptations to the islands, giving the region no single distinctive settlement pattern.

COMPILED DATABASE

Of the forty-eight sites used in this study, island specific analyses were conducted on the cardinal position of the sites on the islands, the geomorphological position of sites on the islands, and the distribution of various sites by period and regional location. (As a general reference, see table 7.1 and figures 7.1 and 7.2.)

In the study of site cardinal position, the islands of Puerto Rico and Trinidad were omitted due to their large size. For all the other islands, 50 percent (seven) of the early-period sites are located in the northeast quadrant of the island, with 35 percent (five) located in the southwest quadrant, 15 percent (two) situated to the southeast, and no sites noted in the northwest quadrant. For the late period, it was noted that one site was found in the northwest quadrant, and only 18 percent (six) of these sites were to the northeast of the islands. The southern half of the islands was clearly the focus for these late-period sites, with 32 percent (ten) to the southwest and 47 percent (fourteen) to the southeast.

It was further noted that the three islands in this analysis with the oldest radiometric dates (St. Martin, Martinique, and Montserrat) all have their earliest sites to the northeast quadrant of the islands. Along with the 50 percent focus on the northeast for the entire early period, this suggests a preference for the northeast position by the earliest settlers, although the reasons for this preference are as yet unknown. Possible roles in establishing such a preference might have been played by wind and water currents, solar or stellar orientation, and the northward trajectory of these early migrations. In the late period, we see a clear cardinal position shift toward the southern half, and specifically the southeastern quadrant, of the islands. But the reasons for this preference too are unknown.

In order to construct an overview of the geomorphological position of site locations in the early Ceramic Age, the entire site list (table 7.2) was separated into early- and late-period sites situated at inland, coastal plain, and coastal strand settings on their respective islands.

The results of this analysis indicated that for the early period, 41 percent of the sites are located on the coastal strand, 45 percent on the coastal plain, and 14 percent at inland settings. For the late period, 52 percent of the sites are on the coastal strand, 45 percent on the coastal plain, and only 3 percent at an inland setting.

From this information we can see that the setting of both the early-period and the late-period sites is very strongly associated with the coastal areas. There were only five sites with true inland positions, three in the early period (Hope Estate, St. Georges, and Cayon) and two from the late period (Tutu and Atagual). However, it is of some interest to note that the distribution of islands with inland sites (except Trinidad) is very localized to the northeast Caribbean (see figure 7.3). Furthermore, two of the three islands with inland early-period sites also have associated early-period coastal sites. This may suggest some specific functional use of these inland sites during the early period of colonization. Whether these specialized functions, if they existed, represent the separation of groups within the community (such as social groups, shamans, or women) or a location oriented toward variable natural resources is as yet unknown.

The focus of this settlement pattern, specifically in the smaller islands of the northern Lesser Antilles, could possibly suggest that some form of inter-island sociocultural system was in effect during the early period. However, it should be kept in mind that perhaps inland early-period sites have simply not yet been discovered in the wider region. These site patterns do suggest flexible adaptations to the different insular environments. On the other hand, the preference in the coastal plain and coastal strand for flowing-water sites suggests a retention of mainland settlement patterns. An argument could thus be made for both the "opportunistic" and the "conservative" views of settlement strategies.

Summary

To summarize the settlement strategies of the early Ceramic Age peoples in the Lesser Antilles, we can suggest that these early colonizers spread rapidly across the Antillean archipelago in the fourth and fifth centuries B.C. Based on data currently available, it seems that the earliest settlers focused more on the northern Lesser Antilles and eastern Puerto Rico. When they colonized the Lesser Antillean islands, it seems the most frequent focus was on the northeast coast of the individual islands, at locations on the coastal plain or strand, where fresh water and good horticultural soils were available. Perhaps there were either social or economic reasons that led them, early on, to establish dual inland/coastal site patterns on some of the smaller northern islands.

By the first centuries A.D., widespread colonization had begun on almost every island in the Lesser Antilles, with a focus on the southern coast of individual islands. Site locations continued to reflect the importance of fresh water and good soils, although with a greater emphasis on coastal resources.

Individual residence sites most likely passed through a transition from gatherings of scattered small hugs with windscreens, to the construction of large, centralized, multi-family *mallocas*.

There also developed, at island clusters and over the region, inter-island interaction spheres of cultural, political, and economic exchange such that, by the close of the Saladoid period in the Lesser Antilles, the entire archipelago had been explored and was being utilized. These events primed the Caribbean for the next major regional effect on settlement patterns—population explosion, a hallmark of the post-Saladoid period.

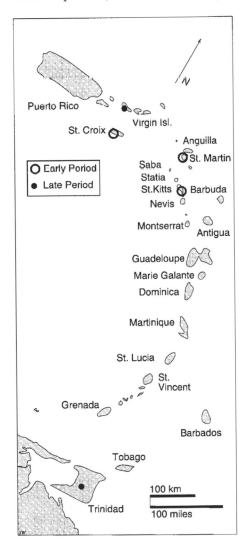

Figure 7.3. Distribution of early- and late-period sites with dual inland/coastal locations. Sites with open circles are early period; those with closed circles are late period.

8

The Ceramics, Art, and Material Culture of the Early Ceramic Period in the Caribbean Islands

Elizabeth Righter

As others in this volume have discussed, our understanding of the early Ceramic-period cultures in the Caribbean Islands is incomplete. However, based upon findings from archaeological investigations in Puerto Rico, Vieques, St. Thomas, St. Eustatius, and other Caribbean islands, a brief overview of the material culture of these groups is presented here. Both organic and inorganic cultural remains allow archaeologists to make inferences about aspects of these peoples' lives.

MATERIAL CULTURE AS AN ARCHAEOLOGICAL RESOURCE

When human beings occupy an area for even a short period of time, they tend to leave behind objects of material culture as reminders of their presence. As archaeologists use the term, "material culture" refers to a wide range of objects that relate to all aspects of human social, economic, spiritual, ceremonial, and personal life. Material remains may be as tiny as a bone needle or as large and impressive as a temple mound. Such objects provide important clues to the archaeologist regarding the cultural patterns of prehistoric peoples, and in cases where we do not have eyewitness accounts of these patterns, our understanding of their cultures must be based largely on our analysis of the residue, both organic and inorganic, that they leave behind. We must rely particularly on two sources: direct information obtained from archaeological excavation, and inference based on ethnographic and ethnohistorical accounts of living cultural groups descended from, related to, or apparently similar to the groups we are studying archaeologically.

For the most part, our knowledge of material culture is obtained from items that do not decay or decay very slowly, such as ceramics, lithics, objects of shell, coral and bone, and remains such as house posts, hearths, pits and burials. For this reason I like to borrow an analogy from biology and think of material culture as the "hard parts" of culture. These hard, durable parts provide a framework from which we may deduce a culture's soft parts, or flesh.

In some areas, climate hastens the rate of material culture decay, and it may virtually destroy all the residue that is composed of organic material—the remains of clothing, for example, or of wooden tools. This is generally the case in the Caribbean. Findings that have existed in dry caves and in other unique conditions of preservation have made archaeologists aware that, in most Caribbean sites, a large part of the material culture inventory has perished. As a result, the items that have survived—the durable, nonorganic items—become all the more important to archaeological analysis. Ceramic remains in particular attract much attention among Caribbean archaeologists and often are used to provide the preponderance of evidence to identify cultural groups.

In addition, many aspects of nonmaterial culture, such as spiritual beliefs, may be inferred from the material items themselves or, in some cases, from the craftsmanship of certain objects or their designs and decorative motifs. Often nonmaterial aspects of a culture are revealed in burial practices and in intangibles such as the alignment or configuration of architectural features such as house posts and rows of standing rocks. In order to identify those objects of material culture that were organic in nature and have not survived, archaeologists may infer their presence from the analysis of subsistence remains or from other clues. For example, the restricted size of atlases of reef fish recovered from the Krum Bay site in St. Thomas led Reitz (1982, 7) to infer the use of fish traps by the occupants of that site.

THE EARLY CERAMIC PERIOD: AN OVERVIEW

In his *The Tainos: Rise and Decline of the People Who Greeted Columbus* (1992), Irving Rouse notes that unlike the Archaic people who preceded them, the cultural groups who "repeopled" the Caribbean Islands during the early Ceramic period produced pottery, hunted and gathered land and marine food resources, and planted and grew manioc and, perhaps, other crops. Rouse traces the origins of these early Ceramic-period people to groups that inhabited the Orinoco River Valley of Venezuela as early as

2140 B.C. Sometime before 500 B.C., he suggests, the people who produced Cedrosan Saladoid ceramics (a subseries of Saladoid series pottery named after the type site of Saladero in the Orinoco River Valley) began moving into the Caribbean Islands.

Ceramics of the Cedrosan Saladoid subseries, and accompanying material culture, have a wide distribution in the Caribbean. They extend along the northern coast of South America from the Wonotobo Valley in Suriname to Margarita Island in eastern Venezuela, and between Trinidad and the eastern tip of Hispaniola in the Caribbean Islands. In the Caribbean Islands, the earliest cultural deposits containing Cedrosan Saladoid ceramics have been radiocarbon dated to 530 B.C. in Martinique, 440 and 260 B.C. at the Trants site in Montserrat, 325 and 300 B.C. at the Hope Estate site on St. Martin, and 430 B.C. at the Hacienda Grande site in Puerto Rico (Rouse 1992, 79). The earliest calibrated (2 sigma) date for levels containing Cedrosan Saladoid ceramics at the Tutu site in St. Thomas is A.D. 65–420.

Within the area of distribution of Cedrosan Saladoid ceramics, there are also assemblages in Trinidad, Tobago, and St. Vincent containing ceramic trade wares of the Barrancoid series, a ceramic series that developed about 1000 B.C. in the lower-middle part of the Orinoco River valley and is represented later in the Ceramic period in the Caribbean. Other early ceramics are those related to the Huecan Saladoid subseries, found in Vieques, Puerto Rico, Trinidad, Guadeloupe, Montserrat, and St. Croix.

Included in the rich material culture found at Cedrosan Saladoid sites are ceramic and other objects of unusual artistic beauty and craftsman-

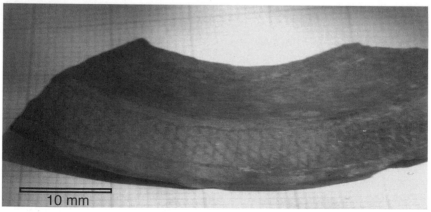

Figure 8.1. Zone-incised crosshatched sherd from the Main Street site, St. Thomas.

Figure 8.2. Inverted bell-shaped, red-painted bowl from a grave at the Tutu Archaeological Village site, St. Thomas.

ship. Of these, the most commonly observed ceramic art styles are a white-on-red painted ware and a zoned-incised crosshatched, or ZIC, ware (figure 8.1), each with its own distinctive material, technology, shape, and decoration. Painted ware, which has received the most attention in Cedrosan Saladoid sites, is characterized by bell-shaped bowls constructed of a fine light-colored paste with plain or flanged rims (figure 8.2), to which D-shaped strap handles were often attached. Among painted wares are those with polychrome designs that may include black or orange paint. In some cases, parts of the vessel surfaces are left unpainted, creating an additional color contrast. Also on some painted wares is found a distinctive kind of incision in which continuous curved and straight lines are used either to outline painted areas or to form purely incised designs. On a variant ware developed in Puerto Rico, curvilinear lines are incised through a red slip and filled with white paint. Other motifs are modeled and incised on flanges, on tabs projecting from rims or flanges and on lugs, where they portray animal or human heads. Undecorated vessels often are finely crafted in sophisticated shapes.

Based on investigations at the Sorce site in Vieques and the Punta Candelero site in Puerto Rico, Rouse (1992, 86) has postulated another subseries, known as the Huecan Saladoid. This subseries also has been identified at the Rio Guapo site on the north-central coast of Venezuela, the Cedros site on Trinidad, Morel I in Guadeloupe, and Prosperity on St. Croix (Rodríquez and Rivera 1991, 46). Among features considered to be distinctive of Huecan Saladoid sites are ZIC decorated ceramic wares, the absence of painted wares, and the presence of bird-head pendants, carved from exotic stone. These pendants have been found at Sorce in Vieques, Prosperity in St. Croix, and Punta Candelero in Puerto Rico. According to Rouse (1992, 87), the Huecan settlement and subsistence patterns are similar to those documented at Cedrosan Saladoid sites, and although painted wares are absent at Huecan sites, there are indications of Cedrosan Saladoid stylistic motifs in Huecan ZIC designs. Rouse also notes that many similar artifacts, including snuffing vessels, three-pointed objects, and simple carved stone pendants are present in both Huecan and Cedrosan Saladoid assemblages. Rodríguez and Rivera, however, observe differences in technology and food procurement strategies between the two Saladoid manifestations.

The relationship of early levels of the Hope Estate site to other early Cedrosan Saladoid components is not yet clear.

Associated with Cedrosan Saladoid ceramic wares are a wide variety of other material objects with functional, ornamental, and spiritual purposes. Among these are stone and shell celts, shell scrapers, stone axes and adzes, grinding stones, stone *metates,* smoothers of *Acropera cervicornis,* and various coral items, including polishing and rubbing tools, *metates,* grinders, and drills (Versteeg and Schinkel 1992, 123–24).

Ornamental objects crafted from bone, stone, and shell include pendants of shell and perforated teeth, both human and animal, such as a drilled tooth of a now-extinct monk seal recovered from the Tutu site in St. Thomas. The presence of drills at the Tutu site can be inferred from the fact that undrilled shell-bead preforms and finished drilled shell beads were found together at the site. Small drilled rectangular shell pieces, commonly found in early Ceramic-period sites (figure 8.3), were probably attached to cloth belts, while beads of shell and stone were made into necklaces. Beads were crafted from a wide variety of semiprecious and other stones including amethyst, quartz, calcite, turquoise, and nephrite. Amulets of semiprecious stone were recovered from the Prosperity site in St. Croix and from Punta Candelero in Puerto Rico.

Chroniclers recorded many aspects of the culture of the Taino Indians who met Columbus, and these ethnographic accounts can often be used in conjunction with archaeological evidence to provide a conjectural "flesh-

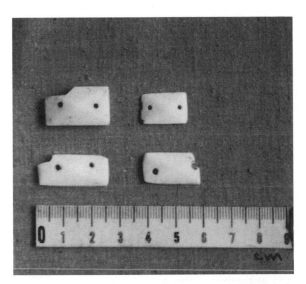

Figure 8.3. Smoothed and drilled rectangular shell ornaments from the Tutu Archaeological Village site, St. Thomas.

ing out" of the prehistoric culture. According to these accounts, the Taino caught fish in nets, stupefied fish with poison, and trapped both fish and turtles, storing them in wooden weirs until they were needed for food. Calabashes were used to carry water, and tobacco was smoked in the form of cigars. Cotton hammocks and baskets were in common use. Although little evidence of these perishable organic items survives in archaeological sites, the study of charred plant remains may indicate their presence in the cultural inventory. Cassava was grated and squeezed through a basketry tube to produce flour from which cassava bread was made and baked. The presence of griddles for baking cassava bread suggests that the technique of removing the poison from bitter manioc was known and that the basketry "matapi" were probably in use during the Cedrosan Saladoid period (figure 8.2; Olsen 1974). It is likely that digging sticks, spears, and other wood poles were used. Atlatl spurs recovered from the Cedrosan Saladoid Golden Rock site in St. Eustatius confirm the use of spear-throwers at that site. The use of canoes for ocean travel is inferred both from ethnographic accounts and from the identification of woodworking tools in archaeological sites.

Rouse (1982, 15) suggests that during the early Ceramic-period formal stone-lined ball courts may not have been in use, but the ball game may have been played on earthen ball grounds that were the forerunners of the later formal courts. With exceptions such as a preserved buried wood post excavated at the Tutu site and radiocarbon dated to be 800 years old (figure 8.4), most wood posts, both above and below ground, decay. Nevertheless, postholes are usually discernible from archaeological investigation, and the location of the former post itself may be evident from a dark organic stain or the configuration of stones that were thrown into the hole to serve as wedge supports. Excavations at the Tutu Archaeological Village site, at Golden Rock in St. Eustatius, and at the Maisabel site in Puerto Rico indicate that during the early Ceramic period, houses were situated in an irregular pattern around a central plaza. At the Tutu site 2,400 postholes were exposed and 1,100 were excavated (figure 8.5). However, the two clearly defined structures date to about A.D. 1100, and structures dating to the early Ceramic period have not yet been defined. At the Golden Rock site in St. Eustatius, Versteeg has uncovered post molds from fourteen structures, seven of which were probably domiciles. Of these, three were circular structures between 7 and 9.5 m in diameter, two were large circular

Figure 8.4. Preserved wood from post 407A of structure 2, Tutu Archaeological Village site, St. Thomas.

Above: Figure 8.5. Overview of postholes at the Tutu Archaeological Village site, St. Thomas.

Left: Figure 8.6. "Malocca" excavated at the Golden Rock site, St. Eustatius. Reproduction from the Historical Society Museum, St. Eustatius.

structures 19 and 14 m in diameter, one was a large structure in the shape of a turtle, and one was rectangular in shape. Each of the two large circular structures was identified by a ring of sixteen outer postholes and an inner circle of eight deep postholes (figure 8.6). In the center were two deep postholes that had contained central supporting upright posts. Using an ethnographic model, Versteeg describes the larger structures as "maloccas" (Versteeg 1992, 157). As at Tutu, windscreens extended from the structures (figure 8.6).

IMPLICATIONS ABOUT NONMATERIAL CULTURE

Finally, material objects can reveal elements of nonmaterial human behavior. Small three-pointed objects of stone, coral, and shell found at early Ceramic-period sites are believed to be figures of gods known in the region as *zemis*. During the early Ceramic period, effigy vessels and figurines in the form of zemis were also produced (Rouse 1992, 121). From ethnohistorical accounts we learn that the term *zemi* was applied not only to the deities themselves but also to idols and fetishes representing them. These idols were made from the remains of ancestors and from natural objects believed to be inhabited by powerful spirits. Zemis recovered from later contexts were composed of wood and cotton cloth also (Rouse 1992, 149).

At Hacienda Grande, Rouse identified three types of modified human bones from which objects had been made: pierced teeth, carved and hollowed humeri (upper-arm bones), and carved and decorated skulls. Using ethnographic comparison, Roe hypothesized that these objects of corporeal art served two nonmaterial functions: the wearing or use of these objects attracted the power of the enemy by contagious magic; and at the same time, it advertised the ferocity of the user. Roe suggests a possible similarity between carved human-skull plaques and artificial copies in ceramic, wood, and stone. Small teardrop-shaped flat-backed polished stone objects recovered from the Tutu site most probably were insets on a wood mask of the latter type (Roe 1991).

The excavation of burials, both human and nonhuman, permits archaeologists to interpret some nonmaterial aspects of human behavior from such evidence as the position and condition of the skeleton, the texture and condition of burial soils, evidence of attempted preservation of the remains, and accompanying grave items. For example, at Tutu, we hope to establish whether or not there is a relationship between the gender and/or age of the interred human body and the presence of accompanying ceramic vessels. At Tutu, two human fetal skeletons were found interred in complete bowls;

and at the Golden Rock site in St. Eustatius, the skeleton of an infant was found accompanied by two pottery vessels, eighty-four quartz and shell beads, and three shell plaques. The shell beads accompanying burials have been interpreted by Versteeg and Schinkel (1992, 180) as prestige items. At the Tutu site, a turtle skeleton was found buried intact. Therefore, while perhaps not fully interpreted, human burials accompanied by material goods and other types of burials can provide glimpses of social, spiritual, and political behavior.

It is evident that the material culture of the early Ceramic period in the Caribbean Islands reflects the nonmaterial as well as the material lives of human cultural groups. Through careful excavation and interpretation, archaeologists continue their efforts to piece together the complete material culture inventory and to understand the complex local cultural patterns of the Caribbean Islands during the early Ceramic period.

9

Religious Beliefs of the Saladoid People

Miguel Rodríguez

The Europeans who arrived in the Caribbean in 1492 were surprised at the complex manifestations of Taino society, but they were not interested in promoting the aboriginal peoples' traditions, religious beliefs, or way of life. On the contrary, the valuable descriptions of Friar Ramón Pané, Father Bartolomé de Las Casas, Dr. Alvarez Chanca, Peter Martyr, and Adm. Christopher Columbus were used to justify the imposition of Western civilization and Christianity on the native peoples. These chroniclers described extensively the Tainos' physical aspect, the production of their handicrafts, and the exotic environment of the Antilles. Yet the intolerance and religious prejudice of these writers' era is evident in their distrust and lack of sympathy. And this bias means that even though their descriptions are extremely valuable documents, it is difficult to reconstruct a clear understanding of Taino religious beliefs from them alone (Pané 1974; Arrom 1975).

A still more difficult task is the study of the religious beliefs of those preliterate societies that flourished before the arrival of the Europeans: the Saladoids or Igneris, who colonized the Antilles twenty-five centuries ago, introducing agriculture and pottery-making to the Caribbean. According to the latest radiocarbon dates, there is scientific evidence of a Saladoid presence in Puerto Rico from around 300 B.C. (Haviser, this volume). Their varied cultural development lasted for almost a millennium, until the seventeenth century A.D. It is quite a challenge for archaeologists to reconstruct components of such a distant past (Siegel 1989).

WHO WERE THE SALADOID PEOPLE?

A preliminary challenge has to do with classification—that is, with determining just who these people were and when they arrived in the Caribbean. In the 1930s, Froelich Rainey, noting the large amount of crustaceans in their diet, named the earliest population the Crab Culture (Rainey 1940). Later, focusing more on ceramics than on diet, Irving Rouse renamed them Saladoid. They are also sometimes known as the Igneri, an ethnographic term in use among Lesser Antillean native peoples.

Since Rouse's work (1948a, b, and c), it has been generally accepted that a single wave of Saladoid settlers began a quick migratory process from the region of Saladero in Venezuela to the northeast of the Caribbean, stopping on the east coast of Hispaniola. The Saladoid population in Puerto Rico has been divided into an early phase called Hacienda Grande and a later one called Cuevas—both of these phases named, in conventional archaeological fashion, for the sites at which similar remains were first discovered. But in the last two decades a series of Saladoid sites that differ from those previously defined have been excavated in the northeast of the Caribbean by Luis Chanlatte Baik and I, among others. This is the case with La Hueca, on the island of Vieques, Punta Candelero on the east coast of Puerto Rico, and other sites in the Lesser Antilles (Chanlatte Baik and Narganes Storde 1984, 1989; Rodríguez 1989).

Some archaeologists believe these discoveries indicate that a separate society had evolved in the Caribbean *before* the arrival of the Saladoids. This allegedly new cultural group has been called variously Huecoid, Agro I, or pre-Saladoid. Others maintain that the chronological and cultural differences that may exist between pre-Saladoid and Saladoid cultures are not significant enough to warrant a new classificatory model. Rouse, still the most acknowledged authority in the archaeology of the region, has offered a solution to the dilemma by suggesting two subdivisions within the Saladoid tradition: the Cedrosan Saladoids and the Huecan Saladoids (Rouse 1992).

This chapter does not offer an assessment of that debate. Rather, I discuss under a wide cultural and chronological umbrella the typical cultural manifestations of both Cedrosan and Huecan Saladoids. We know that these two populations were closely related to each other and that they occupied the islands simultaneously, or nearly so. In addition, they initiated the planting of cassava and the pottery-making tradition in the Caribbean. They incorporated the symbolism of the South American fauna in their artistic representations and developed a sophisticated technology in the carving of semiprecious stones. Both groups of settlers brought to the Caribbean their domestic dogs and plants such as tobacco and cohoba, used in rites and ceremonies. In this chapter I integrate the scarce archaeological information about these two groups that can lead us to general conclusions about the religious beliefs of the Saladoids as a whole.

Inferring religious beliefs and practices from the fragmented legacy of material culture is a challenging archaeological task, for religion belongs to the nonmaterial world of ideas, of the mind, of the feelings of an individual and a community. The task is especially difficult in the Caribbean both because early native life was already "archaeological" when the Spaniards arrived on these beaches at the end of the fifteenth century and because the material legacy—as is true in humid tropical zones generally—is very scattered and sparsely conserved. Fortunately, however, religious concepts are occasionally reflected in the artistic manifestations and the production of handicrafts as well as in the concrete evidence obtained in archaeological excavations.

I present here some observations that may be used as a guide for future studies—conclusions based upon information obtained from almost twenty years of investigation in Saladoid sites in the northeast of the Caribbean, especially in Puerto Rico and the island of Vieques and from more recent reports on other sites in the Lesser Antilles.

HUMAN BURIALS

Saladoid sites frequently contain evidence of human burials that reflect complex funeral rites and a clear ancestor cult. In the majority of cases, the bodies are found in squatting positions; they were also evidently shrouded, being firmly tied with vegetable fibers or hammocks. Eighty percent of the bodies studied in the Saladoid cemetery recently excavated in Punta Candelero, Puerto Rico, had been buried in this manner. The preparation and placing of them in a squatting position is a common religious practice in aboriginal cultures in the Caribbean (see Rodríguez 1989).

According to the reports on the graves that can be associated with the Saladoid culture, no fixed pattern exists with regard to their orientation to the cardinal points. Nevertheless, in Punta Candelero almost two-thirds of the 106 skeletons found were facing east—that is, toward the sea, the island of Vieques, and the rising sun. This orientation has also been identified in Taino burials and cemeteries, and obviously has cultural and religious significance.

In some cases the bodies were interred along with pottery vessels, food, objects of personal use, and valuable burial gifts. In the Caribbean, decomposition makes it almost impossible for us to positively identify such gifts when they are made of wood, cotton, seeds, fruit, feathers, food, or fibers; we can be more certain of their identity when we find ceramic vessels and objects of stone, bone, shell, and other materials that resist decomposition. In any event, the presence of such gifts suggests a belief in an afterlife or reincarnation (Calderón 1985).

Some Saladoid burials at Punta Candelero were accompanied by one or more clay vessels, generally placed upside down over the head or the legs and, on occasion, covering almost all of the body. In the late Saladoid burials of Puerto Rico, such as Punta Candelero, the vessels used as gifts seem to be rough, undecorated domestic containers. It is possible that the vessels' contents, many of them decomposed, had greater ceremonial importance than the containers themselves.

Gifts commonly associated with Saladoid burials include amulets, accessories, necklaces, and strings of stone beads. Beads and amulets of quartz, amethyst, carnelian, serpentinite, jadeite, and other green stones were found inside a small Saladoid vessel, together with a skeleton, at Hacienda Grande. In Punta Candelero, a string of fifty-four beads of milky quartz was found in the right hand of a male adult. Sometimes plano convex and petaloid celts were also used as burial gifts by the Saladoid people (Siegel 1989).

One burial site at Punta Candelero contained a less usual burial item: the shell of a freshwater turtle called *hicotea* by the Indians. The empty shell, with two small polished stones inside, was placed between the legs, in the genital area, and was held by the right hand of the deceased, a middle-aged man. It is possible that in this particular case the shell was a musical instrument buried as among the most valued possessions of the deceased and not necessarily as a ritual gift. Turtle shells are still used as musical instruments among the aboriginal cultures of Venezuela.

The burial of children in Punta Candelero deserves a special mention. There is no evidence of skeletons of newborns or young infants. It is possible that because they were too young to have passed through the initiation rites, they were not considered full members of the society. In some tropical aboriginal cultures, the bodies of infants are disposed of without burial. On the other hand, there are numerous documented burials of infants younger than five years of age. In these cases the child was placed in a large domestic vessel, like a funeral urn. This practice also has been documented in late Saladoid sites such as Monserrat, Luquillo, and Las Carreras.

In Punta Candelero, a green serpentine pendant was placed beside an infant inside of a vessel. At Las Carreras, a buried pottery vessel contained the skeleton of an infant and a shell trumpet.

Archaeologists have found that, in some of the later Saladoid sites, there were specific areas where the majority of the deceased of the community were buried. This seems to have been true, for example, in Tibes, Ponce; Punta Candelero, Humacao; and Maisabel, Vega Baja. In all of these sites the central plaza of the town was selected as the area for the cemetery, establishing as sacred the place where communal ceremonies and festivities, as well as routine domestic tasks, were performed. The Saladoid cemeteries studied are extensive and carefully planned, with few examples found of overlapping bodies. Of the 106 skeletons excavated at Punta Candelero, 80 percent were found in a small zone in the center of the village, with a high concentration of primary burials. The villages of Tibes in Ponce and Maisabel in Vega Baja were planned in the same way.

The early Saladoid sites lack such cemeteries. The human burials associated with the Hacienda Grande phase are scarce and scattered throughout the site, while individual burials or cemeteries associated with the Huecan Saladoid variant have not yet been found. Their absence may constitute a notable difference between the early and late phases of Saladoid culture.

Ceramic Art

According to archaeologist Peter Roe, the Saladoid ceramic styles are among the most elaborate and complex of the early cultures of all the tropical zone (Roe 1989). Saladoid potters included in their ceramic production numerous varieties of containers and decorative techniques, such as the use of paint, delicately crosshatched incisions, incisions filled with paint, relief figures, applications, and combinations of all of these. Using such techniques, Saladoid potters showed a special fondness for the representation of personages, sacred animals, and fantastic creatures. The bodies and heads of zoomorphic, anthropomorphic, and anthropozoomorphic figures and fantastical creatures were used to adorn the recipients and effigy vessels. All of these suggest a complex system of supernatural and mythical representations.

The ancestral sources for this expressive abundance must be in the tropical heart of South America. Yet the plastic representation of individual or combined elements, either realistic or abstract, of the South American flora and fauna cannot be interpreted simply as the desire to conserve ties with the ancestral culture, for the representation of mainland myths and symbols is transformed and adapted to the Antillean environment. Ricardo Algería, for example, has suggested that the South American myths and beliefs may have existed in the Caribbean for some time, but that in Saladoid art we find a replacement of some of their elements by the smaller and less menacing fauna of the Caribbean (Alegría 1978). With the scarcity in the islands of large land mammals, the native amphibians, reptiles, fish, and birds acquired more symbolic relevance.

Among the South American tropical fauna represented on Saladoid effigy vessels, jars, and domestic pottery are several that still have religious significance to the peoples of the continent. These include tapirs, capybaras, armadillos, alligators, turtles, monkeys, snakes, bats, dogs, and jaguars. The mythological connection between jaguar and dog clearly originated on the South American continent, but with the passage of time and the absence of live models, in the Antilles the figure of the dog evolved into a docile jaguar. Its importance becomes more evident when we find in the Saladoid cemeteries the remains of dogs buried in squatting positions, suggesting the same ritual and reverence given to humans.

One phenomenon peculiar to the painted designs of the early Saladoid vessels is the representation of anthropomorphic faces by a combination of geometric elements. Occasionally the repetitive geometric design conceals one or more anthropomorphic, zoomorphic, or anthropozoomorphic figures. Given this peculiarity, we cannot discard the possibility that Saladoid artists employed a variety of artistic codes in different media.

One particular personage is represented constantly in the sample of Saladoid vessels throughout the region. Roe (1989) considers it to be the "god of the hourglass" since in the majority of the examples known, the eyes, nose, and even the head are depicted as hourglasses. The remaining parts of the body and face of this and other personages are defined through the use of diverse geometric forms such as circles, grecques, dotted lines, triangles, and spirals, as well as with applications and incisions filled with paint.

Since very remote times, the aspiration of a powder made from the seeds of the cohoba and from the leaves of tobacco has been a part of the religious ceremonies led by priests and shamans in the tropical region. These hallucinative and narcotic substances were used in the prediction of the future, prophesying, and communicating with spiritual beings. Hence it is not surprising that religious paraphernalia is abundant in the Saladoid sites, particularly in those associated with the Huecan Saladoids such as La Hueca and Punta Candelero. Huecan sites contain a great variety of containers designed for inhaling substances through the nose or ingesting special beverages.

Sometimes these ceramic artifacts are decorated with effigy forms that attain baroque artistic levels. Archaeologists have also excavated *incensaries,* thick-walled clay cylinders for burning herbs. In the later Saladoid sites, the presence of these ritual artifacts is less pronounced.

LAPIDARY INDUSTRY

Saladoid culture supported an active and sophisticated lapidary industry that is characterized by an abundance of small amulets and beads—items that represent a challenge for the artisan and reveal the presence of a complex iconographic symbolism (Chanlatte Baik and Narganes Storde 1984). The utilization of exotic raw materials such as amethyst, carnelian, quartz, aventurine, serpentinite, and jadeite also promoted the development of an extensive trade network between the Caribbean islands and the South American continent (Cody 1991).

It is interesting that in spite of the profusion of early Saladoid amulets, beads, and other adornments, they were rarely used as burial gifts. The small size of these amulets may reflect incipient religious beliefs and practices, concentrated in the diverse family units. As such, their function could have been of an individual protective character and not as a symbolic representation of a religious figure or idea.

HISTORIC CONTINUITY

The continuity over time of some variants and elements of the Saladoid beliefs has been archaeologically proven. These are manifested in pre-Tainan and Tainan cultural components. The Saladoid images of the South American and Antillean fauna—such as the dog, which I have already mentioned—constitute one example of this continuity. They figure prominently in ancient histories and legends of the cycles of the creation of the world, the human interaction with the environment, and other themes. Many of them must have been modified considerably over the centuries. But some of their elements were in existence up until the time of the European conquest and were observed throughout the Antilles by colonial chroniclers.

A particular example of religious continuity is seen in the pre-Tainan and Tainan construction of large plazas and ceremonial centers above ancient Saladoid cemeteries. The pre-Tainan inhabitants of the Tibes ceremonial center in Ponce built their main plaza over an earlier Saladoid cemetery. This phenomenon seems to be repeated in other archaeological sites of Puerto Rico and the Lesser Antilles.

The inhalation of powders and substances like cohoba and tobacco is also part of the Tainan religion. However, Tainan ritual paraphernalia differs slightly from the Saladoid examples. The Tainos incorporated large idols or zemis of wood and stone, spatulas used to induce vomiting, rattles, and other artifacts, a fact indicating a more structured and public religion.

A final example is the presence of small three-pointed figures, carved in shell, coral, or stone, in the early Saladoid sites. These artifacts developed in complexity and size during pre-Tainan times, becoming visible objects of political and religious power of the caciques and shamans of the Taino chiefdoms.

Conclusions

In this chapter I try to bring attention to a cultural and archaeological problem that is difficult but not impossible to resolve: the study of the religious beliefs of the aboriginal society, particularly of the peoples who preceded the Tainos and of whom we have no written narratives. My research model takes into consideration archaeology, art, ethnography, ethnohistoric documentation, and above all conclusions based on facts and common sense.

Let us remember that before the arrival of the Europeans in our world, there existed in Puerto Rico complex societies with authentic worries and concerns very similar to those of modern society: people then as now concerned themselves with the utilization of the environment; individual and collective happiness; relations among communities, islands, and continents; the expression of their creative and artistic capabilities; and the development of a world of religious rites, myths, ideas, and beliefs as complex and as legitimate as our own.

10

Maritime Trade in the Prehistoric Eastern Caribbean

David R. Watters

Native American populations of the eastern Caribbean were well adapted to the maritime nature of their insular world. The surrounding ocean acted as an aquatic highway linking their islands and cultures rather than as a water barrier separating them (see Watters and Rouse 1989). Archaeological evidence for this maritime adaptation is provided by artifactual remains that document the exchange of products through both short-distance trade among the islands and long-distance trade with the South American continent. This chapter examines the archaeological evidence for both types of trade and suggests the applicability for the prehistoric Caribbean of a "lifeline" model of long-distance exchange that has been applied effectively to Pacific Ocean prehistory.

A SEAWARD ORIENTATION

The Caribbean Sea can be conceived as the background of a canvas on which have been "painted" the individual islands. One can focus the eyes either on the painting's omnipresent blue background or on its foreground, where the islands stand out. Most archaeologists, being landlubbers, tend to perceive the world from a "landward orientation," and as a result they emphasize the foreground islands. The worldview of Native American peoples in the Caribbean, on the other hand, focuses strongly on the ocean realm, emphasizing the background of the painting in what I call a "seaward orientation." They see their world, in other words, not as a group of circumscribed individual islands but as an archipelago, whose islands are linked by the ocean. In this chapter I use this native, archipelagic viewpoint to explore maritime trade in the prehistoric eastern Caribbean.

Adopting an archipelagic viewpoint forces one to rethink certain issues. Other essays in this volume explore evidence for the various occupations of the Antilles by Native Americans. Indeed, these events—which are termed population movements, migrations, or colonizations—have long been a major research focus of Caribbean archaeologists (Keegan and Diamond 1987). In recent years, we have even seen the introduction of the "frontier" concept in the Caribbean (Rouse 1986, 106–56), most notably with respect to the Saladoid population movement from the South American continent onto the islands of the eastern Caribbean archipelago.

Inherent in all of these concepts is a primary concern with the onward or forward movement of the colonizers into the archipelago. These concepts intimate that Native American colonizers, as they pushed forward into the Lesser Antilles, turned their backs on the areas from which they originated and never again looked over their shoulders at South America. The possibility that they continued to interact with their South American homelands simply is not considered. I argue that such interaction should not be dismissed. At the close of this chapter, I expand on the idea of the continuation or persistence of cultural interactions with South America.

To examine interaction, I focus on trade and on the discontinuous distribution of resources that is a major factor in the exchange of materials and products. By "discontinuous distribution" I mean situations in which certain resources are present (or abundant) in one area but absent (or scarce) in another. The resource has value for the area where it is present as well as the area where it is absent, and therefore it becomes a commodity for trade or exchange. Here I discuss three examples of archaeological evidence that point to such exchange in the prehistoric Caribbean. The first example is that of Antiguan chert.

Antigua Chert

Chert, or flint, was an important rock material used by prehistoric peoples in the Antilles to make stone tools. Chert is often found in nodules (figure 10.1), and it is the process of reducing the nodule by knapping, or striking off pieces, that provides the tools of what archaeologists call flaked-stone or chipped-stone technology. The knocked-off pieces, called flakes or blades, normally have sharp edges that may be used for cutting or scraping. The nodule remnant is called the core. Remains of the prehistoric flaked-stone industry—including cores, flakes, and debitage (shattered bits of the nodule)—are prevalent and well preserved in archaeological sites.

In the northern Lesser Antilles (the Leeward Islands), the stone tool remnants of the flaked-stone industry are very widely distributed (figure 10.2),

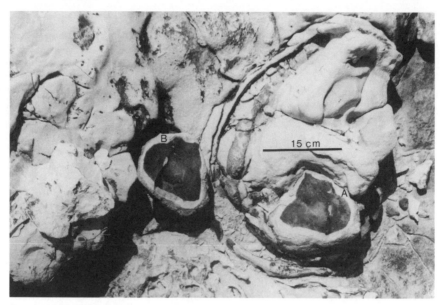

Figure 10.1. A 15 cm (approximately 6 in) chert nodule at Flinty Bay, Long Island, Antigua. The lower portion of the nodule (A) is still embedded in the limestone matrix, while the upper part (B) has split off.

Figure 10.2. An assortment of chert tools from various prehistoric sites on Anguilla.

being found in sites on every island investigated from Guadeloupe to Anguilla (Walker 1980; Bartone and Crock 1991; Crock 1993). However, Antigua is the only island in the northern Lesser Antilles with confirmed chert sources occurring in natural geological deposits. The best-known chert deposit is Flinty Bay on Long Island (figure 10.3), a small island off the northeast coast of Antigua, although other chert sources are known from Little Bay and Corbison Point on Antigua proper.

This is a classic case where the discontinuous distribution of a resource comes into play. Archaeologists have discovered chert tools and cores in prehistoric sites throughout the islands of the northern Lesser Antilles, yet these islands do not appear to have their own naturally occurring chert sources. The raw materials from which the chert tools were made, there-

Figure 10.3. The rocky beach at Flinty Bay, Long Island, Antigua, from which chert nodules are eroding.

Figure 10.4. The white-on-red painting on these pottery sherds from Montserrat is a decorative style characteristic of the Saladoid ceramic series, which is associated with the earliest population movement of ceramic-producing Native Americans into the Lesser Antilles, perhaps as long ago as 500 B.C. Photograph courtesy of James B. Petersen.

fore, must have been brought to those islands by trade or exchange from an external source. Antigua, as the sole source of chert known within the northern Lesser Antilles, is the only logical candidate.

A number of possibilities exist for the process by which the chert raw material moved from Antigua to the other islands. Native Americans on Antigua may have voyaged to other islands to trade chert directly with their inhabitants. They may have traded with people on nearby islands who in turn traded the chert to people on more distant islands. People from the other islands may have come to Antigua to trade. Or people from the other islands may have traveled to Antigua to exploit the chert resources directly, without involving Antiguan Native Americans. The means by which chert was transferred within the northern Lesser Antilles are not known for sure, but it is clear that the process involved its movement across intervening ocean waters.

VOLCANIC TEMPER IN POTTERY

Pottery is the most abundant artifact in the Ceramic Age archaeological sites of the eastern Caribbean. Pottery rarely is found as intact containers;

normally the containers have broken into pieces that archaeologists call sherds. Like chert, pottery sherds preserve well in archaeological sites since they are composed of clay that was baked or fired until hard. Pottery studies have long been a focus of Caribbean research because of the dating information ceramics can provide. Ceramics provide chronological information because ceramic styles (for example, pottery forms and decorations) tend to change through time, so that a particular style can serve as a time marker attributable to a specific period (figure 10.4).

Pottery is composed of clay, which is pliable in its plastic state, and inclusions, which are tiny fragments of rocks or minerals that either occur naturally in the clay deposit or are added to the clay by the potter to serve as binding agents. Once the pottery is fired, the pliable clay becomes hard and the inclusions are trapped within it. Archaeologists usually use the terms *paste* to refer to the clay matrix of pottery and *temper* to refer to the inclusions added by the potter. Both elements may be used to determine the origin and dates of pottery sherds.

Barbuda, a low-relief island of the eastern Caribbean, is composed entirely of marine-deposited limestone formations and modern carbonate deposits. It is perhaps the classic example of a completely carbonate island in the Limestone Caribbees of the eastern Caribbean. Barbuda contrasts sharply with the volcanic islands forming the mountainous inner arc of the Lesser Antilles, which are composed of igneous rocks produced by the volcanoes. It was therefore surprising to discover that all pottery sherds from Barbuda examined under the microscope contained significant quantities of igneous temper (including volcanic rock fragments, plagioclase feldspar, opaque minerals, pyroxenes, amphiboles, and olivine), including in some instances exclusively volcanic inclusions (Donahue, Watters, and Millspaugh 1990).

When one seeks to explain this unexpected finding, the discontinuous distribution of resources again comes into play. Since Barbuda has no igneous rock to serve as the source of the volcanic temper found in its sherds, that temper could have come only from one or more of the nearby islands where volcanic deposits do exist. Either volcanic temper itself was brought to Barbuda and subsequently incorporated into pottery made on Barbuda or the pottery itself was made on one or more volcanic islands, incorporating the igneous temper, and then the ceramic vessels were brought to Barbuda. Whichever hypothesis is true, it is evident that inter-island movement of the materials was involved. Were we able to determine the source island (or islands) of the igneous temper in those sherds, we would have an independent means of tracing the movement of the material to Barbuda. In

Figure 10.5. Undeco-
rated ("plain") pottery
such as these sherds
from Fountain Cavern,
Anguilla, is typical of
the more recent period
of Native American
occupation in the
Lesser Antilles.

theory at least, such determinations are possible. Recent research on other
limestone islands such as Anguilla (Donahue, Watters, and Millspaugh 1990;
Petersen and Watters 1991a) has verified the presence of volcanic temper
in its sherds as well (figure 10.5).

EXOTIC STONE BEADS

The final piece of evidence for maritime exchange involves stone beads,
pendants, and similar ornaments that archaeologists have found in Caribbean sites for many years (figures 10.6 and 10.7). The detailed analysis of
such objects, as a distinct category of artifacts, is a recent development,
spurred on in part because of the concentrations of these objects at sites on
four islands Vieques (Chanlatte Baik and Narganes Storde 1984), St. Croix

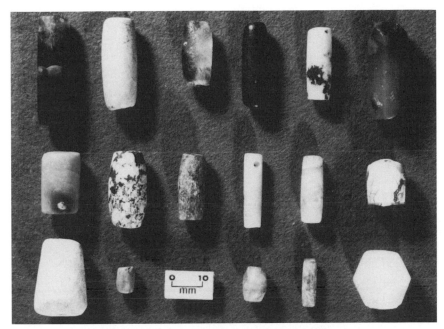

Figure 10.6. Beads from Montserrat exemplifying the varieties of rocks and minerals from which beads were manufactured.

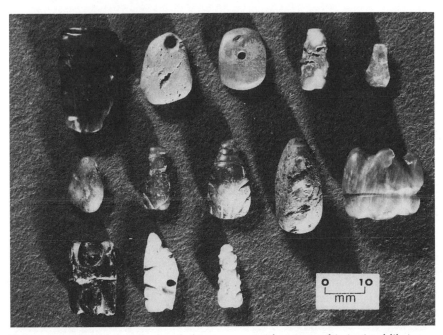

Figure 10.7. Pendants and related objects, some with zoomorphic (animal-like) representations, from Montserrat.

(Vescelius and Robinson 1979), Montserrat (Harrington 1924; Watters and Scaglion 1994), and Grenada (Cody 1991).

The earliest bead assortment to be examined, that of Montserrat, yielded twenty-nine distinct varieties of rocks and minerals. Not one of these varieties can be correlated with geological deposits on that island. Hence, Montserrat could not have provided the raw materials from which the beads were manufactured. The rocks and minerals must have been imported into Montserrat from nonlocal, or what archaeologists call "exotic," geological sources.

The specific sources have not as yet been determined, and archaeologists are still faced with trying to identify the original locations that may have provided the raw materials for the beads. Some of the materials may have come from relatively nearby. For example, deposits of quartz crystals as well as amethyst (a purple-colored variety of quartz) have been reported from Martinique in the Lesser Antilles (Henry Petitjean Roget, pers. comm., 1993). Islands in the Greater Antilles have deposits of serpentine (Wagner and Schubert 1972) and also are likely sources for diorite (figure 10.8).

But other materials in the collection could not have come from such nearby regions. The Montserrat collection, for example, contains certain beads

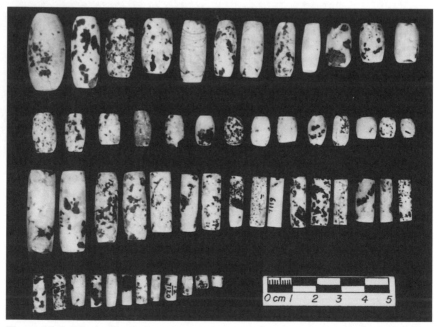

Figure 10.8. Diorite beads from Montserrat are of various sizes and typically either barrel-shaped (top two rows) or cylindrical (bottom rows) in form.

Figure 10.9. The presence of carnelian raw materials (top row) and partially finished bead blanks (undrilled) indicates that beads made from this material were actually manufactured on Montserrat. The island has no known geological deposits of carnelian.

and pendants made from turquoise and minerals of the "jade group." These materials have no known geological sources anywhere in the West Indies. The continent of South America is the closest geographic area with known sources for turquoise and "jade group" minerals, although other possible sources may exist (Rodríguez 1991). Beads and pendants made from these minerals have been excavated from archaeological sites in the eastern Caribbean in association with pottery of the Saladoid ceramic series, which originated in South America. Therefore the South American continent is the likely source for geological deposits of the turquoise and "jade group" minerals and probably for other minerals as well.

Most of the beads and pendants in the Montserrat collection, being fully formed objects, may have been brought to Montserrat as finished products ready to be worn. However, some unfinished artifacts represent earlier stages in the bead manufacturing process. These include raw materials and "blanks," which are partially shaped beads not yet fully polished or drilled. Carnelian is heavily represented in the raw material and blank categories (figure 10.9), a fact indicating that carnelian stone beads actually were manufactured at this site even though the carnelian itself is an exotic. On the other hand, the amethyst objects in the Montserrat collection consist solely of finished beads; there is no evidence of the manufacture of amethyst beads at this site.

Just the opposite situation is evident on Grenada, where amethyst is present in various manufacturing stages but carnelian occurs only as finished beads. This differential distribution of raw materials, blanks, and finished beads suggests that the inhabitants of different islands in the eastern Caribbean may have practiced craft specialization, with certain islands being associated with the production of beads made from particular minerals and with the finished products subsequently being exchanged among the islands through short-distance trade.

CONCLUSIONS

The evidence of maritime trade presented in this chapter deals exclusively with durable materials recovered at archaeological sites. There are other durable items, such as stone axes and shell tools and ornaments, that likely were exchanged as well. These durable materials are emphasized as prehistoric trade items because they preserve well in archaeological deposits. The complete material culture of the Native Americans of the eastern Caribbean also included many artifacts made from wood, fiber, and other fragile materials. Such fragile materials very likely were exchanged as well, but trade in these commodities cannot be archaeologically verified because the items decompose and therefore are rarely preserved in sites.

Based on the evidence reviewed in this chapter, prehistoric Caribbean maritime trade routes could have varied considerably in geographic scale. Resources absent on Montserrat, for example, could be obtained by trade of a short distance (chert from Antigua), a moderate distance (serpentine from the Greater Antilles), or a long distance (turquoise from South America). But regardless of the distance involved, the actual movement of such imported items involved over-water transport.

The probability is strong, therefore, that the Native American populations who settled the Lesser Antilles continued to maintain contact and to interact with peoples in South America. Although this interaction is especially apparent from the persistence of exotic (nonlocal) raw materials and finished products from South America associated with Saladoid period sites in the eastern Caribbean, the contact continued throughout prehistory (Boomert 1987).

Patrick V. Kirch, an archaeologist working in the Pacific islands, has developed a "homeland" or "lifeline" model to explain how the Lapita people, the earliest colonizers of many islands in the Pacific Ocean, continued to interact with their homelands during the colonization process. A central feature of that continued interaction was a long-distance exchange network of materials, especially prestige goods, that were not available on the islands being colonized. Kirch points out that the Lapita colonizers were entering new and unfamiliar territory in which the resource base was unknown. Persistence of social ties and an exchange network with their relatives in the homelands provided a social mechanism for maintaining an essential component of the Lapita colonization strategy. Kirch also mentions local or short-distance exchange among the Pacific islanders in utilitarian commodities of stone, clay, and temper (Kirch 1988, 1991).

Many of the ideas developed by Kirch for the Pacific may be pertinent to the Saladoid colonization of the eastern Caribbean, most notably with regard to the long-distance exchange in exotic materials. Kirch's reference to short-distance trade in stone, clay, and temper materials in the Pacific also virtually parallels the studies discussed above for the eastern Caribbean.

A seaward orientation and an archipelagic viewpoint are integral parts of Kirch's "lifeline" model. As is usually the case, the data analyses supporting the Pacific model have advanced well beyond those of the Caribbean. Caribbean archaeologists have the opportunity to make use of many of the ideas and research strategies developed for the Pacific model in their future research on relationships of maritime trade, social interaction, and the continuation of cultural ties with the South American homelands.

11

Notes on Ancient Caribbean Art and Mythology

Henry Petitjean Roget

The examination in private or museum collections of feather ornaments, basketry, and wood or fiber artifacts still produced today by forest-dwelling societies helps us realize that what has come to us from the ancient societies of the Antilles is but a small part of all that was produced. Insular Saladoid culture, the second ceramic culture to have entered the Antilles at the very beginnings of the Christian era, led directly to the culture of the Tainos of the Greater Antilles. The origins of the Kalina culture—that is, the Caribs of the Lesser Antilles—are still a matter of discussion among archaeologists. In order to focus more precisely on the field of artistic expression among the Tainos or the Kalinas, we nonetheless benefit from several possible approaches. Our first source of knowledge—one essential to our understanding of the ways of life of these extinct societies—is the work of archaeologists whose conclusions are based on the excavations of ancient village sites. Descriptions and information reported by men such as Christopher Columbus, the friar Ramón Pané, Bishop Las Casas, and the French chroniclers of the seventeenth and eighteenth centuries, are our second means of learning about these cultures. Finally, contemporaneous societies that have remained at an archaic stage provide us with comparative cultural data with which to approach the study of the aesthetic productions of Antillean Amerindians.

Not all articles that were fashioned, nor all the artifacts that have been discovered, have revealed to us their use or their meaning. The three-pointed stones still puzzle scholars. And as for petroglyphs, those signs engraved on the rocks—their interpretation still remains difficult.

These plastic or graphic productions do not seem to have any particular direct link among themselves. They nevertheless all belong to a consistent chain of signification closely related to mythological narratives. Among the Tainos or the Caribs, as anywhere else among tribal societies in the world, aesthetic function does not prevail as is the case in Western art. "Art for art's sake" does not exist. The freedom of individual creativity is very limited, and innovation is very slow. Arawak art, from the Saladoids to the Tainos, like that of other traditional societies, is a faithful translation of primeval mythology, that of the creation of the world, of animals, of the arrival of heroes who introduce cultural gifts. Stone tools, body ornaments, carvings, rock art, or rock paintings as well as ceramics are all genuine works of art.

The word *art,* according to art historian Erwin Panofski, designates "the conscious and intentional capability by humans to produce objects in the same manner as nature produces phenomena." The word *art* is also used in reference to a "set of rules or techniques which the mind must follow in order to have access to knowledge and represent reality" (Panofski 1962). Thus, when speaking about the art of the Antillean Amerindians, we simultaneously refer to its practice, to technological skills, to rules and processes that were followed to produce such manifestations as are qualified as aesthetic. Sculptures, decorated pottery, all objects of "primitive art" immobilize the dialogue established between raw materials and those who have gone beyond these contingencies in order to communicate a message.

In order to have any meaning—in order not to lose among the abundance or profusion of its manifestations, any reference to what it is meant to indicate—Saladoid, Taino, and Kalina art must restrict itself to a limited repertory of themes. In its vision of the world, each culture selects from among the infinite themes offered by its natural environment. Associations between the beings chosen and represented by graphic or plastic techniques to correspond to a kind of language must satisfy certain conditions. First of all, they must be found under identical forms or structurally similar variants that are repeated generation after generation. On the other hand, associations among ornamental themes must be realized according to repetitive processes and principles that constitute the rules that regulate the organization of all decoration. The existence of such a language is obvious with respect to the fact that beyond the apparent variability of decoration motifs used by the Saladoids or the Tainos is a restricted but hidden diversity of ornamental themes.

I have shown in previous publications (Petitjean Roget 1973a, 1973b, 1973c, 1976b, 1976c, and 1978) that the decoration of Saladoid and Taino ceramics reveals strict composition rules. To understand what was painted and how it was constituted—and to have access, in other words, to an internal organizational code of ceramic decoration—I have reduced the decorations in a broad sample of whole vessels or sherds to increasingly more simple units. The *elementary motif* is the smallest unit that can be derived. It is not a precise motif but a class of motif that covers all variants determined by the context. A motif may be modulated, transposed, or reversed, without losing its identity. The study of elementary motifs shows there are patterns constituted by particular motif configurations that are repeated through the interplay of symmetry on a single vessel or from one vessel to another. These are *themes*. Finally, these themes are combined into *designs* on the vessels. This approach allows for an emphasis on composition rules and on how these rules are constantly reproduced in order to constrain the plastic impression to a pattern from which it derives its particular characteristics—that is, its "ethnic style," as Leroi-Gourhan would say.

Yet one must not dissociate ceramic art from other cultural productions. Similar motifs may be found on worked shell artifacts or on seals for body painting. Sculptures and petroglyphs also reflect similar networks of expression that intersect each other. There is apparently a constant decoding of information that must be deciphered in order for us to understand what is signified. We must remember that all these products that constitute what we feel as "aesthetic" manifestations actually possessed an altogether different value for their Amerindian authors. When one identifies the beings that figure or symbolize the modelings, the designs, or the paintings, we go forward toward understanding a system of representation in which everything is coherent. We are far, however, from knowing what is represented or the significance of what is figured. Certain adornos, for instance, are unambiguously identifiable. A bird is recognizable by its beak, a fish by the shape of its head, a human face by the typical appearance of the nose. At the same time, a large number of incised or painted designs, as well as adornos, remain incomprehensible. The being that is depicted cannot be convincingly identified. For this reason, vessel decoration may not at first be identifiable. It is abstract and nonfigurative. In fact, I have been able to show that all these representations are codified according to a selection principle based on particular anatomical features. Each being's depiction—

incised, modeled, or painted—is sufficient to represent the being in its entirety.

I have demonstrated (Petitjean Roget 1975) that Saladoid art is based on the recurrent association of the fruit-eating bat and the tree frog. Both themes are not only the most commonly depicted but are also associated according to an immutable order. The frog is always represented in whichever manner, real or metaphorical, above the bat. I therefore had to try to understand why—all over the Caribbean for nearly 1,500 years, from the Saladoids to the Tainos, and under multiple variations—artworks always represent these two beings together in this manner. Decoding an artwork first involves bringing forward the hidden message, then discovering the means to decipher this message. The solution was discovered in the myths collected by Ramón Pané, a Hieronymite friar who was part of Columbus's second voyage. The narratives he recorded as early as 1493, on the request of Columbus, display all the characteristics of myths. They have no precise authors. They describe the origins of human beings, animals, or the sea. Some of the narratives have at first no obvious meaning. Parts of them tell of events that exist only outside the common world: the sun transforms a man into stone, others into trees or birds; bones are transformed into fish; a man is given birth from the back of a turtle. Though the Tainos believed all of them to be true, these tales are actually mythological narratives. Pané's text was first published in Italian in Venice in 1571 as part of the book written by Columbus's younger son, Fernando, *The Life of the Admiral* (Colombo 1571).

It is well known that translations do not alter the internal structures of mythological narratives. I was thus able to apply an approach derived from the methods of structural analysis to the first published transcription of Pané's account (Colombo 1571). In various papers published since then, I have tried to show some of the levels of signification of these myths; I have also attempted to relate them to some of the cultural productions within the material culture of the Tainos. To discover the hidden meaning of these narratives is to reveal what they tell us about the origins of human beings and of social rules and about such events as the discovery of wild honey, the symbol of political power. Other narratives relate the origins of illnesses as well as the ornaments that protect against illness and death.

It is also in the decoding of these narratives that we may be able to derive the meaning of the symbolism found on three-pointed stones and to understand the reasons they were used by women when giving birth. According to Pané, such stones were buried in the gardens to help food grow. Women had to keep them because they helped in childbirth. The symbolic functions of the three-pointed stones are understandable. One of the myths collected by Pané relates how, at the beginning of time, out of the Earth, which was uniformly flat, rises a unique mountain in which there are two caves. Then as the narrative unfolds, there is only one cave in which resides the future humankind. The task of one of the residents is to separate men from women. This he fails to do successfully, and he is condemned to remain at the entrance of the cave, where he is transformed by the sun, a male metaphor, into a stone statue. His name is Marocael; he is to remain immobile, dead, condemned not to ever be born.

The myth unfolds to reveal the long road that led to the existence of human culture. Another phase of this process is reached when men sent fishing are transformed into plum trees. The men had wandered some distance from the cave, the primeval uterus, in which incest was practiced as a matter of necessity because at the beginning of time all human beings were brothers and sisters who had risen out of the same cave, the same womb. Minerals do not move; Marocael remains close to the time of origins, on the side of undifferentiated beings, the zemis. The passage through the vegetable state—that is, the trees that are born, grow, and die—represents the achievement of a new phase on the way toward the emergence of humanity. There remains but one transformation before human beings are fully accomplished. A hero is sent in search of the most valuable magical plant, the *digo* herb, which is a wild tobacco used for purifications. In his quest for the plant, the hero goes even farther away from the cave and is transformed by the sun into a woodpecker, who is endowed with an almost-human voice—he sings, the myth emphasizes. The creation of humankind and human society is near. The bird that sings, that is free, that lives and dies, symbolizes the last stage in the process.

Having returned to the cave, however, the men are desperate without women. The children cry for the breast; they are transformed into frogs. Accordingly, the myth signifies that their mothers must also be frogs. One day the men notice some shapes in the trees that look like women, but they are unable to capture them. They follow the advice of the old wise men and send out four people to look. These are four twins, called *Caracaracols*. They are abnormal beings who were born diseased, by cesarean birth—that is, through a cultural process rather than a natural one. These intermediate beings, born outside of the natural way, are the mediators used to bring extremes closer together. The *Caracaracols* succeed in capturing the shapes in the trees, but are disappointed to learn that they have neither male nor female sexual organs. The elders send for the woodpecker, already seen at the beginning of the myth. And, as Ramón Pané relates it, they tie the bird where the women's sexual organ must be placed. The bird with its beak carves the missing vagina.

The myth has dictated the prohibition of incest. It has narrated the phases—mineral, vegetable, animal—through which humankind has gone before establishing society and its rules. The three-pointed stones by the nature of their material (stone), their triangular shape, and their decoration, as well as the leaf-shaped designs at their apex—or the bird's beak—all recall these stages. They are the Canta Mountains, out of which humanity came; they are the stone guardian Marocael; they are the leaves of the plum tree; they are the beak of the phallic bird that opened up the women. As sacred objects, they belong to the creation myth of mankind. For this reason, while repeating the gestures of the woodpecker that opened the women, through the metaphorical interplay of the symbolic function, the three-pointed stones were considered as favorable to parturition, and women kept them piously. In the same chain of functions, as symbolic phalluses, they are supposed to fertilize the earth and help the crops to grow.

The theme of the frog has also appeared in the myth, already foreshadowed discreetly by the frog children. Frogs belong to a lower level, that of moisture. They symbolize femininity. The connotations of the frog (which comes from beneath the surface of the water) define the character of the animal that must occupy the inverse, meaning masculine, position, which is a dry animal that lives out of water. Thus, art helps to reveal who this being ought to be. It is the fruit-eating bat, *Artibeus jamaicencis jamaicencis,* modeled or painted in Saladoid or Taino art. In the primeval world as depicted in the myths, women were frogs and men were bats.

Another myth relates how a particular zemi known as Opiyelguaobiran had "four legs like a dog." Though he was tethered with ropes, he escaped all the time. It is said that on the arrival of the Spaniards, he had fled to a swamp and has never been seen since. In my study of the Faragunaol myth (Petitjean Roget 1980), I showed that beyond the mere hunting trip during which the men discover a certain animal that seeks refuge in a hollow tree, the myth in reality relates the discovery of the first wild bee (*Melipona* sp.) honey. Faraguanaol is therefore not a single figuration zemi but the metaphor of the cacique's power. In the same manner, by analogy, one can propose an interpretation for the zemi known as Opiyelguaobiran. Zemis are not specific representations but symbolical entities. Like all symbols, they have multiple significations. Because one myth relates that Opiyelguaobiran has "four legs like a dog" and because there are modeled clay dogs in Taino art, some authors believe that the well-known wood statue in the Museo del Hombre Dominicano that has a human head and four legs is in fact Opiyelguaobiran.

Zemis are symbolical realities that, like many symbols, cannot be reduced to a single interpretation. The study of Pané's narratives reveals that sculptures, above all, represent a chain of symbolic significations. When an individual perceives a natural phenomenon, "a tree moving down to its roots," as related by Pané, "he is immobilized by fear. He asks it who he is. The tree replies: bring me Buhitihu and I will tell you who I am." Upon reaching the place where this unusual event has taken place, the shaman (the buhitihu)—through the intermediary of the hallucinogenic drug cohoba, which he sniffs with a *tabaco* tube—establishes contact with the zemis, whose presence he can now experience; "having used cohoba, he rises to his feet and bestows upon the tree all his titles, as he would do to a great lord." The *buhitihu* demands of him: "Tell me, who are you? What are you doing here? Why did you summon me so? What do you want from me? Why did you call me? Tell me whether you want to come with me or whether you want me to cut you down? How do you want me to carry you? Do I have to build you a house with your own land [food garden]?" "Then this tree, Cimiche, either idol or devil answers by saying what he wants to be done" (Pané 1972, chap. 19).

This excerpt from Pané's story tells how the sudden emergence of the sacred in the realm of the secular or profane leads to the production of the carvings known as zemis. These wooden or stone objects are the materialization of the sacred. They are symbolical supports of the sacred. This is why the wooden statue with a human head cannot be reduced by itself alone to all the symbolism carried by the zemi Opiyelguaobiran, which is something entirely different.

Indeed, Amerindians classify many different species of quadrupeds within the *Canidae* (Lévi-Strauss 1958, 76). Many South American myths consider canids and woodpeckers as the masters of honey. By a semantic shift similar to what we Westerners mean when we speak of a "honeymoon," Amer-indian thought places in a symbolic chain both sperm and honey (see Petitjean Roget 1977). In this perspective, Opiyelguaobiran—an unstable zemi carved out of wood, that is, placed on the level of the dry and the masculine, in contrast to stone that belongs to the side of the moist and the feminine, which also has disappeared at the arrival of the Spaniards—is more properly the symbol of political power disrupted by the Europeans.

If particular objects symbolize Opiyeilguaobiran, they are the caciques' seats, the *duhos* made of guaiacum wood (*Guaiacum officinale*), which have four legs like dogs and are always equipped with a penis and usually with a raised back that is representative of the raised tail of a dog.

Other artifacts that also appear to have had a direct connection with the myths related by Pané are the monolithic axes topped with a humpback figure and the clay figurines in the Museo del Hombre Dominicano that also depict a figure with a hump decorated with incised motifs. These axes and figurines undoubtedly refer to a particular moment in the creation of the world. In the myth reported by Pané (1972, chap. 11), Caracaracol—the character who with his three twin brothers was the cause of the flood—is evicted from human society. Sent back to the side of nature, he finds himself pregnant from the blow of a *tabaco* tube filled with cohoba and snot, struck on the back by the old man Bassamanaco, whom he was asking for manioc. The brothers cut open his hump with a stone ax. Caracaracol then gives birth from his back to a live female turtle. The turtle carapace, as we know from other South American myths, is representative of the celestial vault.

As for the petroglyphs, they are representations that are more difficult to interpret as a whole. Some appear to have a significant relation to water, due to their location on riverbanks, and to stone polishers, which are often associated with them. For this reason, some type of petroglyphs seem to have a relation to the manufacture of stone axes and ornaments that call for the use of polishers. They could be like the bats in the myths, the guardians of cultural goods. Other engraved figurations are clear depictions of frog women, identifiable by the motif of the legs folded under the body. The large-eared petroglyphs, common in Grenada and Puerto Rico, of the type known as "swaddled babies" are unambiguously the mythological bat people. A last category of petroglyphs groups those with radiating headdresses. They must be related to the myths about the origins of illnesses. Among the Tainos and the Island Caribs as well as in many Amazonian tribes, the rainbow, considered in their imagination in the shape of a large snake, is the cause of all illnesses and death. Among the Tainos, the rainbow is double. It is evocated by the myths of Badraima and Corocote, the latter being the double of the former. In other words, Badraima is a twin to Corocote (Pané 1972, chaps. 20–21). The rainbow among the Island Caribs is Joulouca, the great serpent who lives in a cave in Dominica. He makes himself at times small, at other times large. He feeds only on fish and colored things. His head, according to Carib beliefs, is decorated by a crest or a "jewel that he covers or uncovers at will," as the chroniclers relate. Only the crest is to be seen; the rest of its body remains hidden. It is probably those myths about the origins of illnesses that are represented by the head-dress petroglyphs that are widely distributed in South America. They would be the representation of the rainbow (see Petitjean Roget 1983).

The artifacts most directly associated with the origin myth of illnesses, however, are undoubtedly the *caracoli* among the Caribs, and *guanin* by the Tainos. A section of the myth (Pané, 1972, chap. 6) tells how all the first incestuous women were abducted by a seductor, Guahayona, who abandons them on the island of Matinino, the islands of the women without men. The myth associates sexual abuse and incest with the disease that strikes the hero. He is cured by a woman, Guabonito, whom he had forgotten in the sea. This shaman woman gives him as a token of his cure some gold guanins as well as ornaments of white and black stones, known as *cibas*. During this commemoration the Spaniards kept asking the Tainos about their most valuable protection against illnesses and death, and they mistook the "guanins" for ghosts coming back from the dead, the place the Taino called *Coaybay*.

It would be beyond the scope of this chapter to pursue any further this survey of the art of the Amerindians of the Antilles. Their art is a message that all knew how to read. This Amerindian art of the Antilles, thus deciphered, strikes us by its immersion in myths. The frog on ceramic decoration is no mere tree frog but in reality Atabeira, the "primeval mother of humankind." As such, in the composition of decoration, she is always depicted above the fruit-eating bat that itself is no other than "the hero who brings to mankind the cultural goods." But the art of ancient Antillean societies has not yet revealed all its secrets. For more recent peoples, the Kalinas or Island Caribs, the chroniclers' narratives enriched by the memories of beliefs that Carib oral tradition has preserved in Martinique or Dominica among the marine or riverine fishermen (see Petitjean Roget 1980) still offer a variety of research potential.

NOTE

This chapter was translated by Louis Allaire.

Part 4: The Taino of the Greater Antilles on the Eve of Conquest

In 1492 the Greater Antilles were densely populated. People lived in large, permanent villages, some of which reportedly housed thousands of inhabitants. They fed their large population by growing cassava and other crops intensively in enriched mounds called *conucos*. Villages—as many as seventy to a hundred in some cases—formed political alliances under the leadership of one person or a powerful family. Dozens of these chiefdoms, or *cacicazgos*, controlled large areas of Cuba, Jamaica, Hispaniola, and Puerto Rico, and perhaps parts of the Lesser Antilles and the Bahamas as well.

More so than any other society in the New World in 1492, the Taino were insulated from the other peoples of the Americas. This is not to say that they had no contact with others at all, for such accomplished mariners as the Taino were not deterred by long sea voyages. But they had for centuries lived without fear of external conquest and had emerged as a society that was unique. Their exquisite stone and wood carvings are richly meaningful, covered with interwoven symbols from their mythology and religion. Their effigy ceramics are made in a realistic but subtly stylized manner that is distinctively Taino. What we know of their traditions of song and oratory suggests that their tangible objects of art are just a fraction of an extraordinarily rich expressive culture. The rapid destruction of Taino society after 1492 is one of the greatest tragedies of the conquest of the Americas. For those who study the indigenous people of the Caribbean, the decimation of the Taino seems even more tragic because they were the first of the Native American societies to be devastated in this way—and because their destruction was so comprehensive.

Focusing on topics ranging from economy and material culture to ideology and religion, the six chapters in part 4 discuss various aspects of Taino society. Most of the essays rely on the integration of historical and archaeological evidence, providing a rich and complex view of the Taino world.

12

"No Man [or Woman] Is an Island": Elements of Taino Social Organization

William F. Keegan

The title of this chapter, "No Man [or Woman] Is an Island," captures the most basic fact of human society: people live in groups. As social beings we define our lives and our identities by our relations with others, and although most cultures share the same basic elements of social organization, the ways in which these identities unfold vary widely. Perhaps the most important characteristic of groups is that they are always changing. The individuals themselves pass though life's stages between birth and death; membership in the group changes as individuals come and go; and the group itself may grow, fission, or even disband. The diversity of such group dynamics means that no two social situations are ever exactly alike; rather, their individualities promote both complexity and subtlety in the norms of behavior.

This chapter begins with a brief introduction to the structural elements of social organization. These categories are then used in conjunction with ethnohistoric and archaeological evidence to develop a general outline of Taino social and political organization.

THE ELEMENTS OF SOCIAL ORGANIZATION: KINSHIP

The basis for all social groupings is kinship, the network of interpersonal relations that arises from marriage and descent. In small-scale societies, kinship tends to dominate both intergroup and intragroup relations. As societies increase in scale, their internal and external operations become increasingly differentiated (Johnson and Earle 1987) and less fully controlled by family connections.

The structure of all social groups reflects adaptations to social and physical environments. In this regard, patterns of residence and descent are especially important because they determine where an individual will live as well as what the individual's rights and obligations will be with respect both to other individuals and to the group's corporate resources.

A rule of descent affiliates an individual at birth with a particular group of relatives through *matrilineal* (maternal), *patrilineal* (paternal), *double* (both maternal and paternal), or *bilateral* (nongenealogical) groups of kin. Descent is especially important in governing the inheritance of property owned collectively by kin relations. Among the Taino, for example, access to communally held land and succession to the office of chief were both determined primarily by descent traced through the maternal line (figure 12.1).

Rules of residence describe the customarily preferred living arrangements for married couples. Of many possible arrangements, five are most common. In a *matrilocal* society, the married couple lives in the same village as the wife's parents. In a *patrilocal* society, the couple lives with the husband's parents. In an *avunculocal* society, they live with the husband's maternal uncle. In a *neolocal* society, they live independent of either set of parents. Finally, in a *bilocal* society, the couple may choose to live with either spouse's parents. A society's residence preference, which anthropologists identify by what most people do rather than what they say they do, in general reflects economic and social conditions.

Customs regarding the relationship of residence and descent are referred to as rules not because they are necessarily recorded or codified but because postmarriage residence behaviors tend to conform to predictable patterns (Goodenough 1955). It is not correct, however, to assume that rules of descent and residence are never broken. Steadfast adherence to the commonly accepted rules may promote stability and order, but in most societies individuals will creatively and actively work to manipulate rules to their advantage. Such latitude can generate flexible responses to changing social and physical environments, even as it provides nightmares for anthropologists who find exceptions to every "rule."

A final category is an indigenous group's own kinship terminology, the set of terms that people in a given society use to address each other. Because archaeologists lack informants who could be asked about terms of address, it would seem impossible to determine kinship terms for preliterate societies from archaeological evidence. It is, however, possible to reconstruct the probable kinship terminology based on other characteristics of the social system.

Anthropologists have defined six main types of kinship classifications: Crow, Sudanese, Hawaiian, Eskimo, Omaha, and Iroquois. Each of these is associated with specific sociological characteristics and developmental histories (Murdoch 1949; Fox 1967; Keesing 1975). Although these terms must be inferred from other nonarchaeological categories of evidence, they are of potentially great significance. For instance, if the Tainos were, as I will argue, an avunculocal society, then it is likely they used a Crow-type kinship terminology (Byrne 1990). In contrast, studies of the Island Carib societies indicate that they probably used Iroquois-type kinship terms. Based on ethnological information regarding the evolution of kinship systems, these differences suggest that Island Caribs and Tainos must have developed separate social identities long before the Antilles were colonized (cf. Davis and Goodwin 1990), a conclusion that is also supported by linguistic evidence (Allaire 1990).

THE SPANISH DESCRIPTION OF TAINO SOCIAL ORGANIZATION

The starting point for reconstructing Taino social organization is the Spanish chroniclers who made the majority of their observations among the Classic Tainos of Hispaniola. Although these reports do not use modern anthropological language, the descriptions of activities and relationships have been used to infer social norms. In addition, the reports have been generalized to other Taino groups, based on the Spanish assertion that all Tainos had similar cultural practices.

The Tainos are reported to have had a matrilineal descent system (Fewkes 1907). In practice, matrilineal descent was expressed in the inheritance of rank through the female line, with females sometimes inheriting chief positions (Sued Badillo 1979; Wilson 1990). Representations of the lineage's ancestors called *zemis* (Rouse 1948a,b, 1982; Fewkes 1907; Stevens-Arroyo 1988) were also passed through the female line, and women are reported to have been both the producers and the distributors of certain high-status goods—for example, wooden stools, household objects, and "a thousand things of cotton" (Las Casas 1951a; see also Wilson 1990; Petersen 1982). Since private property is not reported as an important item of inheritance, even though it did exist among the upper ranks, the common inference is that access to corporate (group) resources was the primary benefit obtained through matrilineal inheritance.

The Spanish also reported that the eldest son would, on occasion, inherit the rank of lineage chief from his father (Rouse 1948b; Alegría 1979). Such inheritance could have resulted from patrilineal descent, or it may have been an exception to general practices that were brought about by the Spanish disruption of the indigenous social system (Sued Badillo 1985; Wilson 1990; Sauer 1966; Cook and Borah 1971; see Rosman and Rubel 1986, 21).

The Spanish reported that the Taino residence pattern was patrilocal (Rouse 1948b). However, this pattern of residence is extremely rare in matrilineal systems (Aberle 1961; Fox 1967). In fact, it has been reported only for societies undergoing extreme upheaval in response to more powerful external agents.

In matrilineal societies, individuals belong first to their mother's lineage, so the most important male in their lives is not their father but their mother's brother. Although this arrangement is difficult to envision in our society, where families are widely scattered, in most matrilineal societies the members of the extended family live fairly close together. Efforts to keep the male members of a matriline together cannot be achieved through patrilocal residence because men are not members of their father's lineage. Only through avunculocal residence can related males be kept together. Avunculocality requires both sexes to change domicile during their lives: adolescent boys move in with their real (or classificatory) maternal uncle, where they are later joined by their wives at marriage.

Thus, Spanish reports of Taino patrilocality are probably a misnomer, referring to a new wife's taking up residence in her husband's village rather than expressly with her husband's parents. What is likely—and consistent with the pattern in other matrilineal societies—is that precontact Taino society was avunculocal, with the new couple residing in the village of the husband's maternal uncle.

Taino Social Organization

The clearest image of Taino society emerges when we examine social relations from the perspective of a single individual, who in the convention of kinship terminology is called Ego (meaning "I"). Ego's membership in groups began at birth. Ego was given a name immediately after birth to identify him or her as a Taino—a human being (Fewkes 1907). Moreover, Ego already belonged to a nuclear family, an extended family, a matri-clan, a matrilineage, and a cacicazgo headed by a cacique.

Membership in these groups had consequences for Ego's entire life. Between birth and puberty, Ego was instructed in the norms and customs of these groups. Life passages were marked by various ceremonies, including a hair-cutting ceremony (Lovén 1935) and a puberty celebration that marked the passage from child to adult. Unless already married at this time, girls remained in the village of their mothers. Boys, particularly those who were expected to participate in leadership roles in their clan, moved to the village of their designated maternal uncle.

Marriage marked Ego's passage into full adulthood. Males of the *naboria,* or commoner, status were expected to compensate the wife-giving lineage by providing "bride service." Ego, the husband, moved to the village of his wife where he worked for his in-laws for several years. (In some societies the end of bride service coincided with the birth of a child—a new member for the wife's clan.) Following bride service, the couple would set up their own household in the most advantageous location. In the years that followed most commoners would pass through various roles and positions within their lineage and other less formal groups. In addition, certain individuals would receive training as craft specialists or as healers and shamans.

Unlike commoners, males of the *nitaino,* or elite, class compensated the wife-giving lineage with payments rather than service. With the help of his clan, the husband would accumulate a variety of wealth items and pay these to the wife-giving clan. The wife would then move immediately to live viri-avunculocally with her husband (that is, with her husband's uncle). High-status males were also polygynous; they were able to take as many wives as they could support. Such multiple marriages had an important integrative effect for the society: high-status women from one clan or lineage were given in marriage to a high-status male from another clan or lineage, thus creating a bond between these groups. The bond was strengthened by the fact that any offspring were members of the wife-giving lineage.

The highest position our high-status Ego could achieve was that of cacique, or chief, which was inherited from his maternal uncle. The Tainos had several levels of caciques, including *matunherí* (supreme cacique), *baharí* (second-grade cacique), and *guaoxerí* (lowest-grade cacique or village headman) (Redmond and Spencer 1994, table 10.1). In preparation, Ego would have joined an assembly of nephews in the village of his uncle the cacique. There Ego would have been instructed in the duties of the position until the moment of succession.

The final passage was death, which was celebrated by a variety of ceremonies depending upon the rank and gender of the individual. Some individuals were believed to live beyond death, and their bones were preserved and cared for in family shrines.

TAINO POLITICAL ORGANIZATION

The principal status ranking in Taino society was between the elite *nitainos* and the common *naborias* (Moscoso 1981). As with other ranked societies, it is likely that there were numerous divisions within these primary ranks. Little is known about the divisions within the *naborias,* but within the *nitainos,* for example, were several orders of caciques, the *behiques* (shamans), and the village headmen or clanlords. The highest rank was held by the supreme cacique, a ruler whose leadership extended over a substantial territory. Among the Tainos, Macorix, and Ciguayos, lineages were grouped into cacicazgos, each headed by a supreme cacique, who had the support of a large number of district caciques and village clanlords. For example, the thirty wives and multiple names ascribed to Behecchio, the paramount cacique of Jaraguá, represent villages allied under his leadership (Redmond and Spencer 1994, 202–4).

Although most caciques apparently were males, there are records of females who achieved this position. More importantly, in avunculocal chiefdoms, women are the power behind the throne. Anacaona, the sister of Behecchio, was married to Caonabo, the paramount cacique of Maguana (Wilson 1990). This marriage cemented the alliance between the two most powerful Taino cacicazgos in Hispaniola. Moreover, Bartolomé Colón reports that Anacaona herself controlled the production and distribution of a wide variety of high-status goods.

The Taino political machine is best described as an avunculocal chiefdom. I use the term *chiefdom* rather than *society* because the fact that a chiefdom is organized through avunculocal residence does not require the entire society to be avunculocal. Avunculocal residence seems to emerge in previously matrilocal, matrilineal societies that have experienced recurring internal warfare (Ember 1974). Because marriage distances are usually short in matrilocal societies, the men of the matrilineage can routinely assemble for political and ritual activities. As internal conflict commences, outbreaks of warfare with neighbors often alternate with periods of alliance and trade, which makes them difficult to anticipate. Constant readiness is required because political leaders must always be mindful of potential threats as well as offensive opportunities. Under these conditions the incentive to assemble the men of a matrilineal group more often and for longer periods increases. However, it is not possible to keep all of the men together constantly, so caciques must attempt to assemble a retinue of capable and loyal followers from among their matri-kin.

Yet Spanish accounts make no mention of inter-cacicazgo warfare. The reason may be that at the time of European contact the *nitainos* were forming marriage alliances among themselves while at the same time increasing the social distance between themselves and the *naborias*. There is tantalizing evidence that the Taino elite intermarried to create a distinct, pan-Taino social class.

My reasoning is as follows. First, avunculocal chiefdoms develop in an environment of intragroup hostility. In other words, it is likely that, at the very least, the Taino, Macorix, and Ciguayo cacicazgos were sociopolitical groups that at one time waged war on each other. Second, there is compelling evidence that the Tainos used the Crow-type kinship terms and practiced father's sister's daughter marriage (see Rosman and Rubel 1986, 44). Third, military and political entrepreneurship were the key elements in the emergence of the avunculocal chiefdom (Keegan and Maclachlan 1986). Faced with a military standoff in which each chiefdom marshaled roughly equal military forces, an alliance among the *nitainos* would foster peaceful relations that would increase the productive capacity within each cacicazgo. Peaceful relations would also facilitate the expansion of Taino influences into Cuba, the Bahamas, and the Lesser Antilles. Recent investigations in the southern Bahamas indicate an Antillean Taino presence beginning as early as A.D. 900 and continuing right up to contact. This Taino presence has a colonial character in which a dominant polity is extracting resources from the surrounding periphery. Hence the notion of "peaceful Arawaks" may in fact be the legacy of competing paramount caciques who manipulated the social and political systems to achieve personal advantage.

13

Taino, Island Carib, and Prehistoric Amerindian Economies in the West Indies: Tropical Forest Adaptations to Island Environments

James B. Petersen

In the ethnohistoric record, the Amerindians who lived across much of the West Indies at the time of contact with Europeans were known collectively as the Taino. During the early historic period, the Taino were apparently present throughout the Greater Antilles, the Bahamas, and perhaps the northern Lesser Antilles (see figure 1.1). However, beyond Hispaniola and Puerto Rico, the area of the socially complex Classic Taino, Taino groups are less well known on the basis of historic records (and as Rouse, 1992, points out, designating the areas best known historically as *Classic* may not be coincidental). To the south, in the Lesser Antilles, lived the Island Caribs, who are better known because of their sustained contact with non-natives and their survival to the present day. In the western Greater Antilles there some is evidence for a third group, the aceramic Ciboney or Guanahatabey (Chanlatte Baik and Narganes Storde 1989; Rey Betancourt 1988; Rouse 1992; but cf. Keegan 1992). Information is woefully incomplete for traditional aspects of all of these Amerindian cultures, however, and archaeology is therefore critical to our understanding of them.

Ethnohistoric information provides an incomplete baseline for an understanding of Taino and Island Carib economies. Nonetheless, when taken in conjunction with economic data derived from archaeology, the available information suggests that prehistoric and historic Amerindians in the West Indies were very successfully adapted to their environments. Their diets combined the native terrestrial and marine resources of diverse island environments with resources brought in by their ancestors from tropical South America (and perhaps Central America). The island groups prospered by combining tropical forest subsistence methods with locally based maritime adaptations. Although nonfood resources were largely obtained locally, non-local or "exotic" materials were also obtained from more distant sources—including mainland South America—through direct acquisition, local trade, and long-distance trade (which seems to be a hallmark of West Indian economies; see Boomert 1987; Chanlatte Baik and Narganes Storde 1989; Cody 1991; Rodríguez 1991; Rouse 1992; Vega 1979; Veloz Maggiolo 1991; Watters, this volume). This chapter summarizes the archaeological and ethnohistoric evidence for these assertions.

West Indian Cultural Evolution

West Indian Amerindian prehistory and history can be divided into five major periods (Rouse 1992; Rouse and Allaire 1978). The first two of these are known as the Lithic (ca. 4000–2000 B.C.) and Archaic (2000–500 B.C.); the latter persisted later in some areas. Both are preceramic and nonagricultural and can be together labeled the Preceramic period. (As noted above, the aceramic, hunting and gathering lifeway may have persisted until European contact; see Chanlatte Baik and Narganes Storde 1989; Rouse 1992; Veloz Maggiolo 1991.) The third period, the Saladoid or Early Ceramic (ca. 500 B.C.–A.D. 600), marked the arrival of larger, more settled agricultural groups who made pottery. The fourth period is labeled the post-Saladoid, or Late Ceramic (ca. A.D. 600–1492), and the fifth is called the contact period—which in the Greater Antilles, northern Lesser Antilles, and Bahamas ran from roughly 1492 to 1550. In this brief period many traditional West Indian native populations were largely destroyed (Keegan 1992; Rey Betancourt 1988; Wilson 1990), while others, such as the Island Caribs in the Lesser Antilles, were later deported (Boucher 1992; Gonzalez 1988; Hulme and Whitehead 1992). For the Island Caribs, the contact period continues to the present.

In the Lithic and Archaic periods, marine resources seem to have been particularly important for the occupants of the Greater and Lesser Antilles. These peoples, who had come from South America and perhaps Central America, apparently were chiefly hunter-gatherers, although they may have been incipient horticulturalists in that they managed native plants (Davis 1988; Veloz Maggiolo 1991; Veloz Maggiolo and Ortega 1976; Veloz Maggiolo and Vega 1982). In any event, they did not practice agriculture and thus were largely if not totally dependent on the native flora and fauna.

Because land animals have always been rare in the West Indies, these hunter-gatherers concentrated on marine resources, especially shellfish.

With the arrival of the pottery-making people of the Early Ceramic period, an economic system more dependent on horticulture was introduced (Davis 1988; Rouse 1992; Siegel 1991; Veloz Maggiolo 1991). A combination of farming, hunting of native and introduced land animals, and utilizing marine resources seems evident for this period. However, it is important to emphasize that only some island environments were extensively used by these first West Indian farmers, particularly the higher, wetter islands in the Lesser Antilles, the Virgin Islands, and Puerto Rico. Other islands were largely bypassed, and most of the larger islands of the Greater Antilles were apparently never settled by Saladoid peoples (Rouse 1992; Tabío and Rey 1966; Veloz Maggiolo 1991).

The rich soils of the higher volcanic islands were most conducive to farming, a fact channeling early farmers to settle mainly on islands such as Grenada, St. Lucia, Martinique, Guadeloupe, Montserrat, Nevis, St. Kitts, St. Eustatius, and St. Martin (Goodwin 1979; Haviser 1991; Mattioni 1982; Petersen and Watters 1991b; Petitjean Roget 1976a; Versteeg and Schinkel 1992; Wilson 1989). Lower, less fertile and somewhat drier islands such as Anguilla and Barbuda were apparently avoided. In the Greater Antilles, cultural rather than environmental factors—such as opposition from resident aceramic peoples—seem to have restricted Saladoid settlement (Chanlatte Baik and Narganes Storde 1989; Rouse 1992; Veloz Maggiolo 1991).

In any case it seems that with time, marine resources became increasingly important to West Indian horticultural peoples during the Ceramic period, and here the maritime adaptation includes use of estuarine, rocky intertidal, beach, reef, and pelagic environments (see Nietschmann 1973 for an excellent ethnographic treatment of the Miskito of Honduras and Nicaragua). This was especially true during the Late Ceramic period. Perhaps this increasing use of marine resources allowed settlement to expand to all traditionally inhabited Antillean island settings during the Late Ceramic period (Davis 1988; Rouse 1992; Watters and Rouse 1989). The Bahamas were also settled at this time, thereby completing one of the most far-flung colonization processes undertaken by native peoples in the Western Hemisphere (Keegan 1992, n.d.). An increased emphasis on marine resources apparently continued into the contact period of the Taino and Island Carib. Aspects of the Amerindian economies may also be seen in more recent Colonial and post-Colonial West Indian systems (see Berleant-

Schiller and Pulsipher 1986; Dunn 1972; Hall 1992; Mintz 1989; Reitz 1986; Rey Betancourt 1988).

PRECERAMIC MARITIME ADAPTATIONS

Because of the long isolation of the West Indies from the American mainland, the islands originally had a relatively impoverished native terrestrial fauna. Paleontologists, in describing the terrestrial fauna prior to and after the arrival of humans, have provided clear evidence that native species further diminished over time as a result of environmental change, over-exploitation, and habitat alteration (Morgan and Woods 1986a; Pregill and Olson 1981; Pregill et al. 1988; Rouse 1960; Veloz Maggiolo 1972). Clearly, modern groups were responsible for such degradation, and Amerindians may have been as well: the topic of human-induced extinctions in the West Indies deserves additional attention.

The evidence is slight for the era of first human settlement, including both the Lithic and the Archaic periods. Significant advances have been made in the past two decades or so, but relatively little evidence is as yet available to characterize preceramic groups. Moreover, the existing evidence is largely related to lithic tool and to a lesser degree shell tool technologies. Thus statements about preceramic subsistence are somewhat provisional at this point.

The available preceramic faunal evidence reflects human use of a mixture of land and marine animals, especially on the larger islands. On some of the smaller islands, site samples of preceramic fauna sometimes consist largely or totally of shellfish, often representing only one or a few species; this is especially so in the later Archaic period (Crock et al. 1994; Davis 1988; Lundberg 1991). These findings may reflect the presence of temporary marine-oriented sites or a preservation bias against other fauna.

In any case, the broad range of demonstrated fauna for preceramic sites includes hutia, a Greater Antillean rodent (including *Boromys*, *Capromys*, *Geocapromys*, *Heteropsomys*, *Isolobodon*, and *Plagiodontia* spp., among others), one or more insectivores (*Nesophontes* spp.), along with other medium-sized rodents, manatees, and birds of various sorts. There were also sea turtles, possible crocodiles (in the Greater Antilles), lizards (including iguanas), snakes, land snails, and land crabs. Whale remains have been found as well, but these may be evidence not of hunting but of the opportunistic use of individual beached whales (Pino 1970a, b; Rouse 1992; Tabío and Rey 1966; Veloz Maggiolo 1976; Veloz Maggiolo and Ortega 1976; Veloz Maggiolo et al. 1977; Veloz Maggiolo and Vega 1982). Although dated as late as the pre-Ceramic period in the Greater Antilles, ground sloths have yet to be conclusively related to human subsistence in this period. Likewise primates such as squirrel monkeys may have been human prey at this time, but this is not certain (Morgan and Woods 1986; Pino and Castellanos 1985; Rodríguez Suarez et al. 1984; Veloz Maggiolo and Ortega 1976; Veloz Maggiolo et al. 1977).

Fishes exploited in some fashion by preceramic groups include parrotfish, snappers, porgies, jacks, grunts, groupers, wrasses, leatherjacks, barracuda, and sharks. All of these species are known from the preceramic Krum Bay site in St. Thomas, for example, as reported by Elizabeth Reitz (1989); only 2.3 percent of the vertebrate fauna from Krum Bay were derived from terrestrial habitats, a fact reflecting a clear marine emphasis. The variable and diverse shellfish remains from across the region include *Cittarium pica,* or West Indian topshell; *Anadara, Arca, Codakia,* and *Lucina* spp.; and *Strombus gigas,* or queen conch (Artiles and Dacal 1973; Davis 1982; Narganes Storde 1991; Pino 1970a, b; Veloz Maggiolo and Ortega 1976; Wilson 1989). *Pinctada imbricata,* or Atlantic pearl oyster, dominates among the species from the Krum Bay site (Lundberg 1989, 1991; Reitz 1989).

Relatively few plant remains are known from preceramic sites, and those that are known have rarely been analyzed. Nonetheless, lithic grinding tools are one of the preceramic hallmarks suggesting, at least in some cases, that native plant foods were indeed important to these early settlers. Preceramic sites on Hispaniola have yielded evidence of the fruits of several palms, including corozo (*Acrocomia quisqueyana*) and royal palm (*Roystonea hispaniolana*); cupey, or false-mamey (*Clusia rosea*); and cycad guayiga (*Zamia debilis*), which has an edible root (Veloz Maggiolo 1991, 1992; Veloz Maggiolo and Ortega 1976; Veloz Maggiolo et al. 1977).

Recently Newsom (1993), working partly from Pearsall's (1989) analysis of samples from Krum Bay, has reviewed the paleobotanical evidence for early plant use. Krum Bay samples show the presence of wild fig, mangrove, mastic-bully, portulaca, and trianthema among food and/or medicinal plants, as well as panama tree (*Sterculia* sp.) and sapodilla, or balata (probably *Manilkara* sp.)—these latter two, possibly home-garden trees. Possible mastic-bully and primrose are also known from the preceramic Hichman's shell-heap site in Nevis, while wild avocado and yellow sapote are reported from Maria de la Cruz Cave in Puerto Rico (Newsom 1993). The panama tree from Krum Bay and the avocado and sapote from Maria de la Cruz Cave are seemingly introductions from outside of the West Indies (Newsom, personal communication 1993). Like some of the finds from

Hispaniola (Veloz Maggiolo 1991, 1992), these latter finds suggest that while preceramic peoples were not likely farmers per se, they may have practiced plant husbandry and long-distance transport of plant species. This important topic obviously deserves additional research.

SALADOID AND POST-SALADOID SUBSISTENCE: THE CRAB-SHELL "DICHOTOMY" REVISITED

One of the early archaeologists to work in the West Indies, Froelich Rainey, identified an important distinction in Puerto Rican sites during the 1930s. Rainey (1940) noticed that the earlier ceramic remains, today labeled Saladoid, were associated with dense deposits of land crabs, while later remains, now sometimes called post-Saladoid, were more typically associated with marine shellfish. Thus Rainey distinguished between an earlier "Crab Culture" and a later "Shell Culture."

The details of this distinction have been the subject of much debate (deFrance 1989; Goodwin 1979; Keegan 1989; Jones 1985; Watters and Rouse 1989; Wing 1989), and although the "dichotomy" is still recognized by some researchers, most scholars now see it chronologically not as the replacement of one resource by another but as a gradual and variable shift in relative usage. The "crab-shell" model thus marks a long transition from more terrestrially dependent economies to more marine-focused ones, in rough correlation with Saladoid to post-Saladoid occupations (although post-Saladoid use of land crabs is notable in some cases—see, for example, Davis 1988; deFrance 1989).

This observation has been refined through recent research by zooarchaeologists over much of the West Indian region. Elizabeth Wing and her students at the University of Florida (especially Betsy Reitz, Sylvia Scudder, and Susan deFrance) have begun to provide the details of island-by-island subsistence for Saladoid and post-Saladoid Amerindians. The following summary is indebted to their work and to the detailed analyses reported by other scholars (Dacal Moure 1986; deFrance 1989; Drewett 1991; Jones 1985; Keegan 1986; Lippold 1991; Mattioni 1980; Narganes Storde 1985, 1993; Reitz 1994; Scudder 1991; Steadman et al. 1984; Tabío and Guarch 1966; Versteeg and Schinkel 1992; Watters et al. 1984; Wing 1969, 1973, 1989, 1991; Wing et al. 1968; Wing and Reitz 1982; Wing and Scudder 1980).

If one accepts the strong likelihood that horticulture was important to the economy (Rouse 1992; Tabío 1989; Veloz Maggiolo 1991; Watters and Rouse 1989), the study of West Indian faunal remains suggests that the arrival of Saladoid peoples into the islands represented a transference to insular settings of a tropical forest economy derived from South America. The term *tropical forest economy* is not without controversy of course (Meggers and Evans 1978; Roosevelt 1980), but as used here, it means generally an economy based on root crops like cassava (manioc, yucca)— an economic strategy similar to that of indigenous lowland South America. Saladoid groups were seemingly less strictly marine dependent than either their preceramic predecessors or later post-Saladoid groups. For example, Wing (1989) has reported that Saladoid sites in the Lesser Antilles have an average of 38 percent terrestrial species, while post-Saladoid sites have only 19 percent. Greater Antillean sites have an overall average of 34 percent terrestrial species, very likely reflecting the presence of much more extensive terrestrial habitats there, as well as the generally later attributions of most such sites (Wing 1989). Values of 62 percent and 89 percent terrestrial are recorded for post-Saladoid sites in some noncoastal areas of Jamaica, however (Scudder 1991). Other, certainly later prehistoric sites in the Bahamas (settled ca. A.D. 800–1000, Keegan 1992) are on average only 17 percent terrestrial (Wing 1989), while in contrast, at one recently studied Saladoid site, Trants in Montserrat, the percentage of terrestrial species is very high, ranging from 44 percent to 57 percent terrestrial (Reitz 1994).

It should be noted again that the distinction between terrestrial and marine resources reflects not an abrupt change in usage patterns but a shift in emphasis, or degree of usage, over time (deFrance 1989; Watters and Rouse 1989). The increased percentages of marine resources in later prehistory may well indicate a greater diversity of settings among later sites, including more coastal occupations. The initial introduction of farming into selected West Indian environments—specifically fertile, well-watered islands—may have allowed Saladoid groups initially to be more selective in using marine resources. Once they expanded to occupy less optimum environments for farming, they became by necessity more dependent on marine resources.

Since this shift over time is seemingly represented at sites both in optimum farming locations and in more marginal environments, it is unlikely that the change was related merely to the use of new environments. Perhaps in both cases population growth necessitated expansion into new environments and the more intensive use of previously exploited terrestrial and marine resources (Keegan 1989, 1992).

Technological intensification may also have accompanied post-Saladoid human expansion. Possibly, Saladoid groups needed to develop additional maritime technologies such as fish traps to more fully exploit relatively rich available marine resources, and thus cultural factors may help account for the change. Recently discovered evidence of post-Saladoid agricultural terracing in the Greater Antilles may reflect intensification of horticulture there during the post-Saladoid period (Ortiz Aguilú et al. 1991) as well as during the contact period (Rouse 1992).

Cultural preferences may have also affected economic use of different fauna by Amerindians in the West Indies, with variability in time and space as a result. It is clear that native and imported mammals as well as fish, bird, and reptile species were important in Amerindian iconography, as ceramics and other material culture testify (see, for example, García Arévalo 1977; Mattioni 1980; Narganes Storde 1993; Petitjean Roget 1976a).

Environmental factors should not be discounted in explaining subsistence variability, however, since both Saladoid and post-Saladoid sites exhibit variable terrestrial and marine fauna, reflecting different island and off-shore environments. At least some of the faunal variety of the Ceramic period, for example, is simply a reflection of local environmental variability. Comparisons of excavated fauna between different settings on the same island (Scudder 1991) and between steep-sided islands with limited reefs and lower islands with substantial reefs clearly show that the frequency of reef habitats and other environments affects the fauna itself (see, for example, Jones 1985; Reitz 1994; Steadman et al. 1984; Watters et al. 1984; Wing 1973; Wing et al. 1968; Wing and Scudder 1980).

On the larger islands, a greater range of fauna was exploited, with hutia particularly important in the Greater Antilles and the Virgin Islands (Scudder 1991). In the Lesser Antilles, the agouti (*Dasyprocta aguti*), a rodent introduced by the Amerindians from South America, may have been comparably important since no hutias were native there. Likewise, several species of now-extinct native rice rats (*Oryzomys* spp.) were heavily used in the Lesser Antilles and elsewhere. The opossum, represented only in the southern Lesser Antilles, is another species possibly introduced by the Amerindians (Lippold 1991; Morgan and Woods 1986; Wing 1991), although it is also claimed to have been native there (Petitjean Roget 1976a).

On the basis of finds in Antigua, the Dominican Republic, and Puerto Rico, it is also possible, although not certain, that guinea pigs were introduced by Amerindians from South America. More certainly, it appears that one of the hutias (*Isolobodon portoricensis*), a native of Hispaniola, was introduced by Amerindians to Puerto Rico and the Virgin Islands, while other rodent species may have been transported from Cuba to Hispaniola and to the Bahamas, in all cases as food sources. The flightless rail may have been raised in captivity and transported to the Virgin Islands, again as a food, while the macaw was seemingly traded to St. Croix from elsewhere (Morgan and Woods 1986; Wing 1989). Remains of the boa constrictor and parrot in Antigua likewise suggest inter-island transport by Amerindians (Pregill et al. 1988).

Ceramic-period groups also extensively used various locally available resources including iguanas, ameivas and other lizards, saltwater crocodiles, and a range of shore and terrestrial bird species, including pigeons and doves. Some of the bird fauna reflect the presence of mangrove and other forested habitats that were extensively cleared during the historic period (Reitz 1994; Scudder 1991; Steadman et al. 1984; Watters and Rouse 1989; Wing 1989).

The common presence of ceramic griddles in Ceramic-period sites, both early and late, has been taken as conclusive evidence of farming among these populations, since griddles are assumed to have been used for cooking cassava bread (Meggers and Evans 1978; Rouse 1992; Tabío 1989; Watters and Rouse 1989). Nonetheless, the paucity of paleobotanical analyses across the region means that there is very little direct evidence of prehistoric horticulture in the West Indies.

Newsom (1993, 1994) and others have begun to correct this deficit by identifying a wide range of wood types now known for different sites and time periods. For example, the Saladoid Golden Rock site in St. Eustatius produced eight types of wood charcoal, and the Saladoid Trants site in Montserrat alone has produced at least thirteen different wood types; various others are reported in Newsom's (1993) regional review, which suggests that a large number of home-garden trees and herbs are demonstrable from Ceramic-period sites in the northern Lesser Antilles and Puerto Rico. Newsom also reports a range of "other food/medicinal plants," including cockspur, wild fig, fish poison, goosefoot, lignum-vitae/guayacan, machioneel, mastic-bully, panicoid grass, trianthema, wild raspberry, and stargrass. Of the twenty species specified by Newsom (1993), at least the Panama tree, papaya, and soursop were not likely native to the West Indies and must have been introduced into the region by the Amerindians.

In spite of the promising inventory reported above, evidence of cultivated crops is still scant, with cassava tentatively identified from only one or two prehistoric sites in the West Indies. Unequivocal evidence of Amerindian maize has been identified only at En Bas Saline, a Late Ceramic and possibly early contact site in western Hispaniola. This site also includes evidence of cassava, possible cassava bread, sweet potato, and a possibly related "starchy tissue" tuber (Newsom and Deagan 1994; Newsom, personal communication 1993).

Maize kernels are also reported to have been found at the Saladoid Sugar Factory Pier site in St. Kitts (Davis 1988), but the details of this find have not been published. In addition, isotopic analysis of human skeletons from post-Saladoid burials in the Bahamas (and one Saladoid individual from Puerto Rico) by Keegan (1989, 1992) and others suggests that maize may have been consumed there, in conjunction with various other foods, but this is only indirect evidence. Nonetheless, isotopic analysis of human remains is a very promising method for defining prehistoric diets, and it should be more broadly applied in future West Indian research. Obviously, much more work remains to be done in the analysis of Amerindian diets for the full span of prehistory across the region.

Contact-period Economies: Ethnohistorical Data for the Taino and Island Carib

Ethnohistoric evidence for the Taino is largely confined to Hispaniola and Puerto Rico, the area of the so-called Classic Taino—with few, if any, comments about subsistence (or other issues) available for other probable Taino groups, especially those that might have lived beyond the Greater Antilles. In fact it is very difficult to prove that the people of the northern Lesser Antilles were indeed Taino, although this seems likely (Rouse 1992). Similarly for the Island Carib, little information about traditional subsistence is available for the period before the mid-seventeenth century, the time by which economic changes had certainly occurred as the result of contact. Early Spanish chroniclers such as Las Casas and Oviedo indicate that the Taino were very dependent on horticultural crops—particularly cassava or manioc, of which six varieties were recorded in the early 1500s. As summarized by the ethnologist Sven Lovén:

> The islands the Tainos lived on, were for the most part a veritable ... paradise. The soil was suitable for yucca [cassava] and other plants that they cultivated. There was an abundance of edible fish in the rivers and above all along the coast. Meat played a less important role in the diet. . . . Big game did not exist.
>
> On the savannas and in the woods were to be found great quantities of small rodents . . . and also certain birds were easily captured. . . . But as also in the other Arawak tribes, it was nevertheless the soil that

provided the Tainos with cassava, their staple food together with certain other culture-plants especially suitable to Indian requirements.
(Lovén 1935, 350)

The primacy of cassava among the Taino was reflected in the fact that one
of their two supreme deities was *Jocahu,* or *Yucahu,* the lord of cassava
and the sea, while the other was *Atabey,* his mother, the goddess of fresh
water and human fertility (Arrom 1975; Bourne 1907).

From the early accounts, it is obvious that the farming technology was
relatively simple, largely limited to a digging stick—a fact leading some to
regard Taino farming as horticulture, or gardening, rather than as agriculture proper. However, evidence suggests that sizable earthen mounds, or
conucos, were used for planting over extended periods and that irrigation
was practiced in arid areas such as southwestern Hispaniola (Rouse 1948a,
b, 1992; Tabío 1989; Veloz Maggiolo 1972). Evidence of prehistoric terracing further supports the idea that farming in some areas was more complicated than simple horticulture. Rouse (1992) suggests that farming had
been intensified in Hispaniola and Puerto Rico in the area of the Classic
Taino as well as in Jamaica but that the western Taino of Cuba and the
Bahamas as well as the eastern Taino were slash-and-burn horticulturists;
he correlates this distinction with greater and lesser degrees of social complexity. This issue too bears further investigation.

In any case, after cassava, sweet potato was apparently of secondary importance to Taino farmers, along with a host of other crops such as maize,
squash, beans, arrowroot, peppers, and peanuts. Pineapples were cultivated,
as were various fruits, tobacco, calabashes, and cotton. The latter two were
used for a variety of utilitarian purposes, with cotton especially valued for
weaving. A wide variety of native plants were also used as foodstuffs and
for other purposes (Guarch Delmonte 1973; Keegan 1987; Rouse 1948a,
b, 1992; Siegel 1991; Tabío 1989; Veloz Maggiolo 1972, 1991).

Besides plants, the chroniclers report a wide variety of Taino nets, weirs,
and other fish-catching devices. Hutias were apparently caught in corrals
and kept penned until needed, while iguanas, parrots, other birds, manatees, and various shellfish species were also used as food (Guarch Delmonte
1973; Rouse 1948b, 1992; Veloz Maggiolo 1972). Unfortunately we do
not know which of these foods were of the most importance; it seems likely
that the available information underestimates the role of marine resources.

In many ways, traditional Island Carib subsistence was similar to that of
the Taino, although it seems to have been somewhat less intensive—and
our reconstruction of it does suffer from a paucity of precise details. To

begin with, the word *Carib* has often been equated with the Spanish word for cannibal, *canibal*, suggesting that these people were man-eaters. The latter point has been widely contested in recent years, not only by scholars (Boucher 1992; Hulme and Whitehead 1992; Moreau 1992; Petitjean Roget 1976a) but also by the surviving Island Caribs in Dominica (Chief I. Auguiste, personal communication 1993). Only one plausible ethnohistoric account documents this practice, and even that account suggests that Carib "cannibalism" may have been less a gastronomic than a ritualistic practice—as appears to be the case among modern Amerindians in South America. It seems likely that this attribution was largely a myth promulgated by the Spanish and others as a justification for their harsh treatment of the Island Caribs and other native peoples.

Details about Island Carib subsistence suggest that land crabs and shellfish were particularly important native foods, along with agouti, birds, lizards, manatees, sea turtles, and fish. Among the plant resources, cultivated cassava was a staple, as it was for the Taino. Other crops included maize, sweet potatoes, yams, beans, and peppers. Bananas, plantains, papaya, pineapple, and other fruits were also important, with at least the first two in this list being contact-period introductions. Tobacco and cotton were important nonfood plant resources. Gardens were placed in protected locales, sometimes at great distances from Island Carib habitations. Inter-island travel for stored-food resources such as found in fish pens and contingency garden crops was apparently a traditional practice (Allaire 1977; Boucher 1992; Moreau 1992; Petitjean Roget 1976a; Rouse 1948c).

In sum, the subsistence practices of the Taino and Island Carib peoples was broad-based and much like those of their prehistoric predecessors, at least as represented in the Greater Antilles. Additional details derived from the ethnohistoric record and more certainly through excavation of unequivocal contact-period archaeological sites may help to refine this general reconstruction in the future.

Summary and Conclusions

This brief review of Taino and Island Carib economies and those of their predecessors suggests that all Amerindians in the West Indies shared a broad-based dependence on diverse food resources. Preceramic inhabitants of the Lithic and Archaic periods, and the later post-Saladoid (Late Ceramic) groups seem to have been more marine resource-oriented than Saladoid (Early Ceramic) populations. Saladoid subsistence was seemingly more reflective of the South American tropical forest settings in which it originated; as such it may have been less adapted to the rich marine environments of the islands.

Judging from their limited technology and their propensity to occupy a relatively restricted range of environments, it is also possible that Saladoid groups enjoyed little if any population pressure. Saladoid groups seem to have favored the higher, well-watered islands, which have more consistent and plentiful water sources and fertile volcanic soils. In contrast, peoples of the Preceramic and Late Ceramic periods seemingly occupied a broader range of West Indian environments. Contact-period Amerindians in the region, whether Taino or Island Carib, are best known from sketchy ethnohistorical documents, and these confirm that they also had broad-based economies derived from cultivated crops and land and ocean resources.

Although this review of traditional Amerindian economies raises more questions than it answers, it does demonstrate the long-term versatility inherent in West Indian subsistence practices. The overall range of food (and other) resources used in a particular time and place was largely dependent on local environmental conditions, but cultural practices and preferences were also relevant. Continued zooarchaeological and paleobotanical research is needed to further unravel the archaeological record, while additional ethnohistoric research may also contribute details about economic issues, particularly the relative importance of environmental and cultural considerations. Obviously much work remains to be done in these important areas.

14

The Material Culture of the Taino Indians

Ignacio Olazagasti

At the moment of the European encounter, the Tainos were a large ethnic group who inhabited the vast territory of the Greater Antilles and who produced a vast and varied material culture. In this chapter, I discuss the diverse objects and artifacts that the Tainos made using wood, stone, shell, bones, corals, cotton, and various fibers, and I examine the various uses—technological and artistic—to which these materials were put. As far as possible, I use the original words of the chroniclers as they described what they saw.

AGRICULTURAL IMPLEMENTS

In order to facilitate the planting of cassava roots in their *conucos*, or mounded fields, the Tainos used the *coa*, a long, hardwood digging stick. In his *Apologética*, Las Casas describes this instrument and its purpose: "for this God provided for them, giving them what they needed for their labors by granting them rich lands, so fertile that with a strong fire-hardened stick they could easily dig and break the ground and prepare their fields. They had all these things necessary to support life, these true natural riches, as I have said, in great abundance" (Las Casas 1967).

This passage illustrates the importance to the Taino agricultural process of various clay objects, including the *buren*, or clay griddle, on which they baked cassava bread, and the supporting *topias*, or rounded cylinders. Another important cooking implement was the *cibucán*, a basketry tube that was used to squeeze the poisonous juice out of the cassava. The Tainos also employed a variety of other implements to hold the cassava roots, the baked bread, and other products.

To aid them in the various stages of the agricultural process, the Taino used different types of axes. The petaloid axes are the most common found in the sites. The ax heads, which vary in size and types of stone, were generally grooved and tied to a wooden handle. The Tainos were masters in the process of ax making. With the help of stone instruments such as burils and hammerstones, they produced remarkable examples of lithic craftsmanship. Their expertise in this area is also shown in their production of mortars and pestles, often adorned with human and animal forms. Ceremonial pestles, which are very common in Santo Domingo, are particularly known for their exquisite carving.

WEAPONS

Although some authors refer to the Tainos as peaceful, they were in fact, as many chroniclers indicate, equipped with a wide array of weapons to defend themselves and their villages from invaders. In addition to the petaloid axes, they manufactured bows and arrows, harpoons, spear-throwers, and most importantly a heavy club called the *macana*. Las Casas describes it as follows: "a spade of palm wood, which is extremely hard and very heavy, made in the following way: not sharp, but with a flat handle and uniformly thick, with which, since it is hard and heavy like iron, although a man wears a helmet on his head, one blow will sink his skull into his brains" (Las Casas 1951a).

The spear-thrower, or *atlatl,* was a composite weapon made of a wooden handle and a small shell piece used to hook the end of a feathered wooden shaft with a stone projectile point:

> they had bows and arrows and shafts like darts, which they threw with great force and accuracy, in the following way: they had a throwing stick, well and finely made, four palms in length and at the end it had a small piece of shell with a notch, where the dart-like shaft was seated, and the hilt had well-made cotton as a strap, into which the elbow was placed, as a brace to prevent it from slipping; they placed the shaft in the notch or foot of the throwing stick, and grasped the dart with their fingers on the hilt, and with great force threw the dart better if they were driving it a great distance. (Las Casas 1967)

FISHING AND HUNTING IMPLEMENTS

In addition to the bow and arrows, the spear-thrower, and the *macana,* the Taino used a variety of wooden traps and textile nets for hunting and fishing. These tools were so efficient that they have passed the test of time and are still being used today by Caribbean peasants:

> they fished with nets, very well made, in the rivers and in the sea, those that were near enough, with fishhooks made from fish bones, and also with arrows for large fish. They were great and marvelous swimmers. They had their boats, as has been said, made from hollowed out wood, which they called canoes, which carried fifty or a hundred men, and these were used throughout the Indies. The oars are like long handled bakers' shovels, but sharp, and very well made. (Las Casas 1967)

> There still grows in these islands an herb, tall like tough feathergrass [espata] or hemp, which they card, tan, and spin, and they make fishing nets with it, as fine or thick as they like; it is a strong, pretty thread, and instead of lead weights they put stones on the nets, and use lightweight wood instead of cork. (Cuneo 268)

To anchor their fishing nets, the Taino used stone weights called *potalas*. They produced a great variety of stone and shell hooks to fish the mangrove areas and rocky beaches that surrounded the islands. To aid in the fishing process, they also built large, oceangoing canoes. These huge dugouts, which the chroniclers say could hold up to eighty people, were the Indians' principal means of transportation from the South American mainland to the Lesser and Greater Antilles. Later they became a means of communication for maintaining kinship ties among the islands:

> On this island of Española, and in all other parts of these Indies known up until now, along all the seacoasts and on the rivers that Christians have seen to the present time, there is a kind of boat that the Indians call a canoe, with which they navigate the great rivers as well as these seas, which they use for war and plunder, and for their business from one island to another, or for fishing or for whatever they need them. Each canoe is of just one piece, either a single piece of wood or a single tree, which the Indians hollow out with blows from stone hatchets, hafted as they are shown here; and with these they cut or pound the wood, hanging it, and they continue burning what is beaten and cut, little by little, killing the fire, cutting and beating again as in the beginning. And continuing in this way, they make a boat in the form of a canoe or trough, but deep and long and narrow, as large and thick as the length and width of the tree from which they make it

permits. And the bottom is flat, and they do not use a keel like our boats and ships. I have seen these carry from 40 to 50 men, and they are so wide that one could comfortably place a cask crosswise between the Indian rowers, because these latter use these canoes, as big or bigger as I have described them. The Caribes call them *piraguas,* and navigate with cotton sails, as well as rowing with *nahes,* as they call their oars. Sometimes they paddle standing, sometimes seated, and when they want, on their knees. These *nahes* are like long shovels, and the prows are shaped like a crutch, worked and painted along with the paddles and the rest of the canoe. (Fernández de Oviedo 1959)

I saw between the trees of this port a canoe thrown up on the shore, beneath a covering of branches, made from the trunk of a tree, and as big as a *fusta* [small Spanish vessel] of twelve benches. (Fernando Colón 1984)

RELIGIOUS OBJECTS

Many examples of Taino craftsmanship were associated with their religious practices. At the time of the encounter, the most significant of these were the three-pointed stones known as *zemis,* first classified in Jesse Walter Fewkes's classic work, *The Aborigines of Porto Rico and Neighboring Islands* (1907). The zemis were one of the most important elements of Taino material culture. Their magical powers were associated with all aspects of their daily and cosmogonical activities. Zemis were made out of wood, shell, bone, clay, stone, and cotton. Fewkes presents a wide array of these amulets, which were generally hung on the body. The only remaining example of a cotton zemi, a piece originally found in a cave in Santo Domingo and now housed in a Turin museum, is a fine example of Taino weaving skills.

The zemis are also associated with the *cohoba* ritual, an important and complex religious ceremony in which a considerable number of objects with religious and political power—including wooden idols that contained snuff powder and *espatulas vómicas,* or vomiting sticks—were used. In addition, as Fernando Colón related, "most of the caciques have three stones, towards which they and their peoples show great devotion. The first, they say, is good for the grains and vegetables they have planted, the next, so that the women may give birth without pain, and the third, for the water and the sun, when they are in need of them" (Colón 1984, 204).

OTHER POWER OBJECTS

Of the varied personal objects that caciques and nitainos wore to show their political and religious status, the most significant were the objects of hammered gold alloy called *guanins*. Other things that denoted power were the *duhos*, or wooden stools, used by caciques and high-ranking officials. Some chroniclers refer to them as "thrones." Judging by their descriptions and by the few remaining examples, these stools were very elaborate pieces made of wood or stone, and sometimes decorated with shell or gold foil inlays.

COTTON CLOTH MATERIALS

Cotton was a wild crop used by the Indians to weave a variety of implements:

> [T]rees bearing very fine wool have been seen, such that those who know the art say that they would be able to make good cloth from it. There are so many of these trees that the caravels could be loaded with their wool, although it is laborious to pick, because the trees are full of spines; but surely some ingenious method for picking could be found. There is an infinite amount of cotton from perpetual trees as big as peach trees. (Chanca 1949, 64)

> [The cotton plants grow] in the fields, like the roses, and open by themselves when they are ripe, but not all at the same time, because on the same plant one could see a small bud, and another opened, and another fallen from ripeness. From [these] plants the Indians took great quantities to the ships, and for a strap of leather they would give a full basket, although to tell the truth, none of them used them for clothing, but only to make their nets and their beds, which they call hammocks, and to weave the skirts of the women, which are the clothes with which they cover their immodest parts. (Colón 1984, 122)

> These people practice a very singular industry: with cotton thread they know how to make a great variety of nets which they use for fishing, for carrying objects on their shoulders, and even for sleeping. Those which serve as beds are very large. They are suspended by their ends to the walls of the house. We have all tried this way of sleeping. These beds have the great advantage over ours of not taking up space.

I have acquired one for virtually nothing. They call them hammocks. In this country the married women wear a sort of loin cloth, but the girls do not. (Cosa 1957, 121)

They cultivate a great deal of cotton and even gather it in a wild state. In one house they had a quantity that our people estimated at 500 *arrobas* [an arroba is about 25 lbs.]. They know how to work it marvelously. (Cosa 1957, 136)

Although the Taino wore few clothes, cotton was used for the headbands worn by unmarried women, for the *naguas,* or short skirts, worn by married woman, and for various ornamental bands. Cotton was also used to weave decorative belts and hammocks. The following accounts give several examples of how cotton was grown and used:

Their beds were like a net, hung like a sling, in the middle of which they would throw themselves, and they tied the ends to the posts of the house. (Colón 1984, 116)

The beds in which they slept, which they called hammocks, were made like a sling, with a width of one and a half to two *estados,* the height of a man, and one *estado* in length, and with all the cotton threads twisted, not crossed over like a net, but extended lengthwise. (Las Casas 1967, 316)

It is well that it is told what kind of beds the Indians had on this island of Española, a bed which is called a hammock, and it is as follows, a blanket woven in part and in parts open, crossed with a checker-board pattern like a net (so that it is cooler). And it is of cotton spun by hand by the Indian women, [and the hammocks are] more or less 10 or 12 palms long and of whatever width they preferred. (Fernández de Oviedo 1959, 117)

He sent with his servant and messenger a belt from which instead of a bag hung a mask which had two large ears of hammered gold and a tongue and a nose; this belt was woven with something like fine stones, very small, like pearls, which were made of fish bones, white, with some colored ones mixed among them, almost like a kind of needlework; it was so well sewn in cotton thread, and with such beautiful skill, that on the side where the thread showed and on the reverse of the belt it appeared to be such beautiful work, although all in white, that it was a pleasure to see them. [It looked] as if it had been woven on a frame and by the technique that the Castillian weavers make the chasuble [sleeveless outer garment] of a priest's garment in Castile, and the [belts] were so hard and so strong that without doubt I believe that an arquebus [firearm] could not shoot through them, or not without difficulty; these were four fingers wide, and they were like those formerly used by the kings and great lords in Castile, made on a frame or woven of gold, and I managed to see one of those. (Las Casas 1951a, 1:272)

HOUSES AND BALL COURTS

To protect themselves from the tropical climate, the Indians constructed two types of wood and fiber dwellings, the *caney* and the *bohio*. The villages, or *yucayeques,* composed of these structures were so well organized that they impressed the Spaniards quite favorably:

The towns of these islands did not have streets, rather, the house of the king or lord of the town was in the best or most favorable place, and in front of the royal house in every town there was a large plaza, more cleared and levelled, and long rather than square, which they called in the language of these islands *batey,* pronounced with the last syllable long, which means ballcourt, because it was played as I will describe below, if God wishes. There were also houses near this plaza, and if it was a large town, there were other plazas or ballcourts smaller than the principal one. (Las Casas 1967, 244)

[H]aving walked 12 leagues by land and having reached a town of 50 very large houses, all of wood, roofed with thatch, made in the form of tents, like the others; there might be there some 1,000 hearths [or nuclear families], because in one house lived all the members of a family [extended family or clan]. (Colón 1984, 120)

On that voyage he passed through many Indian towns, whose houses were round and covered with thatch, with a small door, so that to enter one had to bend over considerably. (Colón 1984, 177)

The houses are of wood and straw, very long and narrow, made in the form of a tent, narrow at the highest point and wide at the lowest, and with a capacity for many people. They leave an opening above where the smoke escapes and on top they have finely worked and well-proportioned ridges or cornices, which are, as the Admiral says, made in the manner of tents or pavilions, and both are good comparisons. Finally, as to the wood and thatch, they could not be more graceful nor better made, more secure, cleaner, or healthier, and it is a pleasure to see them and inhabit them. (Las Casas 1951a, 214)

We have navigated towards the west, following the coast. We can make out houses which are the most important of those we have seen up until now. We do not stop. We discover a river that the Admiral calls *de la Luna*. We go ashore and reach a town whose buildings, very well built, are distributed without plan. They have a thick layer of palm leaves for the roof which give them a certain character. These houses are called *bohío* in the language of the country. Sensing our approach, everyone flees. We find nothing but dogs that cannot bark. As always, the cleanliness of these homes is notable. We also marvel at the ability with which these people weave their nets and other fishing tackle. We have found in some of these houses figurines of women and masterfully sculptured heads. They resemble our carnival masks. Are they idols or objects they enjoy keeping with them? We do not touch anything and make for the sea. (Cosa 1957, 128)

The Tainos were also adept at constructing plazas or ball courts, typically composed of earth embankments and/or stone slabs. Sometimes the stone slabs were decorated with carvings of human and animal forms, or petroglyphs. The courts were oval, rectangular, or long and narrow in shape and could be used either as ball courts or dance grounds:

It was interesting to watch when they played a game with a [rubber] ball, which was almost like our light balls in appearance, but bounced six times higher than ours. They had a plaza, generally in front of the entrance to the house of the lord, very well cleared, three times longer than wide, enclosed by some low ridges, one or two palms in height, which when the ball left, I believe, was a fault. They placed themselves 20 and 30 on each side along the length of the plaza. Each one wagered whatever he had, not considering whether it was worth much more what one or the other was risking to lose, and so it happened, after the Spaniards arrived, that a cacique bet a large cape full of grain and another an old scrap of cloth, and this was the same as if he had put in 100 *castellanos* [gold coins]. One of those on one side threw in the ball to those of the other side and the closest one returned it, if it came high, with his shoulder, with which he returned it like a lightning bolt, and when it came in close to the ground, quickly, placing his right hand on the ground, he hit it with his hip, until, according to the rules of that game, one side or another committed a fault. It was a joy to see them playing when they got really excited, and much more when the women played against each other, hitting the ball, not with their shoulders or buttocks, but with their knees, and I believe with their closed fists also. The ball is called batey in their language, with a long "e," and the game and the place are also called batey. (Las Casas 1967, 350)

Among the best examples of the ball-court system is the Caguana court at Utuado, Puerto Rico, a fine illustration of ancient engineering. Located at the mountain heart of the island, it served as both a religious and a political center. Also associated with the ball-court activity are the *aros líticos* (stone yokes), *codos líticos* (elbow stones), and *esferas líticas* (stone balls). Although the use of these implements has been explained in various ways, to judge from the care shown in their carved and detailed surfaces, we can safely suppose that they were very special ritual objects.

Musical Instruments

The Tainos produced a variety of musical instruments of different materials: wooden drums; shell, clay, and wood flutes, or *ocarinas;* maracas of wood and higueras gourd containing small stones as rattlers; *güiros,* or gourd rattlers; and little drum sticks called *palitos.* All of these objects had ceremonial uses, and their importance has survived to the present day in Caribbean musical folklore.

Conclusions

The Tainos were important craft-makers who used any material available—especially wood, stone, shell, bone, and clay—in order to express their view of the world. The analysis of their craft and material culture provides clues that might help us understand the social, political, economic, and religious aspects of our vanished island ancestors.

15

The Taino Cosmos

José R. Oliver

THE ORDINARY WORLD OF THE TAINO: ORDER AND CHAOS

The day-to-day experience of life in the world of the Taino centered in all the ordinary things and events all humans are confronted with in tropical islands. The Tainos lived and participated in a physical, tangible, and concrete world. They were keen observers of the rhythms of nature, for it was only through such knowledge that they could aspire to master their environment, to anticipate what the future had in store for them and develop strategies to handle it successfully. They strove to maintain harmony, or at least coordination, with the motions of nature and the events that took place from day to day and from season to season. The body of knowledge that is developed from an observation of the behavior of the world and all the things in it, living or not, and the explanations that are formulated about why the world (system) is organized (structure) the way it is and works (function) the way it does is called *cosmology.* Certainly, the Tainos' cosmological views are paramount in understanding their religious beliefs and practices.

The Tainos were just as sharply aware of the fact that while a harmonic relationship between humans and nature is a highly desirable goal, the world in which they lived rarely behaved in such a stable, predictable manner. Like all of the other inhabitants of this planet, they were witnesses to concrete, physical examples of a world gone "mad." There are, for example, such things as sporadic droughts, seasonal hurricanes, disease, and floods that can threaten the stability of an entire community. But not all destructive forces are the products of nature; some are also the result of one's own

actions or those of other human beings. War, the violation of sexual taboos, the breaking of laws, falling prey to witchcraft, and a myriad of similar circumstances could also throw the Taino universe into chaos.

And so the cosmology of the Tainos reflects an awareness that the world
is not a static but a dynamic one—a universe in which there are pendular
swings between order and entropy (Adams 1975, 109 ff.; Reichel-Dolmatoff
1975, 1976). The dynamics of cosmos were understood by the Taino as
being driven by antagonistic, contrasting forces: those that are beneficial
and those that are deleterious to cultural order. The Taino "captured" the
numinous qualities of these antagonistic forces and personified them in the
çemí (zemi, cemí, semí).[1] Explanations about the nature and functioning of
the forces that drive the universe, that introduce stability and change, are
at the core of Taino cosmology and religion. These views are codified in a
belief system called cemíism.

It is not unreasonable to imagine that the Taino wished that the cosmos
would always remain unchanged, for it was only in this way that the forces
and events affecting their lives could become entirely predictable and therefore manageable. By knowing the outcome of a set of circumstances, they
could exert full control over their destiny. But the Taino also knew by personal experience that such a view is hopelessly utopian, that the world
does change and often in unexpected ways. In a formulation not unlike our
own Western concepts of physics (the laws of thermodynamics, for example), the Tainos recognized that there is an inherent tendency toward
entropy, or disorder, in the cosmos and that a lot of energy must be ex-
pended to either maintain, promote, or restore stability and order in it. A
great many of their rituals and ceremonies—such as the areíto (ceremonial
dances and chants), batey (ritual ball games), and ceremonial mock battles—
were designed precisely to deal with disorder and to produce social integration.

INTERPRETING THE TAINO MYTHS OF CREATION

Like all peoples, the Tainos had definite ideas about how the universe, the
cosmos, was created—and therefore they had not only an explanation of
the roles that humans play in it but also a moral blueprint to guide their
conduct in it. Much of our understanding of Taino belief comes from our
study of their myths as they were recorded by the Catalan friar Ramón
Pané. (Pané 1974) And though not all Taino myths have been preserved in
such a manner, themes pertaining to their mythology are also symbolically
encoded in their ritual material culture—objects such as charms, seats (duho,

turén), wooden sculptures, rattle gourds, and petroglyphs—and it is therefore possible for us to reconstruct some of the lost elements of these myths. (Roe 1993). On rare occasions it has been possible to decode entire "statements" regarding Tainan religious beliefs from such ritual artifacts.

Tainan myths, of course, ought not be perceived as primitive superstitions with no basis in reality. To the contrary, myths are profound philosophical statements about the universe based on both concrete and perceived experiences (including dreams and hallucinogenic visions; see Reichel-Dolmatoff 1975). The myths of the Tainos are presented in terms of a kind of "narrative" where the events and the actors belong to the past, to a remote, primordial cosmos. The events are presented not in a historical (chronological), linear sequence but rather in sacred time and space, and therefore the normal rules of the passage of time and of the movement from one place to another do not apply. In this primordial world rocks, plants, and animals can "speak" to each other—but in sacred, nonhuman language. Moreover the actors can suffer transformations from one state (for example, "human") to another (for example, plants, rocks, or animals), usually after a specific behavioral act that changes their role. Some characters are portrayed as neither human nor animal but rather as being simultaneously human-animals (anthropozoomorphic personages). All of these personages must be "fantastic" because if ordinary, natural laws applied, these individuals could not belong to the *extra*ordinary sphere of the cosmos.

This mythical, sacred part of the universe is quite often expressed by the Taino myths (and art) as being an *inverse* of the ordinary and concrete world. Thus night (the absence of light), when humans ordinarily sleep, is the appropriate time for the "awakening" supernatural forces. It is the magical, sacred moment when the ordinary, physical world is more susceptible to experience the numinous powers of the universe, from ghosts and cemíes to mythical personages and spiritual beings.

While the protagonists in this primordial world were supernatural entities that "lived" in the remote past and in a place that was the inverse of the ordinary world, they nevertheless possessed all the knowledge necessary for establishing social and cultural order. They had knowledge of the shamanistic practices and the artifacts used in religious rituals. They possessed the magical *guanín* (tumbaga gold), *çibas* (stone beads), and feathers that transform mere individuals into powerful caciques. They understood cultivation and crops, fire and cooking; they knew how to bake cassava bread, how to weave cotton nets, and how to make hooks for successful fishing. In a word, these supernatural beings had all the knowledge necessary for the establishment of human culture.

The first humans—still not mere mortals—had to wrestle, even steal, the cultural secrets from these mythical personages and, through trial and error, to learn how to make use of them for the benefit of mankind. This is not surprising, since giving away religious knowledge to mortals is tantamount to betraying the ways in which humans can exert some control over the supernatural. Most important, the myths told the Tainos that their culture, who they were, was ultimately derived from the divine. As happens in other religions, the Taino considered themselves a "chosen" people.

There is one feature common to Taino myths of creation that requires some clarification. Even when the obvious objective of a given Tainan creation myth is to explain the origin of the sea, or women, or whatever, the characters in the plot act and react according to a code, to a set of rules concerning what is proper and improper behavior. These social "laws" are expressed in Taino myths in one of two principal ways. Either the characters behave in an opposite way from what it is expected of an ordinary Taino (that is, what not to do—reverse psychology), or their behavior establishes—usually for the first time ever—the codes of proper Tainan behavior to be followed henceforth (that is, the correct way to do it).

Often a myth will exhibit an interplay of both kinds of behavior. This is because what is permissible for a given character in the supernatural domain is often the exact opposite of what is acceptable in the ordinary world. In other words, in the supernatural domain the order that reigns is the inverse of the ordinary world and vice versa. The Taino myths creatively manipulate these contradictions (oppositions) to explain and describe the processes of creation (life~order~stability) and degeneration in the world (death~disorder~instability or change).

THE CREATION LIFE AND THE PRIMORDIAL OCEAN, OR BAGUA

The birth of the ocean (*bagua*), and of living creatures it nourishes, is the first act of creation of the Taino universe. The tale is told in two different but closely related myths from Hispaniola. The same myths have also been artistically encoded in a sequence of petroglyphs located in the central precinct (plaza) of the famous ceremonial center of Caguana in Puerto Rico (see Oliver 1992a,b), so that it is fair to say that the same myth collected in Hispaniola or close variants of it was shared by the all Tainos, including those who lived in Puerto Rico and the Virgin Islands. The two myths can be briefly paraphrased as follows.

144 / José R. Oliver

The Origin of the Ocean, Fish, and Life in the Universe
Version 1

> There was a man called Yaya, whose name no one knows. His son, Yayael, was ostracized for wanting to kill his father. Thus, Yayael was banished for four months [forever]. Afterwards [upon Yayael's return] his father killed him, and placed his bones inside a gourd and hung it from the roof of the house, where it remained for some time. One day, wishing to see his son, Yaya ordered his wife, "I wish to see our son Yayael." Filled with joy, she took down the gourd and emptied it to see the bones of her son. From the gourd many large and small fish gushed out. Seeing that the bones were transformed into fish, they resolved to eat them.

Version 2 (Abridged)

> Hungry, Deminán and his [three twin] brothers entered Yaya's house to eat [steal] food because they were hungry. As they ate from the gourd where Yayael's bones were placed, Deminán sensed that Yaya was returning to his house from the *conucos*. While hastily trying to hang-up the gourd back on the roof, Deminán did not secure it well, and thus it fell onto the ground and broke. So much water came out of the gourd that it covered all the earth, and from it many fish came out. This is how the ocean was created. (My paraphrases and synthesis of Pané 1974, 28–30; and Stevens-Arroyo 1988, 88, 103.)

As Stevens-Arroyo (1988, 89–90) correctly argues, Yaya is none other than the supreme being of the Taino. For this reason it "has no name" and, as its namesake indicates, it can be understood only as the reflection of a spiritual essence[2]. Yaya is the primal, causal force of creation that presides the universe. Yaya causes the cracking of the gourd and the emergence of *bagua,* the first ocean, which is teeming with fish. Let us examine the myth more closely, for in it Yaya is anthropomorphized (made humanlike), playing the multiple functions of supreme being, cacique, and father.

The first act in the myth is by Yayael, who wants to "kill" his father/ cacique. His father, Yaya, reacts by banishing Yayael from his household/ chiefdom for "four months"—that is, forever.[3] The intent to "kill" the father and cacique manifests a clear transgression of social norms, and yet the punishment does not seem to match the apparent severity of the violation. Why? Yayel's intent to "kill" is symbolic. It implies a desire to remove the Yaya from his rightful role and position as both head of the household (father) and as a chief (cacique). The intent to permanently remove ("kill") the father/cacique implies Yayael's desire to usurp political and religious power as well as parental authority. The transgression is, therefore, Yayael's attempt to steal power that is exclusive to the chief or the head (father) of household. Chiefly power is to be acquired only according to prescribed norms of inheritance and certainly not by stealing. To usurp power is the same as stealing, which is nothing else than acquiring something that right-fully belongs to someone else. Stealing was regarded by the Taino as the most serious of all social sins. Oviedo y Valdés, a sixteenth-century chroni-cler, emphasizes the severity with which the Taino dealt with the offender: he would be impaled without mercy (in López-Baralt 1985, 92).

Punishment by banishment not only removes the threat of usurpation of chiefly power and authority by an aspiring, presumably greedy, heir but also presents the social mechanism (norm) by which such circumstances of potential "theft" can be minimized or even eliminated. In the myth Yaya prescribes that children of the head of the family or cacique must be ban-ished from their natal home. Their remaining at home and growing into adulthood would obviously place the son and the father (or the heir and the chief) at odds, for the young adult will eventually want to "steal" (de-sire) the status and prestige that rightfully still belongs to his elder. But, as is evident, the desire to become like one's father/cacique is quite a natural one, for it is an integral part of the social life cycle. It is necessary for the continuity of chiefdoms that the heirs develop a desire to acquire such chiefly status and functions, so that the office can pass from one generation to the next, perpetuating the Taino sociopolitical organization.

Due to ambiguous evidence in the historical documents, anthropologists are not sure of whether the Taino practiced patrilocal, matrilocal, or avunc-ulocal postmarital residence rule (see Keegan 1992; Stevens-Arroyo 1988, 106).[4] Nor is it certain whether the Taino traced their group (lineage) mem-bership through female (matrilineal) or male (patrilineal) relatives. For the sake of argument let us assume, as William F. Keegan (1992) and Jalil Sued Badillo (1975) have proposed, that the Taino were a matrilineal society whereby, upon marriage, the newlyweds had to reside in the village of the groom's maternal uncle (mother's brother). This being the case, Yaya's ban-ishment establishes the social norm of avunculocality, which states that once the son is initiated into the responsibilities of adulthood (puberty/initiation rites), and upon contracting marriage, he must move with his bride away from Yaya's household to reside in his maternal uncle's village.[5] With this rule, Yaya removes the potential for trouble (social disorder) that naturally ensues when a son grows up and assumes full membership among the adults: the natural desire to become a father and to assume the power of his father, a cacique.

It is Yaya, the supreme being, who establishes the rule of postmarital residence away from the parental household that maintains social order by removing potential disorder (Yayael's asocial desires). The desire for power and authority is perceived as a "natural" weakness but one that is easily controlled by conformity to the social norm. For this reason, banishment and not death is the appropriate solution to the problem.

The second set of actions and reactions, however, do result in death. Yayael returns home, and Yaya kills him. Why kill him now? By Yayael's returning to his parental or natal household, the threat of usurpation of power and authority is reinstated. Moreover, Yayael has purposefully and with knowledge of the law defied his father's authority. While in the first instance the jealousy (wanting to kill, in the sense of wishing) is a natural desire that is socially resolved by obedience to the norm of postmarital residence (banishment), in the second attempt the improper desire to steal is premeditated, for Yayael had been forewarned not to return to his natal/ parental household. This is, therefore, Yayael's real transgression. And this is why Yaya (the cacique) has no other recourse but to kill him—that is, to permanently remove Yayael and the threat of usurpation of chiefly power. But punishment by death, however necessary, is always traumatic, bringing deleterious consequences to the smooth functioning of society.

Once Yaya kills the son, another series of events is put in motion, each of which is designed to redress death and reestablish order. First of all, the permanent removal of a member of a household entails the elimination of someone who positively contributes to the stability of the family unit and to the social group as a whole. The loss of a son, whether by marriage or by death, introduces a measure of disorder that is not altogether beneficial to the social unit. The loss of a member of the household by marriage is counteracted by other norms in which some form of service or payment for the loss incurred by the family must be made. We are not sure what rules the Taino had about postmarital bride/groom service, but they most certainly had them. Loss by death, however, is eminently more traumatic since it is permanent and irretrievable. The family and dependents of the deceased will now become a burden, economically and emotionally, to other members of the village. The stable, normal, and predictable functioning of the daily routines are thus shattered. And so the Taino also had a series of practices designed to reestablish the normal workings of everyday life. These practices involve funeral rituals and ceremonies.

The next act of creation by the supreme being precisely entails the prescription or rule of proper funerary rituals by "burying" his son's bones inside an *higüero* (*güiro*), or gourd, and hanging it from the roof of the house. This is the origin of the Taino custom of burning (desiccating) the deceased and selecting the skull and long bones to "bury" them inside a gourd or a woven basket that is to be hung from the roof of the house—exactly as Columbus himself describes it for the Taino of eastern Cuba during his first voyage (see Dunn and Kelly 1989, 188–89).

But establishing the norms of this funeral rite, while an important step, was not enough. Yaya established yet another very important ritual that lies at the core of Tainan society. In the myth Yaya asks his unnamed wife to "see" his dead son's bones. The act of "wishing to see" is a metaphor for the establishment of the cult to the dead and, by extension, to the ancestors. This is the most crucial act of creation, for it is his homage to the ancestral spirits that triggers the chain of events that culminate in the birth of the first fish (flesh) and, implicitly, of the first life in the primordial oceanic universe. In the myth Yaya's demand to see his son causes the unnamed woman to empty the gourd, from which all sorts of fish come out. The theme is rather clear: through the observance of religious ceremonies, nonliving spiritual essence is transformed into life; from dead bones (Yayael's), living flesh is created. In this respect, *Yaya-el*—whose name means "son-of-Yaya"—is simply another manifestation of Yaya himself because the "son" is what Yaya creates, what comes from him/it: bones, which upon entering the cosmic uterus (the gourd) impregnate the universe with life.

As many other Amerindians, the Taino considered bones not simply as symbols for the dead, death, and sterility; quite the contrary, they were the source of life itself. Among the Taino, bones were the symbolic substitution for the supreme being's phallus. The placement of the bones into the gourd symbolizes the penetration of the phallus into the uterus and the insemination of it with life.

Some time passes before Yaya asks to see his creation, since every Taino knew that there must be a period of gestation. The emptying of the gourd/uterus by the unnamed woman is a metaphor for birthing. Now one can understand why the woman/wife is never named and why the exact nature of "her" relationship to Yaya (wife, consort?) is never made clear in the myth. It is irrelevant because the supreme being requires no woman—as Taino did in the real world. Rather, the mystery of birthing—not of the creation/insemination life—is simply reduced to the gourd-woman metaphor. The natural container or receptacle we call a gourd is the ideal analog for the concept of an enveloping, protecting, dark cavity symbolizing the feminine aspect of the universe, which in the myth is parlayed into an "unnamed [gourd-]woman" and, therefore, an undefined feminine entity. To put it as simply as possible, Yaya impregnates with life the dark, hollow void of the universe—which, "logic" dictates, must be feminine. The gourd symbol, therefore, not only operates as a uterine metaphor but also embraces the idea of the universal dome (*domus universalis*).

At another level, the cult to the "bones" (deceased/ancestors) established by Yaya also explains the continuity of created life from nonlife. That is, from a spiritual, inseminating essence (bones~phallus) not only fish and oceans are created but all living matter. Above all, bones are literally someone's deceased relative and ancestor. The very existence of living humans presupposes the prior existence of a progenitor that is no longer among the living. More important, living humans are able define their relationship to their fellow kin and their membership in a given lineage or community only with reference to deceased, that is, through their mutual genealogical connections to a common ancestor. Whether matrilineal or patrilineal, the Taino of a given village could determine who were (or were not) the members of his/her lineage by their kinship ties to a founding ancestor, who was often a mythical personage.

In sum, ancestors formed the basis by which the Taino defined themselves in the world of the living and served as their only real, personal linkage with the sacred other-world. Without ancestors, there could be no social order because the roles performed and the positions occupied by individuals in the present society were strictly defined by those ancestors. By definition, ancestors were life-giving, for they possessed the power to order and to organize the ordinary world into a coherent, functioning society, just as Yayael's "dead bones" have the power to create ordered life in the universe.

This conceptualization of the process of generation (life, creation) and degeneration (death, nonlife) was the ultimate paradox for the Taino, as it is for all humans: all life and the things we experience are ultimately created from nonlife and from nonmatter, whatever it might be. To have living humans organized into a community, there must be ancestors to define the social relations of this world.

At this juncture we come to the results of this monumental process (and mystery) of creation. The symbolic, magical insemination (bones) of the cosmic gourd-woman (uterus) results in the birth fish. That is, from nonlife (bones) Yaya creates life symbolized by fish. Fish were the main source of proteins for the Taino and thus were essential for the health of the population. Fishing was not just a subsistence task but a highly prestigious economic endeavor among Taino. It is easy to see why fish were used as a symbol of nourishment and the very essence of life itself. It is only then Yaya and his "wife" are able to eat fish. And this act of eating one's own "flesh," of deriving sustenance from it, has yet other implications. To eat means one must "kill" and ingest what is created from the same essence that created everything in life: from the transformed bones of Yayael and ultimately from Yaya himself.

As Stevens-Arroyo (1988, 98–100) notes, the act of Yaya's eating his own son (the transformed bones of Yayael) is a direct reference to endo-cannibalism—a ceremony during which the powerful spiritual essence of a deceased person is passed along to the living in a beverage made with his or her ground and burned bones, which all the participants drink. As other South American Indians still do today, the Tainos practiced endocannibalism. It will be recalled that the death of an individual brings chaos and disorder to social stability. Yaya provides the ceremonial means through which the loss of a living human can be transformed into sacred forces that can restore order to society. Through endocannibalism, the beneficial, spiritual forces that inhabited the living person are not lost but kept among the living. It is worth recalling that bone is the symbolic phallic instrument that impregnates the universe producing life. Thus upon ritually ingesting the ashes of the bones of the deceased—who is now, in effect, an ancestor—those who take part in the ceremony receive the gift of the continuity of human life and social order. The bones are transformed into food for the living, just as much as the bones of Yayael are transformed into fish-food for Yaya and the unnamed woman. Herein lies the seminal power of bones.

In short, the ceremony of endocannibalism, symbolized by Yaya's consumption of the bones, is nothing more than the transmission of sacred power from ancestors to the living. And bones are the physical, tangible, yet numinous matter that transmits such forces of creative life between the living and the nonliving (spiritual) domains.

The second version of the myth adds an explicit reference to the emergence of the ocean that is only implicit in the first version (see the paraphrase above). In this version, the cracking of the gourd (~uterus) results not only in the creation of fish (~life) but in the pouring of water, a deluge that fills the world. And here we have the second symbolic power of creation. The symbolic bones are essentially a metaphor for the masculine qualities of the universe. Water, on the other hand, is a metaphor for the

feminine qualities of the cosmos. Obviously, if bones are the sacred seminal forces that impregnate the universe and transmit life from ancestors to
descendants, then water is the stuff that nurtures or gestates life. Just as the
amniotic fluids (~water) of a woman nurture the life of a fetus, the water
contained within the cosmic gourd nourishes the bones that are transformed
into fish and, hence, life. Upon rupture of the uterine sack, amniotic fluids
come out; the cosmic uterine gourd, upon cracking open, releases the primordial ocean. Thus the concept of reproducing or "gestating" (creating)
involves not just women or a feminine principle but the interaction of both
the masculine and the feminine. From the very inception of the cosmos, it
is evident that two opposing but complementary forces are required in order for life to be established and to move on: the interaction of the feminine and masculine. Thus, for the Taino, everything in the universe was
constituted and characterized by these dual priciples, both of which must
be possessed in order for life (and social order) to be created and maintained.[6]

While seemingly a different story, the second version of the myth dupli-
cates the same basic structure of the first one. Only the outcome for the
four culture heroes' actions is different. Bagua (ocean) was created as a
result of Yaya's causing Deminán and his twin brothers to drop the gourd
and thus to "crack" it open. Like that of Yayael, Deminán's transgression
lies in the act stealing (food) from Yaya. The driving force is hunger, for the
culture heroes do not yet possess the cultural knowledge of agriculture,
fire, and cooking. Upon reaching adulthood, the Tainos were expected to
prepare and harvest their own *conuco* (garden plot) and derive sustenance
from their own efforts. That is what made for a responsible adult Taino
man and woman. But the Taino were able to do so only after the culture
heroes made culture accessible to humans.

As in Yayael's case, their "punishment" for attempting to steal food is
permanent banishment from Yaya's land/chiefdom. They are condemned
forever to live away from the domain presided by the supreme being. And
thus the same rules of "postmarital residence" apply. The prescribed banishment is what causes the mythical culture heroes to begin the long journey that leads to the discovery of the secrets of culture for the ultimate
benefit of humankind. It is they who first learn about fire for cooking,
about how to plant and harvest and to make cassava bread. They are also
the ones who wrestle from the mythical Baymanaco (see Pané 1974, 30–
31), the proverbial wise old man/*behique,* the rituals and secrets of sha-

manism, curing, and magic. And it is they who, led by Deminán, "discover" the proper (ceremonial, ritual) use of *tabaco, digo,* and *cohoba.*

The centerpiece of a religious ceremony crucial to the Taino, cohoba is a plant (*Anadenanthera peregrina*) whose seeds, when crushed and mixed with an alkaline substance (like lime or ground burned shells), produce a powder that can be sniffed to induce hallucinogenic experiences—the effects of which have been brilliantly discussed by Gerardo Reichel-Dolmatoff (1971, 1975). It was therefore regarded by the Tainos as a sacred substance that permitted the ordinary person to transcend into the extraordinary world of the supernatural. The acquisition of these cultural goods from the divine by Deminán and his brothers took place thanks to Yaya's causing their banishment.

Unlike Yayel, who returns home in defiance of Yaya, the four mythical brothers remain ostracized. Because of their compliance with the norm of banishment, the acquisition of culture was possible. Once Yaya enforces the "banishment" law, he is never heard from again. He has created the most important elements of world life and order, the oceans teeming with fish, the principles of masculine impregnation and feminine reproduction (fertility), the rules of residence (moving out of the natal household), the funeral customs and ceremonies (endocannibalism), and the cult devoted to the ancestors. With all this accomplished, his job is finished. Like the God of Old Testament Christianity, "He rested." It is left to other subordinate mythical beings, like Baymanaco and the culture heroes, to complete Yaya's creation.

The synthetic explanatory power of myths is quite evident here, for in a few sentences and with the skillful use of symbols, the initiated and educated Taino encapsulated his complex conception of creation of the cosmos. When they were considered old enough to be allowed to hear the myths, the Tainos were taught by their elders and ritual experts about the deep social, political, philosophical, moral, and economic meanings that such a seemingly simple story had.

CONCLUSIONS

For the Taino, religion was not a body of knowledge separate from that of politics, or economics, or even the knowledge derived from the observation of behavior in nature. Theirs was an integrated, interactive universe within which all things and persons had an important role to play. Yet the very fact that they were chosen by the divine and placed at the center of the civilized universe was a serious burden and responsibility. By accepting such function in the universe, they also assumed the awesome responsibility of making it work for all generations to come.

The Tainos are no longer amongst us; their genes have been diluted among new Old World populations. Their culture—as an integrated holistic system, as a mode of interacting with the natural and supernatural surroundings—is for all practical purposes gone as well. All that seems to remain are remembrances and a few artifacts here and there. But their legacy can and should be retrieved from the pages of historical neglect, if we are only willing to look for it and to learn how to "read" it. It is inscribed in the magnificent rows of petroglyphs in Caguana; it is expressed brilliantly in the Cruzan site of Salt River; it can be appreciated in the intricate designs seen in pottery, in magnificent wood, shell, and stone objects.

NOTES

1. The term *çemí*, or *semí*, is etymologically related to the Lokono terms *seme* and *semehi*, which mean "sweet" or "having the taste of honey." Lokono apply this root to the term *semichichi*, which means "shaman," "medicine man," or "cure" (Bennett 1989, 39). The Tainos, for example, establish in their myths a close relationship among guavas (that is, "sweetness") and hog plum (*jobo*) trees—as well as the bats that eat their fruits—and the supernatural spirits of the nonliving (*opía*) that roam the forest at night. Night and sweetness then are essential qualities of the sacred domain. That is why the Lokono shaman is denominated *semichichi*, for he possesses the qualities of the sacred and magic: sweetness, honey. Thus the three-pointed objects known as cemíes are so called because of their sweet/honey qualities, which are exclusive to the sacred. The supernatural forces are collectively designated as *cemí* (*zemi, semí*) for the same reasons.

2. The term */ia; iatá/* among the modern Lokono (Arawak) of Surinam means "likeness, portrait, a photograph, resemblance, or reflection"; */iatáhü/* means "a picture, a sculpture or image" that captures the reflection or essence of a being (Bennett 1989, 16). It is not a person but a reflection (a "photograph") of it, and hence it is an intangible, nonconcrete being: a spiritual essence. The repetition and alliteration of */ia→iaiá/* functions in Taino language as a superlative (double emphasis) and thus can be literally translated as the "reflection or image of a superlative being." The suffix *el* added to Yaya, as Pané himself observes, denotes "son of" or "descendant" of Yaya.

3. The number four is of extreme symbolic importance in Tainan thought. Four is what it takes to be a complete, functioning whole. There are four culture heroes. The first protowomen are four in number. And there are four spheres in the sacred domain, as well as four spheres in the profane world (see Oliver 1992b, 1993).

4. *Matrilocal* means that after marriage the son must leave the household and reside near his wife's relatives. *Avunculocal* (from the Latin *avunculus,* meaning "mother's brother," which is also the root of the word *uncle*) residence means that both son and daughter leave their natal home and settle with or near the groom's maternal uncle. *Patrilocal* means that the son remains in the household while the bride/wife leaves the natal household to reside permanently in her husband's village.

5. If the rule among the Taino was instead patrilocal residence, then the reasoning would be as follows. Patrilocal residence requires the son to remain in his father's household and thus to bring his bride to live there with him. In such case, the banishment from the household would constitute a true punishment for Yayael because he would be dispossessed of the inheritance of the office of chief and of the garden plots (*conucos*) that would be his upon the father/cacique's death. Yayel would then be, so to speak, a man without a country. It would therefore be a powerful reminder to the Taino of the price to be paid for the intent or act of usurping the authority of the chief.

6. The close association between the feminine and water is the reason why women in Taino mythology are often portrayed as the mythical analogs of frogs, turtles, eels, fish, and other creatures of the aquatic and semiaquatic environments. In fact, Peter Roe (1993) has pointed out that in lowland South America, women are associated with the fauna and flora of lower strata of the forest, while men are associated with those of the high canopy and above. This "high : men :: low : women" relationship is also observed in the etiquette of seating arrangements between sexes; men are seated above on duhos, whereas women sit below on the ground or on mats. It is in the upper forest canopy that the more colorful birds are found—birds whose feathers are an important accouterment in the men's dress code.

16

Some Observations on the Taino Language

Arnold R. Highfield

The coming of the first Europeans to the New World was followed not only by a clash of peoples but by a conflict of cultures and languages as well. The invading Spaniards superimposed their Castilian language onto those of the indigenous populations whom they encountered, first in the West Indies and later in Mesoamerica and in South America. In a number of those areas, however, native languages, such as Nahuatl, Quechua, and Guarani, managed to survive, albeit in a subordinate position to Castilian, in most instances as a result of pure demographics—that is, their massive numbers served as an effective *contrepoid* to the military superiority of the invaders. In other cases, indigenous languages survived due to the influence of geography and the relative inaccessibility it created. The language of the Yanomami, for example, endured simply because its speakers did not at that time inhabit those areas coveted by the invaders (Ruhlen 1987). However, Taino—the very first language encountered by the Spaniards in the islands of the Caribbean and the one that made the initial and, in many ways, the strongest impression on Castilian—became effectively extinct within about a century of the initial contact with the Iberians. This chapter first looks in general terms at the linguistic situation in the Caribbean on the eve of conquest and then considers in some detail what is known of the Taino lexicon.

Since our most important sources for the indigenous languages of the Caribbean are the ethnohistorical ones written at the time of the initial encounter between peoples of the Old World and the New World, as well as in the years immediately thereafter, our story then begins in the late fifteenth century with the arrival of the first Spanish ships in the West Indies. What exactly was the linguistic situation encountered by Columbus on his early voyages? (For overviews, see Highfield 1993, 1995; Taylor 1956, 1957, 1977; Goeje 1939.)

In the Greater Antilles, Taino was the predominant language, forms of which were spoken in the Lucayos (Bahamas), eastern Cuba, Jamaica, Haiti (Española), and Boriquen (Puerto Rico). The archaeological record as interpreted by Irving Rouse and others points to the division of these islands into major cultural zones, including the following: Classic Taino (Haiti and Boriquen, with nearby Ayay (St. Croix) included, before the Carib intrusion; Western Taino (Cuba, Jamaica, and Lucayos); and Eastern Taino (the islands of the northern Lesser Antilles, to the east of Boriquen and the Virgins). The ethnohistorical data generated by European observers who were present at the earliest contact, and supported by the archaeological evidence, argue that the people of those zones, with the exception of certain recess populations, spoke closely related forms of one and the same language: Arawakan-based Taino (Arrom 1980, 1992; Brinton 1871; Vivanco 1946).

Scattered through the islands of the Greater Antilles, adjacent to and among these Taino-speakers, were small pockets of non-Taino speakers, about whom little is known. It is assumed, for example, that the Guanahatabey of western Cuba were the remnant of a preceramic, Paleolithic people who may have migrated there earlier from Central America and that they evidently spoke a language other than Taino. Nothing, however, is known directly of those people and their speech beyond a few vague references and these general suppositions (Rouse 1986, 5–19; Tejera 1977).

The Spaniards also encountered pockets of other non-Tainos in northeast Haiti (Española). Known as the *Ciguayo,* they inhabited the *cacicazgo,* or chiefdom, of Macorix; they are mentioned in the early literature by Las Casas, Peter Martyr, and Oviedo (Tejera 1977). However, very little beyond a couple of words is known about their language. Were they also the remnants of a Paleolithic people who inhabited the Greater Antilles before the arrival of Arawakan-speaking populations, or were they communities who migrated to the island, perhaps from the north, at a later date? A paucity of both ethnohistorical and archaeological information may leave this question forever unanswered. It is a telling commentary that one of the two words preserved from their language during the initial contact with the Spaniards was *tuob,* or gold (Fuson 1992, 172).

*   *   *

Farther to the east lived the Igneri, an Arawakan-speaking people who settled in the smaller islands of the eastern Caribbean as the main thrust of the pre-Taino, or Saladoid, migration proceeded over several centuries toward the west, into the Greater Antilles. Apparently they were forced into the recess areas of various of the islands of the Lesser Antilles upon the arrival of Carib-speaking migrants from South America sometime in the second half of the first millennium. According to some, the first of the Arawakan-speaking women taken by the Caribs came from this group (see Breton 1978, 52–53). However that may be, very little is known directly of their language, beyond the supposition that it was Arawakan and that it played a significant role in the formation of the Island Carib language (Taylor 1977, 26–27).

Farther to the south, on the island today called Trinidad (Chaléibe), several Arawakan languages were spoken into historical times: Lokono, Jaoi, and Shebayo (Taylor 1977, 14–16). Although all that is known of those languages are several short word lists, the data they offer are sufficient to establish their relation to the Arawakan family of languages, as well as to Taino.

Many centuries after the migration of Arawakan speakers into the Caribbean area, there occurred another migration from South America: the Kalina (or Karina), later the self-styled Kallinagos and better known today as the Island Caribs. Originally they spoke Galibi, a language related to the larger family of Cariban languages in South America (Durbin 1986; Boucher 1992; Hulme and Whitehead 1992). The expansion of that warrior society into the Caribbean archipelago and its practice of bride capture, particularly those women taken from the ranks of Arawakan-speaking peoples, led in time to the Caribs' adoption of a form of speech that soon came to be essentially Arawakan, though embedded with numerous Cariban lexical survivals. That linguistic transition occurred as captive Arawakan-speaking mothers, taken from Igneri, Taino, and other Arawakan-speaking communities, communicated in their native languages with their sons and daughters engendered by Carib men. That language, paradoxically enough called Island Carib, was the one spoken in Caloucaéra (Guadeloupe), Oüáïtoucoubouli (Dominica), and Iáhi (St. Croix) at the time of the second voyage of Columbus, 1493. According to Taylor and others, the remnants of the original Carib language, Galibi, came to be used exclusively as a ritual men's language in that warrior society (Taylor and Hoff 1980). Under those circumstances, that mixed form of Arawakan—but principally Igneri, laced heavily with Cariban words—became the everyday language of Island Carib societies.

In very broad strokes, such was the linguistic state of affairs in the Caribbean region at the time of the encounter and subsequent prolonged contact, first with Spaniards and later with other western Europeans. It can be summarized in the following manner. First, Arawakan, in one form or another, was by a wide margin the dominant indigenous language of the Caribbean area at the time of the initial contact with people from Europe at the end of the fifteenth century. Moreover it had occupied that position for a considerable period of time, and its speakers most probably numbered in the hundreds of thousands. Second, even though the language was intelligible over wide areas, it nevertheless had dialectal divisions, not only among the various islands but also within some of the larger islands as well. Third, the language—perhaps by dint of its numerous, well-established population of speakers and its relatively advanced culture—had expanded, by one means or another, into areas where other languages had previously been established. In the Greater Antilles, for example, it became established in areas where the languages of the preceramic peoples (both Casimiroid and Ortoiroid) had been previously spoken. In the Lesser Antilles, it became the basis of Island Carib. And fourth, only a few other, recess languages were in evidence at the time, and either they were much older languages that had been forced into marginality by the growth of the Taino domain or they had only recently been established in the region and were therefore of minor status in their presence and influence. The former seems the more likely scenario. What emerges, in the final analysis, is a picture of the dominance of one linguistic group Arawakan based, in one form or another covering the area from Trinidad in the south to central Cuba in the west.

Given such an advantageous position at the onset of the fifteenth century, Taino, one would likely conjecture, might well have had at least an even chance of surviving the coming Spanish onslaught just as did other indigenous languages on the mainland in the years that followed. But such was not to be the case. In the short span of just several generations, the Taino language was completely extirpated. Several questions arise in the context of any attempt to explain that abrupt and unpredictable fate. Who were the Taino people, and where did they come from? What was the essential nature of their culture? What is known about their language and its correspondence to that culture? What were the circumstances that resulted in the disappearance of the Taino language? And finally, how, if at all, did that language leave traces of its existence on the peoples and cultures with which it came into contact?

* * *

The following is intended as a cursory description of the Taino lexicon, drawn from the primary ethnohistorical documents. It is presented here for descriptive purposes, with an eye for showing something of the language itself in the context of the culture that it represented. We must assume that like all languages Taino had lexical resources adequate to serve the needs of the Taino people's material and nonmaterial culture. That is to say, since the Tainos had, as one example, a strong interest in agriculture—indeed their very survival depended on it—then one would expect their language to have been fully formed in this regard, altogether capable of describing the concepts, artifacts, practices, and so on, that were fundamental to agricultural pursuits. What is actually known today about those lexical resources, however, is another matter—one constrained and defined by the perspectives and limitations of the contemporary mind-set of those Spanish writers who were present at the time of the initial contact with the Tainos.

The Spanish chroniclers focused their attention by and large on those things that were new and unknown to them, or most immediately apparent, in the physical world of plants and animals. Root crops such as *yuca* and *age,* animals such as *hutía* and *manatí,* and cultural artifacts such as *canoas* and *zemis,* to mention only a few, were both new to them—that is, beyond their peninsular experience—as well as readily apparent. As a result, they dutifully recorded the names of those categories of creatures and things: terms for plants and animals as well as geographical regions and locations (toponymy); the names of prominent people, caciques in particular; the terms related to agriculture and mining; and the terminology and lexicon of religion and mythology (for example, priests, myths, spirits, deities, rituals).

To understand fully the nature of the remains of the Taino lexicon, it is equally important to know what the Spaniards did *not* record, that is, what they ignored or omitted for one reason or another. Plants and animals that had apparent counterparts in the Old World were often referred to using the familiar Spanish word. Avifauna, for some reason, seemed to attract scant attention. The same is true for the Taino terms for the parts of the human face and body, which, obviously enough, could have been referred to by the use of Spanish equivalents. Similarly little attention was paid to Taino verbals, most probably because the Spaniards' own verbs, especially those signifying common actions, could be effectively employed, along with signs or gestures and thereby effect the minimal necessary understanding. Adjectives too attracted little attention, perhaps for the same reason. In the final analysis, the Spaniards were attracted primarily by concrete objects and the terms for those objects. Not surprisingly, it is also this element—substantives—that has persisted in the Spanish of the islands today.

The following is a brief descriptive overview of that part of the Taino lexicon that has survived by one means or another and has come down through the sources reviewed in other essays in the volume, especially that of Alegría. In perusing the lexicon, one should recall that its fragmentary nature is a direct result of the manner in which it was collected. Not only does it render a partial, incomplete perspective of Taino culture and the words that described that culture; it also illustrates a good deal about the way the invading Spaniards viewed the people whom they were in the process of conquering and eventually exterminating.

The Taino lexicon, as it has survived to the present time, is top-heavy with nouns, which far outnumber adjectives, verbs, and other word forms. Nevertheless some adjectives are in evidence, as in the following examples: *cynato,* "irritated"; *estarei,* "shining"; and *manicato,* "strong," "of great spirit." Verbs are equally sparse in the sources. The few that are attested appear to have been formed by adding the suffix *-a* to certain stems: for example, *cama,* "to listen"; *macaná,* "to kill"; *teitocá,* "to be quiet"; and *serra,* "to exchange." A negative particle *ma-* could be prefixed to verbs—as in *mayanimacaná,* "Don't kill me."

Even a quick perusal of the abundant substantives that have been preserved in various texts reveals the presence of numerous roots, prefixes, and suffixes as the means through which the dynamics of the Taino language expressed itself. Although even a brief overview of these linguistic resources would extend far beyond the intent and scope of the present study, the following examples give an idea of the nature of those linguistic means (Tejera 1977).

A great number of roots occur throughout the Taino lexicon. As one example, the stem *-caira,* or *-caera,* "island," appears in the names of several islands, such as *Calocaéra,* "Guadeloupe"; and *Cibuquiera,* meaning "rocky islands," apparently the present St. Croix. The root *-heri,* or *-hari,* "man, person," appears in several terms of address, including *matunheri,* "exalted person." The root *-arima,* "end part, anus," is present in the place name *Guaccaiarima*, "the extreme southwestern part of *Haití*." And finally, *-aco*, or *-caco*, meaning "eye," occurs in the terms *xeiticaco*, "black eyes"; and *hicaco*, "fruit in the shape of an eye" (see also Arrom 1992).

The language is rich in prefixes, of which the following is a sampling: *ay-*, place-names such as *Ayay*, "St. Croix"; *Ayaibex*, "place in Santo Domingo"; *Ayqueroa*, "a place in Guaccaiarima"; *ma-*, a negative particle meaning "not," "without," or "lacking," which may be prefixed to a substantive as in *mahite*, "missing a tooth." The prefix *ni-* is an oft-used form that may be either an article or perhaps the first-person singular pronoun, as in the following examples: *Nibagua*, "a cacique"; *Niti*, "a place in *Haití*"; *Nizao*, "a river"; and *nitaino*, "a Taino noble."

*　　*　　*

The language is also richly endowed with suffixes, of which only a sampling is offered here: *-bo* is in some instances a shortened form of *bohio*, meaning "house of" or "place of," as in the example of the name of the cacique *Caonabo*, "Lord of the House of Gold," according to one interpretation (Arrom 1992, 56). The same underlying meaning may be present in such words as *ceiba*, "the giant silk-cotton or kapok tree" (*Ceiba pentrandra*); and *cobo*, "conch" (*Strombus gigas*). The suffixes *-bo* and *-coa* both appear to be locatives, the former in particular being present in the names of a number of rivers, as in *Maunabo* and *Bucarabon*, both in *Boriquen*, and in *Cayabo*, "an ancient province in *Haití*." Examples of *-coa* are available in *Cibacoa*, "place of rocks"; and *Baracoa*, "near the sea." The suffix *-nacán* carries the meaning "in the middle of," as in the place name *Cubanacán*, "settlement in the middle of Cuba." Several other suffixes worthy of note are the following: *-el*, added to personal names, means "the son of," as in *Jayael*, "the son of Jaya"; and *Guavaoconel*, "the son of Guavaenequín"; *-ex*, as added to the names of numerous caciques, is perhaps an honorific particle, as in *Guarionex*, *Yamarex*, and so on; and *-quin* or *-quen*, which may mean "numerous, abundant," as in *Boriquen*, "Puerto Rico"; and *Duiheyniquen*, "a river."

It now remains to have a look at the general lexical resources of the Taino language in relation to the principal elements of Taino culture. The Tainos developed a sharp awareness of the physical world in which they lived. They kept a regular eye on the *turey*, "sky" (cf. Perea and Perea 1941, 18–22) and on the *bagua*, "sea." They traveled over the latter and had a broad knowledge of the *cayos*, "islands," which they encountered there. They were most certainly aware of the great forces of nature to which they were subject, in particular the *huracán,* "hurricane," that descended on their islands from the Atlantic. Their islands were covered with *arcabuco,* "forests"; *sabana,* "savannah"; and *maguá,* "vegas" or "fertile plains." Depending heavily on lithic industries, they were concerned with *cibu,* "stones," and other minerals. It is a result of the Spaniards' quest for gold, however, that we have been left with a disproportionate number of terms for that mineral, namely *nozay* among the Lucayos, *caona* in Haiti, and *tuob* among the non-Taino Ciguayo. The *yari,* "ore," that produced the gold and items made from it—such as *guanín,* "low-grade gold jewelry"— were also of interest to the Spaniards.

That the Tainos traveled widely and readily in their waters is evident in the names they assigned to both nearby and distant islands and places. The very first of their lands that Columbus happened upon, *Guanahaní,* was only one of a larger group known as the *Lucayos.* There were a host of others in that group—*Bahama, Caycos,* and *Ciguateo,* to mention only a few. All the larger islands of the Greater Antilles had Taino names—*Cuba, Jamaica, Haití, Bohío,* and *Boriquen*—as did the smaller islands and cays lying off the larger islands, *Camito* off the northern coast of Haiti being one example. In spite of the efforts by the Spaniards to give these islands Christian names, a surprising number of the original Taino names have survived to the present day. The island located just off the eastern coast of *Boriquen,* presently called St. Croix, had two recorded names of apparent Taino origin—*Ayay* (cf. Iáhi) and *Cibuqueira.* To the east of the Taino domains lay several islands inhabited by Caribs *Caloucaéra, Caribe,* and the fabled *Matinino.* And far across the waters, etched in their ancestral memory, lay a region of unlimited land, which the Tainos called *Caribana* or *Caribata* and which the Spaniards would later call *Tierra Firma,* the mainland.

The islands of Haiti, Boriquen, and eastern Cuba were especially rich in toponyms. Nearly all the rivers in the Dominican Republic today have retained their Taino names, the *Agmina* River, which empties into the *Yaque,* and the *Jaina* River, which empties into the sea, being only two of many examples. Likewise, names for valleys such as *Hathathiei* and for mountains like *Hybahaino* and *Macaya* abounded in these islands. Those that attracted the attention of the chroniclers, for whatever specific reason, were duly recorded. The designations for various other geological features have survived in the colloquial Spanish speech of those islands.

The Tainos called their settlements *Yucayeque,* and numerous of these have survived, including *Guanahibes,* "Gonaives"; and *Hincha,* "Hinche," in Haiti. In similar fashion, the Tainos had names for provinces such as

Agueybana and *Baoruco* in Haiti, regions such as *Cibao,* and cacicazgos such as *Xaraguá, Maguana, Higüey, Magua,* and *Marien* in Haiti, in present-day Hispaniola.

Taino people depended heavily on plants, both cultivated and unculti-vated, for a large portion of their food supply. And since the newly arrived Spaniards were also interested in the plants of the new lands as an impor-tant element in their own adaptation and survival, it is not surprising that the words for numerous plants found their way into the written record, especially since many of them were new species with which the newcomers were completely unfamiliar. Among the trees that were important for the construction of dwellings and other elements of material culture were the *caoba,* perhaps mahogany (*Swietenia mahogany*); *damahagua* (*Hibiscus tiliaceous*); the *manaka,* "a variety of palm"; the *ceiba,* "the silk-cotton tree" (in the Bombacaceae family), which was considered sacred by the Tainos as well as by many of the African peoples who arrived later in the West Indies; the *corbana,* "a large hardwood tree," (*Pithecolobiun be-teroanum*); the *guao,* "a caustic tree" (*Rhus metopium*); and the guaiacum (*Guaiacum officinale*), whose heavy wood is known as *lignum vitae,* "the wood of life." This list, like the ones that follow, is by no means exhaustive but is rather intended to present a general overview of the manner in which the Taino marshaled their ecological resources and represented those re-sources in their language.

Fruit trees were both plentiful and important in the Taino economy. Fore-most among them were the following: the *jagua,* "the genip tree" (*Genipa americana*); the *hobo* and *hikako* (*Chrysobalanus icaco*) "varieties of West Indian plums"; the *mamei,* "the mamey tree" (*Mamea americana*); the well-known *papaya* tree and its fruit; the *guannaba,* "soursop" (*Annona muricata*), a fruit supposedly eaten by the dead (the *opia*); the *guayaba* (*Psidium pomiferum*); the *casina,* "edible apples," according to some au-thors. In addition to these, there were other plants and their fruits, includ-ing the *yayagua,* "pineapple," as well as the terms *boniama* and *yayama* for other varieties of the same fruit. The presence of multiple names, both here and elsewhere in the Taino lexicon, points to a certain level of sophis-tication in their practice of horticulture.

Central to Taino agriculture was the cultivation of several root crops, the most important of which was the *yucubia* plant which produced *yuca* (*Manihot esculenta*), "the manioc root," from which *casabi,* "cassava," was produced. There were several varieties of this plant, including *diacanan, hobos,* and *tubaga,* as well as *boniata,* "a sweet variety of the plant." The food provided by yucca and its varieties were supplemented by *age*, or *aje*, "a species of sweet potato," the very first food plant encountered by the Spaniards in the islands (Fuson 1992, 137). According to Oviedo, *athibuineix, aniguamar, guaraca, guacarayes,* and *guahanagax* were all names for different varieties of *age*. Other edible tubers were the *lerén*, or *lirén* (*Calathea allouia*), the *yahutía* or *yautía*, "any one of several species of edible tubers of the genus *Xanthosoma,* such as *Xanthosoma sagittifolium*" and the *maní* (*Arachis hypogeae*), "a plant and its edible fruit." In addition to these, the Taino fields were planted with *mahíz*, "corn"; *ector*, "tender corn"; and *aji*, "a pepper."

Additionally the Taino economy made use of several important "industrial plants," from which products were consumed by the local communities and also used in trade. In addition to the food-producing trees referred to above, the tropical forests produced large hardwood trees from which the Tainos fashioned *canoas*. Other trees provided utensils—the *hibuero* tree (*Crescentia cujete*), whose fruit, the *hibuera*, the "calabash," was used as a vessel, for example. Another plant, the *cabuya* (*Furcraea tuberosa*), produced cord or thread. Cohoba was the name given to the pulverized leaves of yet another plant, as well as the term for the religious rite in which the powder was inhaled through the nose by means of a bifurcated tube called a *tabaco* to produce a hallucinatory effect. The Spaniards' confusion between *cohoba*, the powder, and *tabaco*, the tube, resulted in the loss of the former term and the misapplication of the latter. Consequently, the misnomer, *tabaco*, spread into a number of languages as the word for the plant. Bixa (*Bixa orellana*) was an important dye plant; *digo* was a plant used in washing. Cotton was in general use among the Tainos, but curiously enough, the Spaniards did not record the indigenous name, most probably because they were well acquainted with the plant in the Old World, as well as with the fiber that it produced. This omission is instructive as to the manner in which the Spaniards viewed the Taino culture and language.

Animal life received less attention from the early writers than did plant life because fauna did not exist in great abundance or variety to begin with; but, perhaps equally important, the role of native fauna in Taino life itself was less important than was agriculture. The most important of all the animal groups were the mammals, particularly several varieties of small quadrupeds that resembled rabbits or large rodents and were hunted as a source of food. Among these were the *curics*, or *cori*, the *hutía*, the *guaminiquinajes*, the *mohics*, and the *quemí*. The *aon*, "a small, barkless dog," was perhaps a semidomesticate. And the large marine mammal, the *manatí* (*Manatus americanus*) was hunted in the estuaries and in the shallows around the larger islands.

Several reptiles were prized as a food source, namely the *iguana* (*Cyclura carinata*) and some turtles, particularly the *carei*, which was valued in particular for its shell and the *hicotea*, "a small turtle" (*Pseudemys palustris*). The *caiman*, or Caribbean crocodile, inhabited streams and waterways near the sea. Among the avifauna were the *giahuba-bagiael*, a bird that "sings like the ruiseñor"; the *guaraguao*, "a species of raptor"; and the *higuaca*, "a parrot valued for its feathers" (*Chrysotis vittatus*).

From the sea, the Tainos took the *cohobo*, or *cobo*, "a large conch" (*Strombus gigas*), which provided meat and a prized shell. The Tainos were expert fishermen, taking a selection of fish, including the *biajaiba*, "a sea fish." They also utilized the *xayba*, "an edible crab"; and the *guabina*, "a river fish." Although limited mention is made of insects and other lower life-forms, there were the *cocuyo*, "a flying insect"; and the *xixén*, "a small stinging insect," perhaps the sand fly.

The Tainos had names for the various other peoples that lived around them, including the *Ciguayo*, the *Caribe*, the *Caniba*, and the *Guanahatabey*. The names of their highest leaders, the *caciques* and *cacicas*, were well-known throughout the islands over which they ruled. *Amanex, Behechio, Cotubanamá*, and *Guacanagarí* are but a few examples of these names. *Anacoana, Cabomba*, and *Higuanamá* were all female chiefs, or cacica. Though the names of nonrulers are less abundant in the records and sources, we nevertheless know of a certain *Ganauvariu*, one of the first persons encountered by Pané, as well as *Guaticavá*, the first Indian who died baptized, and *Nabeca*, an Indian in Haiti. A rather extensive collection of Indian names has survived in the legal documentation of Puerto Rico (Hernández Aquino 1993).

The remains of the vocabulary of the human body and person are curiously lacking. This may be attributable to the fact that Spanish, like all languages, naturally had a complete set of terms for these features and therefore few inquiries were made about them. The term for "man" was *eri* or *ari*, as embedded in certain honorific titles such as *guaoxerí*. In Island Carib, the term for "man" was *eyeri* (Breton 1900, 204). Some words, did, however, attract the direct attention of the Spaniards. The term *goeiz* referred to a "living person," who at death (*operito*) was transformed into a *hupia*, or *opia*—that is, a "dead person's soul or spirit." The term *aco*, or *caco*, designated "the human eye" and was present in several expressions such a *peiticaco*, "a man with black eyes"; and *buticaco*, "man with light blue eyes." Among the scant number of other words in this category are *yarima,* "anus or end part"; and *ahi,* which probably meant "tooth." *Caracaracol,* "an infirmity of the skin, a rash," was one of the few recorded diseases.

The Taino social and political order attracted greater attention, especially those elements that reflected hierarchy and power. The *cacique* was the chief or leader of the tribal unit. There were numerous of these caciques, as well as undercaciques or subcaciques, who ruled over provinces and smaller areas in a universally recognized hierarchy. In general, Taino society was sharply stratified between the privileged aristocratic *nitainos* and the *naborías,* the latter being commoners who obeyed the former and did their bidding. The title *guamiquina,* meaning "great lord or person," was the term used by the Tainos in referring to the greatest of men; it was the title the Tainos used in reference to Columbus. The aristocratic order was also organized in an internal hierarchy with appropriate terms of address for individuals in accordance with their rank and position in society. The term of highest respect and honor among the nitainos was *matunherí,* which translates as "your highness" and was reserved for the very highest caciques. The title *guaoxerí* referred to the intermediate category and *baharí* to the least of them. Social bonding and great friendship were expressed by the use of *guatiao,* or *daihao/datihao,* that is, "the exchange of names between two persons, as a sign of great friendship."

Of all their economic activities, agriculture was the most important in that it provided the basis of all daily life as well as the rest of their material culture and the foundation of much of their religious belief. The principal food plants *yuca, aje, yahutía, maní, lerén, mahiz,* and *ají* have already been mentioned above. These were cultivated through swidden agriculture and, in many instances, in *conucos,* small mounds of loose earth in which the tuber crops grew rapidly and well. The existence of a variety of names for different kinds of *yuca, aje,* and *yayagua* point to an intensive concern with and understanding of island horticulture.

The fields were cultivated by the simplest of means. A dibble stick, called a *coa,* was employed to make holes in the worked mounds of loose earth, *conucos,* into which seeds and stalks were manually inserted. In several months, a crop of tubers, small ears of corn, and small peppers were harvested. The crops from the fields were converted into several simple foods, the most important of which was *casabi,* "a bread, or biscuit," made from a coarse flour derived from the yucca root. After the *hyen,* "poisonous juices," had been extracted from the crushed tubers by means of a long, flexible sieve, the dough was cooked on a *burén,* "a flat ceramic griddle." *Xabxao* was a kind of fine *casabi.*

The village, or *yucayeque*—a collection of thatched structures situated around a central plaza—was the center of Taino life. The *bohios* were the common dwellings of the naborias, while the *caney* were larger structures reserved for the caciques and the higher-ranking nitainos. We are told by Oviedo that there was also a type of bohio called an *eracra.* In the interior of the dwellings, *hamacas,* or "hammocks," were strung between the structural posts of the dwellings by means of *hicos,* "cords," which allowed the inhabitants to sleep well above the ground and the annoyance of insects and other pests. *Duhos,* or "ceremonial stools made of wood and sometimes inset with carvings," were used by ranking members of the society. The *barbacoa* was a platform on poles used for storage and perhaps the smoking and drying of foods. The Tainos wore scant clothing, principally the *nagua,* "a short loincloth."

The *batey* was the central plaza in the village, where a ceremonial ball game of the same name, it is believed, was played and where other cultural activities, including, most prominently, the *areitos* (see below), took place. In warfare and battles, known as *guazábara,* the Taino warrior fought with a *macana,* "a simple wooden club." Otherwise the *coa,* "a sharpened and fire-hardened all-purpose stick," was used for a variety of purposes.

The Tainos were able to exploit the rich marine resources of the surrounding seas as a result of their manufacture and adept use of *canoas,* "large canoes made from the hollowing out of large trees." The *cayuco* was a "small canoe," perhaps of Carib origin, suited for one or several persons. Both were propelled by a *nahe,* "a paddle of simple design."

Taino cultural activities were all closely associated with their religious practices. The cohoba rite was enacted by the cacique or the *behique,* the shaman. It involved, first, the inducement of vomiting for purposes of purification, then the inhalation of the powder or smoke of cohoba, "powdered tobacco" (*Nicotiana tabacum*), through the tabaco, the instrument designed for that purpose. The cacique thereupon fell into a trance, during which he communicated with zemis, or "spirit forces in the other world." He returned to consciousness with a message and instructions from the spirits. Positive responses from the deities were followed by the convocation of areitos, which consisted of singing, dancing, and chanting on the part of the people—activities that communicated among the members of the group the central cultural and religious repertory of the tribe. These events were accompanied by the playing of drums, *maiohauay* or *baiohabao*, as attested by Pané, and *maguey*, by Martyr. The ceremonial culture also included the employment of *guaizas*, or masks.

Taino religion was marked by polytheism, animism, shamanism, and fetishism. The cacique acted as a kind of "pontifex maximus," while the behique performed healing and other ritual duties. The Tainos believed in an all-powerful god, *Yocuhu Vagua Maorocoti*, whose name meant "the giver of Yucca, the Sea, the one without a grandfather," according to Las Casas. His mother, *Atabey*, or *Atabeira*, had five names in all, which, according to Pané, were *Apito*, *Guacar*, *Yermao*, and *Zuimaco*. Beneath the mother and son in importance were other deities, all represented by the idols called zemis, or *cemis*—many of which were seen to reside in incised, three-pointed stones of the same name. In general, those zemis originated and dwelled in the primal forces of nature. For example, *Guabancex* and *Guatauba* were zemis associated with hurricanes, whereas *Boiniael* and *Maroho* were related to rain. And there were numerous others. The principal rites of the Tainos were the cahoba rite and the areito (mentioned above), which were aimed at interpreting the will of the deities and then venerating them. Ritual purification by vomiting and fasting were a means of ritual sacrifice through which the caciques and behiques approached the zemis. Additionally, they maintained certain beliefs, such as the notion that humanity—that is, the Indian peoples—originated in a cave called *Cacibagiagua*. A certain mythological figure, *Machochael*, was the guardian of the cave whence issued those first humans. *Jouanaboina*, another cave, was believed to have been the source for the sun and the moon. Another legend had it that there was an island in the sea, *Matinino*, where only women lived. As rich as the Taino religion appears to have been, it is certain that the early writers, especially Pané, Las Casas, and Martyr collected only a part of the Taino lore and, at that, imperfectly. Christian writers, after all, had no real interest in promoting "pagan" belief and ritual.

Not a great deal of the Tainos' knowledge of the physical world and its workings was recorded by the early observers. Since such information would have been viewed by the chroniclers as nonproductive and unusable toward any specific end, it was neither solicited nor recorded. But certainly it must have existed. It is difficult to imagine, for example, that such intrepid seafarers had no knowledge of the secrets of the seas and the heavens so important in navigating those seas. Yet we know little of the intellectual content of their culture beyond the fact that they had a system of counting that did not extend beyond twenty—the first four numbers of which are supplied by Las Casas, namely *hequetí, yamocá, canocúm,* and *yamoncobre* (Las Casas 1909, 538).

Summary

The Taino language had flourished in the Caribbean area for nearly two thousand years before it came into violent contact with Spanish culture at the end of the fifteenth century. In less than half a century, the Taino people, their culture, and language were effectively destroyed as independent, autonomous entities. Yet in spite of that sudden catastrophe, traces of the original peoples of those islands and elements of their culture have survived by having been ultimately assimilated and absorbed into the colonial establishment of the conquerors. As that was occurring, the process of assimilation of the vanquished effected a partial transformation of the conquerors. In the first place, the Taino bloodline mixed with European and African elements, giving rise to new physical types, particularly in the larger islands. Running parallel with that biological process, certain salient aspects of the Taino culture (discussed above) were selectively adopted by generations of successors in the Indies, along with those linguistic elements that gave those cultural features expression. In time, new people and new cultures appeared in the West Indies, identified by the Spanish word *criollo,* or "creole," a term that takes on its full meaning only when it is contrasted to other designations—"peninsular," "Spanish," "European." The Taino contribution to that creation of a creole identity and lifestyle, not least in the area of language, has been considerable.

Note

This chapter is excerpted from a longer manuscript of the author, which deals more extensively with Taino language and culture.

17

The Taino Vision: A Study in the Exchange of Misunderstanding

Henry Petitjean Roget

Upon arriving in the Caribbean in the fall of 1492, Christopher Columbus learned from the local Taino people that neighboring islands were inhabited by man-eating warriors called *Calinas*. For Columbus these Calinas— he transcribed the name as *cariba* or *caribe*—were obviously the subject people of the Great Khan. His misreading of the situation sent him hurrying back to Spain, where he informed his royal patrons that he had reached the Indies.

It has long been acknowledged that the admiral's mistake constitutes one of history's great misrecognition scenes. What has received less attention is a parallel misrecognition on the part of the native peoples whom he erroneously identified as "Indians." If Columbus interpreted them according to his own preconceptions, they did the same to him in turn, providing him and his men with a false identity that conformed to their own preconceived cosmology. In this chapter I explain certain Taino beliefs that helped to guarantee this second misunderstanding.

When the Spaniards descended on the populations of Haiti and the Lucayos, the native peoples must have experienced a veritable shock—one that forced them to seek for these strange beings' origins and to fit them into the universe of Taino beliefs. They first imagined that the strangers were the *cannibales*, "cannibals" from beyond the island of Bohio. But when the Spaniards so freely distributed gifts among them, the Taino abandoned this view and realized that the benevolent visitors had come from a world unknown to them. As we shall see, the Tainos were convinced that this world was *Coaybay*, the land of the dead, which they believed to exist in a region known as Soraya. The "Indians" thus concluded that the Span-iards were revenants, or returning ghosts.

In order to reach this conclusion, they relied on two related pieces of evidence.

EXHIBIT 1: STRANGERS BEARING GIFTS

In order to befriend the natives, Columbus distributed trinkets. To him and his men, these were items of almost no value. To the Tainos, however, the Spaniards' baubles and beads were rich with magical, supernatural signifi-cance—objects validating the belief that the newcomers were otherworldly.

The misapprehension began within days of the admiral's first landfall. Columbus describes how on October 15, an Indian who had tried to es-cape from the Spaniards in his canoe was recaptured: "I sent for this In-dian, and I gave him a red cap, some green glass beads that I put on his arm, and two bells that I tied to his ears, then I returned his canoe which was in our boat, and sent him back to shore" (Navarrete 1828, 55). En-couraged by the obvious success of these gifts, the admiral repeated his generosity: "He made them be given small bells, brass rings, and yellow and green glass marbles which made them very happy" (157). Later, he exchanged a few pieces of Taino gold for another bell, "because nothing pleased them more . . . they are literally mad about them" (238).

In this seemingly minor gesture of diplomatic good will, Columbus had forged the first link in a chain of misunderstanding, for unbeknownst to him two of the objects he had just given away, the cap and the bells, held great symbolic value for the Taino people. The cap was red, the color of the seeds of the *roucou* plant (*Bixa orellana*), which the people used to paint themselves red. The color red also recalled the red feces of the Rain-bow Serpent, it was seen as a protective covering against bad omens and illnesses. As for the bells, the Tainos were greatly attached to them for two reasons. As sonorous objects, they were analogous to the shamans' mara-cas, while their yellow color and brass material made them analogous to the gold ornaments known as *guanins*, whose origin is described in their myths (Pané 1972).

Taino thought referred constantly to myth and its nonlinear conception of time, in which "events supposed to be taking place at one moment in time also form a permanent structure which simultaneously relate to the past, the present, and the future" (Lévi-Strauss 1958, 231). Such a manner of apprehending duration could not be assimilated to the Europeans' own concepts of time. Taino perception of a closed and circular time—coupled with their constant expectation of a particular event, the arrival of those whom they called *Cannibas*—led them to an inescapable interpretation of the Spaniards' actions.

In the context of significance attributed by the Tainos to cultural goods, the gifts offered by the Spaniards were anything but trinkets. Accordingly the Tainos assessed those who distributed these gifts in reference to myths that accounted for the origins of similar goods. Because they were unable to place these strangers within the mundane context of their own society, the Tainos concluded, logically enough, that they were supernatural.

Exhibit 2: The Origin of Gold

The Island Caribs in post-Columbian times were still involved both in raiding and in trading with Puerto Rico (Moreau 1992). Among the most important objects they traded with the Tainos were the *calloucouli* or *caracoli* (Breton 1665, 106), which were called *guanins* by the Tainos. These were ornaments made of low-quality gold obtained by the Caribs through trade with Amazonian tribes who practiced metallurgy. (The indigenous populations of the Antilles did not know how to work metals by smelting.)

As soon as they landed, the Spaniards became interested beyond reason in these guanins, which they found Taino men and women wearing in their noses and ears. This interest created a further misunderstanding, for the guanins, as I have shown elsewhere, had a symbolic, prophylactic function for their wearers. Among the Tainos, guanins were the materialization of the double or twin zemis Badraima and Corocote, the rainbow to whom the Tainos attributed the origin of all illnesses (see Petitjean Roget 1985). Among the rarest and most precious of objects, they also represented the crest of the great Rainbow Serpent, known as *Joulouca* among the Caribs and *Boyusu* in the Amazon; in that aspect, they provided magical protection against disease.

The Spaniards' interest in the guanins was quite differently motivated, for Columbus and his men were obsessed with gold—a fact his reports endlessly verify.

Beginning on Saturday, October 13, in Guanahani, he noticed men wearing small pieces of gold suspended from their noses. He managed by signs to "learn from them that around their island and sailing south, [they] would find a land whose king had large vases of gold and a great quantity of that metal." The name of this island was written variously as *Samaot* or *Samoeto*

(Navarrete 1828, 60, 63, 67). Columbus believed that he understood from the Indians that the island where he landed on Friday, October 19, was Samoeto. Disappointed at not finding gold, he named it Isabella.

On Monday, October 15, a mere three days after his first landfall, Columbus was already able to state, "I landed near the said point to learn if there was gold there, because the Indians I had taken in the island of San Salvador had told me that the people there wore very large gold bracelets on their legs and arms" (Navarrete 1828, 53). He continued, "I left . . . to pass to the other island which is very large, and where all the men I took from San Salvador indicate by signs that there is a lot of gold, and whose inhabitants wear it as bracelets and chains on their arms, ears, nose and neck" (56).

Similar information was reported on Sunday, November 4. After Columbus displayed some gold and pearls, "several old men answered that there was gold in great quantity in a place they call Bohio whose inhabitants wear it on their neck, ears, arms, legs, and that pearls were also found there" (101). The diary for Monday, November 12, reports that the "Admiral left the harbor . . . to sail towards an island which according to the Indians who were with him, was called Babeque, and where according to their signs, the inhabitants gathered at night, on the beach, to collect gold with lighted candles, and made them into ingots with a hammer and that to get there one had to direct the ship east and a quarter southeast" (111). The diary is replete with similar mentions of alleged sources of gold that were, in reality, guanins.

Having arrived on the coast of Hispaniola, Columbus looked again for gold mines. He writes that the Indians "gave us indications on the presence of mines in that island . . . and in other places they indicated as producing this precious metal, citing Cipango, which they call Civao: they insisted that there is gold in quantity there, and that the cacique wears a banner of hammered gold, but that this place is very far" (Navarrete 1828, 229). On December 29, the young nephew of King Guacanagari "told him that at a four days distance, there was towards the east an island named Guarionex, and others named Macorix, Mayonix, Fuma, Cibao and Coroay, which contained much gold" (246).

On January 13, Columbus encountered some Indians armed with bows and arrows. One of them described to him what he takes as "the island Matinino, all peopled with women without men." "They find there," writes Columbus, "much 'tuob,' which means gold or copper, and it is located east of Carib. He also talked about the island of Guanin, where there was much Tuob" (Navarrette 1828, 279). Always seeking more gold, Columbus on January 14, gave a cacique "a red cap, a piece of cloth of the same color, and glass beads; he then gave pieces of red cloth to the Indians among his followers. The king said that on the following day he would bring him a gold mask, assuring him that there were many in that land, in Carib as well as in Matinino" (283). On the following day, Columbus mentions again both Carib and Matinino, fearing that "entering and staying on Carib would prove difficult because the Indians say that the inhabitants eat human flesh . . . from that island the Admiral would go to Matinino which is said to be peopled by women without men."

Columbus's references to the origins of gold were interpretations of the Indians' responses to questions that had to have been asked not in the Tainos' own tongue but haltingly, by gestures and signs. It is clear that there was a serious problem of translation here. The words that Columbus heard he interpreted as place-names; he believed that, in response to his queries, the Indians were directing him to nearby gold-producing sites known as *goanin*, *cibao*, and *coroa*. They even gave him, so he thought, sailing directions to reach them. Hearing what he wanted to hear, the admiral invented a connection among gold, islands called Carib and Babeque, and the Calinas of the Lesser Antilles.

When Columbus took Babeque and Carib as place-names, he was guilty of a misunderstanding that nevertheless provides interesting evidence for the probable location of the area where guanins were traded. The island of Babeque, as has been shown by José Arrom (1970), was none other than Boriquen, that is, Puerto Rico. Moreover the Western Tainos (those from the Bahamas), who provided the information about Babeque, the golden ornaments, and the Boriquen or Caribs whom Columbus believed to be the subjects of the Great Khan, also account for a real fact: the Caribs or Calinas of the Lesser Antilles came to Puerto Rico to trade with the Tainos for guanin of gold alloy procured through trade with Indian tribes of the South American continent (Prato-Perelli 1983).

What do we really know of such islands as Babeque, Carib, and Matinino or of places like Civao, Coroai, and Goanin? One of the myths collected by Columbus's linguist cleric, Father Pané, provides an answer. The Taino myth transcribed by Pané, tells of the province of Caonao in the island of Hispaniola, in which there is a mountain called Cauta. In that mountain are the two caves out of which, the Tainos believed, human beings emerged. The myth tells of the hero Guahayona, who, after killing his brother-in-law the cacique and seducing all the women, brought them with him at night to the island of Matinino, where he abandoned them. He then left for another place, which was called Guanin "because of what he brings back from there; Guahayona acquired thus all the women for him alone, and left them behind at Matinino where they say that only women are now found" (Pané 1972).

Pané further says that the dead go to a place called Coaybay, situated in a region of the island known as Soraya. There is no mistake possible; all these names are those heard by Columbus during the first moments of the encounter. He inquired about gold, but the Indians understood that he was interested instead in their guanins. And they concluded, not irrationally, that he was a revenant seeking not the European version of gold—that is, wealth—but a prophylactic to be held against his doom.

Other elements of the myth were also misinterpreted by Columbus as the names of geographical places. The island of Samaot or Samoet, for which he searched so assiduously, as well as Civao, which he believed to be Japan or Cipango, were none other than the Canau mythical province. The admiral understood that some of this information was related to the sea; thus he writes that they gathered gold on the beaches at night. Other island names in Columbus's narratives did not actually refer to islands at all: *Guarionex* was the name of a cacique; *Macorix* was a distinctive Taino group in Hispaniola.

One conclusion is inescapable: faced with the Spaniards' insistence on learning about the origins of gold, the Indians consistently repeated to them the mythical story of the origins of gold ornaments, or guanins. The island of women without men Matinino, of women covered with copper plaques for protection, that Columbus sought beyond the land of Carib, was none other than the island where, in the myth, the hero Guahayona abandoned the women he had seduced.

It is important to note that after leaving the women on Matinino, Guahayona returned to Medicine Woman, who gave him the insignia of his cure, the "guanins and the cibas to be worn tied on his arms." This was the Tainos' mythically constituted belief that golden guanins provided supreme protection against illness and death, reinforced by the Spaniards' constant efforts to find gold, that convinced them these strangers had risen out of nowhere, as beings returning from Coaybay, the land of the dead. Alert to their visitors' fascination with gold, the Tainos undoubtedly insisted on knowing whether they had come from the land of the dead. Their inquiries were not understood by Columbus, and the Taino word for the land of the dead, *Coaybay,* was recorded in his diary as a place-name.

RETURNING THE RETURNED

As Columbus was sailing hastily toward Spain in January 1493, convinced that he had reached the shores of China, the men left behind at La Navidad became so obsessed with gold and women, and proved such a burden to their hosts, that the Tainos soon killed them all. In addition, they ritually mutilated them to ensure that they would be sent back to Coaybay, the land of the dead, where they thought these evil men had originally come from. The same punishment that the Tainos would have inflicted on bad shamans, they now inflicted on the invading Spaniards.

Father Pané gives us a description of this punishment. When a sorcerer had failed in his cure, Pané writes, they seized the medicine man, and to kill him so that he would not return, they "pull out his eyes and crush his testicles." The eyewitness account of Michel de Cuneo, who reports that the Spaniards killed by the Tainos had their eyes pierced, here finds its proper meaning. The Tainos had sought to send the invaders back definitively to their proper home, the land of the dead.

It is thus clear that gold and trinkets were only the most visible elements that were exchanged between Columbus and the Taino people: a much more critical exchange was that of misunderstanding. By bestowing certain gifts on the Tainos, Columbus reenacted the immemorial gestures of their founding hero, unwittingly making himself and his companions figures of a myth. The Tainos had no alternative but to fall back entirely into the world into which Columbus had unsuspectingly drawn them. Faced with the clear evidence of the Spaniards' symbolic gifts and their obsession with gold, the native people concluded with perfect logic that the invaders could only have come from the land of the dead. And it was to that land, with fitting irony, that the Tainos returned them.

Part 5: The Island Caribs of the Lesser Antilles

One of the greatest points of disagreement among Caribbean historians and prehistorians concerns the identity of the Lesser Antillean people called the Island Caribs. Early European observers, influenced by partially understood accounts offered by the Taino, came to view the people of the Lesser Antilles as all the same—and all dangerous. One of the questions surrounding the Island Caribs concerns their origins. In the Island Caribs' accounts of where they came from, written down in the mid-1600s by French missionaries, they are said to have come very recently from the South American mainland. According to these accounts the Island Caribs maintained relations with mainland Carib groups, and the men spoke the Carib language. However, many archaeologists, historians, and linguists have argued that the Island Caribs are closely related to the Taino and other Caribbean groups, and that the Carib language spoken by men was a trade language that was used to communicate with trading partners from the mainland.

Louis Allaire's discussion of the ethnohistoric and archaeological information on the Island Caribs provides a good overview both to Island Carib culture and to some of the complexities of this debate. Vincent Cooper looks at the issues of identity and culture in the Lesser Antilles from a linguist's point of view and offers new insights concerning Island Carib society and history.

18

The Caribs of the Lesser Antilles

Louis Allaire

So much has been written about the Caribs, especially in the context of the Quincentenary, that trying to discuss questions of their identity and of what they did or didn't do is not an easy task. Not only is there confusion surrounding these issues, but the emotionally charged debate about their identity and origins must also be taken into account.

The Caribs of the Lesser Antilles, known to anthropologists as Island Caribs, have long been closely associated with the European discovery of the New World, although they were not encountered until Columbus's second voyage of 1493. Yet a romantic vision has pervaded research on the Caribs ever since, tending to depict all aboriginal remains found in the islands they occupied as having been produced and left by them (Rouse 1948c).

If we are to believe the Columbian chronicles, especially the accounts of Dr. Chanca, of the 1493 voyage (see Columbus 1988), the island of Guadeloupe then was already in the hands of ethnic Island Caribs. This is indicated by some distinctive particularities of their costume, such as the woven garment worn by the women below the knee. Linguistically the Guadeloupe natives appear to have been different from the Tainos, and the name *Turuqueira* for Guadeloupe, already appearing in Peter Martyr's *De Orbe Novo,* was also the name recorded by the French there in the seventeenth century. They also were already raiding for captives to be later castrated and eaten, and from what we may gather from descriptions reported by Martyr, the pottery found in the Carib dwellings in 1493 may have been consistent with Island Carib pottery as described in the 1650s. We may even suggest that large beer-making pots were actually seen there, whereas the Tainos of the Greater Antilles did not make or drink manioc beer—that Carib cultural trait of such significant social implications.

We learn little else about the Lesser Antilles peoples following this initial and brief encounter of 1493. Caribs appear by name throughout the sixteenth century in connection with enduring hostilities toward the Spanish colony in Puerto Rico, when the island of St. Croix seems to have been used as a base for their raids (Anderson-Cordóva 1990). It is true that occasional encounters were reported, such as that of the chronicler Girolamo Benzoni (1857), who had landed briefly on Dominica in the 1530s on his way to Santo Domingo. He was greeted there by naked and *red painted* Caribs. This feature, which is not reported in 1493, was certainly another typical ethnic characteristic of all the Caribs and related peoples of the South American lowlands, but it differs from Taino practices in the Greater Antilles.

It is not before the middle of the seventeenth century, in the writings of several French missionaries established in Dominica, Guadeloupe, Martinique, and St. Vincent, that we start learning more about the Island Caribs—or, as they called themselves, the *Calinago* (for the men) and *Callipuna* (for the women). (See Hulme and Whitehead 1992 for several of these sources in English translation.) Essentially, what anthropologists and historians know today of Island Carib culture, language, and society is based almost entirely on these documents. In other words Island Carib culture is essentially a seventeenth-century phenomenon. By that time, almost five generations separate them from the year of the discovery, and for over a century, there had been no Tainos left to raid or trade with. Indeed it seems that the Tainos were by then entirely forgotten, by both the missionary writers and the Caribs.

On the basis of this evidence let us try to answer the question of who the Caribs were. Establishing this fact involves identifying this group in relation to neighboring peoples of the Caribbean, and there is major disagreement among historians concerning this identity. The best approach would be to ask the Caribs themselves who they are as an ethnic group.

The Caribs, who by the seventeenth century were only found in the Windward Islands and possibly St. Kitts, shared a strong national character and ethnic identity. They claimed openly that they were of the same ethnicity as their Carib-speaking neighbors of what is today French Guiana and Surinam; they knew these people as the Galibis, claimed them as their ancestors, and even used a common ethnic name, *Kalina* or *Kalinago*. For the French missionary Father Breton, the greatest ethnographer of the Caribs, this was like someone's calling himself a "Frenchman from Paris" as opposed to a "Frenchmen from the city of Lyons" (Breton 1892).

This ethnic consciousness was further reinforced by the Caribs' contrast to their traditional enemies, the Arawaks from Trinidad and adjacent areas of the mainland, with whom they fought, raided for cannibal victims, and conducted seasonal trade. By the 1650s, obviously, there were no Tainos to contend with, and there is no way to learn how the Caribs would have related to the Tainos of the Greater Antilles before 1492. Along with every anthropologist working before a decade ago, I find no evidence whatsoever to suggest that the Caribs were in reality a group of Tainos living under different socioeconomic conditions and mistakenly identified as a different race by the Europeans to justify their raiding them for slaves. This idea is currently expressed in several publications about the Caribs. It can only be assumed that their authors have failed to properly interpret the cultural and linguistic evidence.

Everything indicates—as Rouse was able to demonstrate in the 1950s—that Carib culture, including its pottery making and its language, belongs essentially to a type of culture common to the Guianas. It is reasonably well established that the language of the Tainos, known as Taino, was an early manifestation of the Arawakan linguistic family (Taylor 1977). It is also well established that the Island Caribs, despite their name, did not speak a Cariban language as their Galibis allies did but an Arawakan language close to some languages of the Guianas. This is so despite the well-known fact that the men used between themselves a Carib-based pidgin that was a widespread trading language in South America (Taylor and Hoff 1980). This fact cannot be construed to imply that Caribs and Tainos spoke a same language.

This question of identity is closely related to the issue of Carib origins. The alternative is simple: the Caribs found in the islands by the Europeans were either recent intruders, as they actually claim to have been, or descendants of earlier prehistoric populations. Some of these issues must be discussed in the context of the archaeological evidence that I review in chapter 3 of this volume. On the basis of the historical situation alone, the oral traditions accounting for a recent migration should be given some credence, as should the differences at all levels between Caribs and Tainos and the similarities between the Caribs and the peoples of the mainland, where local Kalina societies still survive today. These contrasts and correspondences strongly suggest a mainland origin. Strong continuities with the earlier encounter by Europeans cannot allow for a later or seventeenth-century movement from the mainland. I like to think that the fear the Caribs inspired in Taino chiefdoms is sufficient indication that they were a foreign and threatening reality, not just belligerent cousins.

Carib life is fully described in the chronicles of the French missionaries of the 1650s. By that time, obviously, the Caribs had maintained some distant relationships with Europeans for over a century, first with the Spanish, then the French and English, and even the Dutch. Even before the French and English attempted some effort at colonization in the Lesser Antilles, beginning in the 1620s, this European exposure undoubtedly had an effect on Carib culture, altering its prehistoric or truly traditional conditions. Yet by modern standards, the seventeenth-century Caribs were certainly still close to their ancestral ways of life.

The Caribs were essentially a farming people. They planted small manioc and sweet potato gardens in the surrounding rain forest near their villages, which consisted of a series of round huts for the women built around a larger rectangular men's house (see Petersen, this volume). Their settlements were found in the more humid and fertile islands, and although they certainly fished and collected shellfish (especially topshells of rocky shorelines) and trapped land crabs, they cannot be characterized as a society of fishermen. There was certainly little to hunt in the islands, but techniques developed on the mainland were used to capture agouti, rice rats, and iguanas. Turtle hunting was also a major subsistence activity.

Their foods are well known. As on the mainland, manioc was baked as cassava bread, and the pepper pot was the common meal, with it bits of meat and fish stewed in manioc juices and spiced with lots of hot chili peppers. There is no doubt that beer making was a major food activity among them, serving to animate major intervillage gatherings at which political events were debated and prestige positions were assumed.

Island Carib society was of a type anthropologists usually call egalitarian or tribal. The village community was ruled by a headman, but no chiefs ruled over groups of villages or entire islands, as was the case among the Tainos. For purposes of war, however, some war leaders were able to assume leadership over warriors from various islands and to lead expeditions all the way to the coasts of the Guianas or Venezuela. Often these war chiefs were singled out by the Europeans as representatives of their tribes for the purpose of negotiations. This practice, in colonial times, may have led to these generals' being vested with a greater political authority than that power they originally enjoyed within their own societies (Dreyfuss 1977).

The arts and crafts of the Caribs are also consistent with a simple type of society; this is again in sharp contrast with the more sophisticated Tainos. Their domestic crafts included pottery of a style closely related to the early historic ceramics of the Guianas as they were still being produced until recently. As such it is unlike most late prehistoric ceramic styles in the Lesser Antilles but which may be related to the historic Cayo ceramics of St. Vincents mentioned in chapter 3, which belong to a mainland ceramic tradition. They made ample use of calabash containers, however, as well as wood—especially for their canoes, which were sufficiently seaworthy to take them from Puerto Rico to the mainland, and for the little stools on which they sat in their huts. They were also expert weavers, and although they wore little clothing, their cotton beds—or hammocks, as we would call them today—were greatly appreciated by the Europeans. Basketry was another art in which they excelled; their only furniture except for the stools was basketry containers (Allaire 1984; Rouse 1948c).

The Caribs who are known to us from the seventeenth-century sources already knew how to use metal objects. European tools and utensils such as knives, needles, sickles, hoes, and axes had long been a medium of exchange in trade with Europeans. The griddles used for their manioc bread were made of iron. Native metal objects had been limited to the small crescent-shaped gold-copper pieces known as *caracoli*, which may have come from the mainland. Greenstone pendants were also much valued, and the Caribs used parrot feathers as ornaments or garments to wear in their public ceremonies. They had otherwise no major artistic representations. Even their pottery seems to have been largely undecorated, with the only decorated utensils being the calabash bowls they painted in red and black.

Among the Caribs, who are so much remembered as a belligerent group, weapons were a major element of material culture. The all-purpose weapon was the longbow, accompanied by arrows tipped with wood or stingray spine and poisoned with manchineel juice. Another major weapon was the war club, or *boutou*, often illustrated and decorated with incised designs. This fact is usually overlooked, but the Island Caribs, according to Father Breton, also used the blowgun—an unmistakable indication of the mainland origin of their culture. Their tactics were surprise attacks, and they are known to have used noxious gases (smoke from hot chili peppers) in their battles.

The simple Island Carib religion lacked the diversified deities or zemi worship of their Taino neighbors. An evil being or devil named Mabouya may have been their major spiritual preoccupation, but shamanistic practices were very much part of daily life and were used for healing by a specialist known as *boye,* similar to the *piaye* of their Guiana neighbors.

Much has been said about the notorious Carib cannibalism. The word itself derives from *cannibales,* a name the Taino used to describe the Caribs to Columbus. That this practice, which was so abhorrent to the Spanish and French, may have been overstated in the European effort to justify slave raiding is a reasonable notion to consider, for there are few eyewitness accounts of cannibalistic activities. Anthropologists are agreed that the practice was to a degree quite widespread in the lowlands of South America, as among many non-Western societies. Here anthropologists must avoid making value judgments and stick to the cultural relativism that has always been a backbone of the profession, especially when living people are no longer involved in these practices. Those who were the closest to the living Caribs, and the most sympathetic to their cause—Father Las Casas in the sixteenth century and Father Breton a century later—recognized that the eating of human flesh was indeed practiced. Its precise role, whether ideological or purely nutritional, is still widely debated (Myers 1984; Whitehead 1984).

Traditional Carib culture, as described by French missionaries in the early part of the seventeenth century, brings us back to the ethnographic situation at the very eve of European contact. As mentioned above, I strongly believe that Guadeloupe in 1492 was already both ethnically and linguistically Island Carib (see Allaire 1980). There are, however, indications that a greater cultural diversity existed farther west in the Leeward Islands (Wilson 1993). This evidence is based on the famous occurrence at Salt River on St. Croix as described in most trustworthy chronicles of Columbus's second voyage, and especially by Chanca. There, the marked difference in appearance between the natives encountered in the Leewards and the other Caribs was evidenced in the type of hairstyle displayed by the Indians of St. Cruz. Whereas the Island Caribs of Guadeloupe wore their hair long or in a ponytail with bangs on the forehead, "like the women of Castille," as one chronicler remarked: the Santa Cruz population favored short cropped hair, cut in various designs "decorated . . . in a great number of different patterns each according to his fancy. They make these patterns—crosses and such like devices—with sharpened reeds" (Chanca 1949). Incidentally, this unusual description is very much reminiscent of a similar hairstyle that survives today in the southern Amazon, such as that among the Mehinaku, described by Thomas Gregor (1977)—yet another indication of a continental origin for the Caribs.

The identity of the original early historic population of the Leeward Islands, as well as of the Virgin Islands, is a matter that still remains to be precisely determined. Differences from the Island Caribs of Guadeloupe have already been noted in this paper. That they may be an entirely different people is suggested by a seldom-cited statement in Chanca's letter (Columbus 1988) relating to some hearsay about a recent depopulation or extermination of the island of Montserrat by the Guadeloupe Caribs. This may signify that different hostile populations had clashed shortly before the coming of the Europeans. If so, the event would give further credence to the theory of a recent Carib migration from the mainland.

Another misconception that has received considerable attention concerns the presence of Taino refugees in the Lesser Antilles in the early 1500s, following upon the initial Spanish colonization of the Greater Antilles, and especially Puerto Rico, as contributing to the ancestry of the later Caribs described by the Europeans. The idea is simply not supported either by historical facts or by Carib traditions.

Finally, the cultural and ethnic picture becomes more complex with the probably late addition of mainland (and Cariban-speaking) Caribs, those known as Galibis, on the islands of Grenada and Tobago, where they were found by 1650 and where they maintained separate ethnic communities alongside those of the Island Caribs proper. At the same time, St. Vincent was beginning to witness the emergence of the Black Carib ethnic group, a people who until their ruthless deportation from that island in the 1790s by British colonial authorities had come to symbolize native resistance to European invaders. Indeed, many small surviving Carib groups both in the Windward Islands and the Guianas at this point came to share this warlike destiny (Watts 1987). By then, however, populations had shifted, and the Carib world was now entirely different from what it had been on the eve of Columbus's arrival. The Caribs' world was no longer simply their own; from the point of contact onward, they belonged to the history of early colonial South America—no longer the subject of anthropologists but more properly of historians.

19

Language and Gender among the Kalinago of Fifteenth-century St. Croix

Vincent O. Cooper

When Columbus arrived at Salt River, St. Croix, in 1493, there were perhaps 3,500 Kalinagos, or Island Caribs, living on that island. Irving Rouse (1992) suggests that these Amerindians may have actually been of Taino rather than Kalinago background, but scholars still disagree on the details of this matter (see Morse, this volume). As the Arawak name *Ayay* suggests, Tainos had inhabited St. Croix at an earlier time, although *Cibuqueira* seems to have been the name used later by the Island Caribs. Whatever the terminology, in 1493 there were approximately twenty villages of these people, averaging sixty or so inhabitants each. During the sixteenth and seventeenth centuries, the Kalinago also occupied St. Kitts, Barbados, Dominica, Martinique, Saint Lucia, St. Vincent, Grenada, Tobago, and other islands southeast of Puerto Rico, although by 1590 the St. Croix population was virtually extinct.

Rouse hypothesizes that, unlike the Tainos, the Kalinagos arrived in the Caribbean recently enough to have retained traditions of their mainland Carib origin. Rouse describes them as a marginal subgroup of the Taino family who left the South American mainland later than the main group and who, upon conquering another Amerindian group, the Igneri, imposed on them the masculine aspects of their ancestral Carib culture (Rouse 1992, 21–25). (During the seventeenth century, and perhaps as early as the fifteenth century, the males lived in separate houses from the women, many of whom they had captured from the Tainos in warfare.) Douglas Taylor (1977) supports this assessment of Kalinago origin, as does Hilary Beckles (1990), who places the arrival of the first wave of Kalinago from South

America at approximately A.D. 1000 and adds that they were still arriving at the time of the encounter.

THE IDENTITY OF THE KALINAGO LANGUAGE

A number of scholars have speculated on the relationship between the Island Carib language, spoken by the Kalinago, and the Island Arawak language, spoken by the Tainos, during the period from the fifteenth to the seventeenth centuries. The identity of the Kalinago language, like that of the people themselves, remains controversial. Some scholars suggest that the Kalinago originated in South America and continued to maintain communication with the Caribs of Guyana up to the fifteenth century; according to them, the Island Carib language would therefore probably be closely related to the Carib language spoken in Guyana. Other scholars, however, suggest that at the time of Columbus's arrival, the Kalinago spoke both a variety of Arawak and a Carib-based trade jargon, or pidgin.

This latter conclusion follows from widely corroborated reports that for probably as long as five centuries, the Kalinago maintained an ancient ritual of taking as wives the women they captured in wars against Taino males. Over time, the particular Island Arawak language of the mothers was passed on to their children, eventually displacing the Island Carib language and relegating it, by the time of European contact, to the marginal status of a trade and warfare pidgin. Taylor (1977) allows for the possibility that the women used Island Carib when speaking to peer males and Arawak when speaking to their children and other women, with their sons speaking only Island Carib to their fathers.

Taylor's conclusion is based on two assumptions: that the extended contact between Island Carib and Island Arawak resulted in language transition from the former to the latter, and that all communication between the Kalinago men and Kalinago boys was restricted to the subject of trade and warfare. This line of reasoning would lead one to dismiss the quite real possibility that these males conversed in Island Carib during hunting and fishing expeditions.

Another reason that we need to be careful about such conclusions is that the Kalinagos and Tainos had oral traditions, not written ones. Hence we should be cautious when making distinctions between what is assumed to be a stable Island Carib language and a residual pidgin, which, unlike a creole, is not a native language. It is even conceivable that what some European observers assumed to be evidence of pidginization simply reflected the normal variation caused by the Kalinagos' frequent contact with other

Amerindian groups—a contact that perhaps dates back to the South American past.

An examination of the role of the Kalinago and Taino systems of kinship, descent, age distinction, and class/caste distinction would also provide useful insights on language use and status. One would also need to consider the relative gradual or abrupt nature of the language transition process on the various island communities, the relative structural similarities and differences between the varieties of the two languages that came into contact at a given time, and the ethnic and political relationships that obtained throughout the duration of the contact period.

Although empirical data on the actual language spoken by the Kalinagos have not been adequately reconstructed, I use here the methodology provided by comparative linguistics and sociolinguistics to offer a tentative hypothesis on the social and linguistic status of the Island Carib language and the relative roles of women's language and men's language on St. Croix.

PIDGINS AND CREOLES: DEFINITIONS AND DEBATES

A pidgin is not a native language. According to the commonly accepted definition (Taylor 1977; Thompson 1961; Whinnom 1971; Stewart 1962; Navarro Tomás 1951; Cassidy 1971), a pidgin is a makeshift trade jargon derived from limited contact between people of politically unequal influence whose own native languages are mutually unintelligible. Pidgin grammar is unstable, and its vocabulary is restricted to terms relating to specific activities such as trade and war.

A creole, on the other hand, is a pidgin that has evolved into the mother tongue of a community. Traditionally pidgins have been called adult languages and creoles called child languages or first languages. Both pidgins and creoles are said to derive 80 percent of their vocabulary from the language of the politically dominant group in the contact situation. Although most pidgins have a short life span, it is possible for some of them to survive for long periods of time without becoming native languages—as in the case of Tok Pisin, spoken in Papua, New Guinea.

In a revision of this definition, Derek Bickerton (1981) views pidgins and creoles as two separate, unrelated systems. Pidgins are considered grammatically too inconsistent and undeveloped, too confusing and elusive, to serve as adequate language models for young children. A creole is therefore not merely an expanded pidgin but a completely new and independent creation, generated by the child's innate ability to create language. Creole languages, therefore, are created by all children who are not socialized into learning the dominant language of their particular environment. Children would create and speak a creole in New World plantation communities, where the institutions of slavery prevented teaching the colonizer's language to Africans. According to this theory, Caribbean creoles developed during one or two generations in those cases where Africans outnumbered Europeans by a ratio of four to one in the early stages of contact.

A common feature of these two theories is their insistence that the members of the subordinate group in the contact situation speak a minimum of three or more mutually unintelligible languages (Whinnom 1971). For political reasons, members of the subordinate group do not find it feasible to select any of their native languages as the common medium of communication; hence they turn to an external, politically neutral language, such as one of the European tongues. In the Caribbean, however, this did not always occur, for European exploitation prohibited the teaching of European languages to African slaves. In fact Africans caught trying to become literate were severely punished because this practice would enhance the Africans' ability to challenge the status quo.

Theory number one regards the emerging creole as the result of syncretisms between, for example, Bantu, Kwa, Mande, and Ibo grammar and English, French, Hispano-Portuguese, and Dutch lexicons (Alleyne 1980), depending on the particular European and African groups involved. Theory number two, however, regards the African language influence as incidental to the creation of Caribbean creoles. Supporters of this second theory point out that some creole languages originating in places without African populations share many grammatical features with Afro-Caribbean creoles. The grammatical influences attributed to African languages are thus assumed to be universal tendencies evident in varying degrees in all creole languages. All creoles, for example, have similar verb conjugation patterns (Bickerton 1981).

Noting the lack of consensus regarding the relationship between pidgins and creoles, Mervyn Alleyne (1980) suggests the use of a more flexible term, *contact languages*. The use of this term would make it unnecessary to establish an absolute dichotomy between a pidgin and a creole, and it would enable linguists to see pidgins and creoles not as static systems but as stages in a dynamic process.

ISLAND CARIB: HOW MANY LANGUAGES?

Some linguists suggest that when the Kalinago conquered the Igneri, they simply adopted the conquered peoples' language. In fact some linguists even prefer to refer to Island Carib as Igneri. Rouse also speculates that the invaders, being numerically smaller than the Igneri, were able to impose on

them only their own name and a pidgin language. He draws analogies between the Carib invasion of the Igneri, the Norman invasion of England,
and the Moorish invasion of Spain. However, these analogies are inexact.
The Normans were partially assimilated into English culture while maintaining partial allegiance to their place of origin. The same holds for the
Moors in Spain. However, the Normans succeeded in imposing French on
England for over two centuries, while apart from contributing to the Spanish vocabulary, the Moors were never able to impose Arabic as the official
language of Spain.

This essay assumes that the variety of Island Carib language spoken on
St. Croix at the time of the encounter shares an early relationship to the
Carib language of Guyana or Venezuela (between 200 B.C. and A.D. 1200)
and a more recent one to the Arawak language spoken in neighboring Puerto
Rico (between A.D. 1200 and 1400). Linguistic data recorded by Las Casas,
Pané, Oviedo, and other clerics based on the early contact period amount
to only a few hundred words and a few sentences, but this limited cor-
pus—the only evidence that survives from an oral language now extinct—
suggests that the language of the Taino belonged to the Arawakan family
of languages (note the distinction between Arawak and Arawakan). I follow Taylor in believing that Island Carib was also a member of this language family, distinct from but distantly related to the language spoken by
the Tainos to the north and the mainland Arawaks to the south (Taylor
1977).

The current debate over the relationship between Island Carib and Island Arawak vocabulary and structure perhaps tends to view in static terms
what may actually be a dynamic process of lexical borrowings between
ancient linguistic cousins. However, such a relationship does not necessarily imply mutual intelligibility between the two historically related languages.

Research in historical linguistics has established that language "drift" or
change is inevitable and that within a given community, the spoken language varies according to differences in class/caste, age, and gender; language use also reflects social and regional differences within a given speech
community. Some varieties of a given language may also be reserved for
religious or other ceremonial functions, and in some cases, select groups of
community members are responsible for preserving certain secular-religious
speech traditions—as with the Yoruba of Nigeria, for example. In addition, oral languages tend to exhibit more variation than scribal ones. The
language spoken by the Island Carib on Ayay (St. Croix), St. Kitts, St. Vincent, Dominica, St. Lucia, and Martinique during the fifteenth century was

an oral language and therefore must have varied considerably from island to island.

As we have seen, one common explanation for the alleged pidginization of Island Carib is that over a period of years, the Arawak-speaking women taken as wives by the Carib warriors passed on their Arawak mother tongue to their children. In time the Carib language was transformed to an Arawak one, leaving behind a residual pidgin (Taylor 1977). The standard accounts also report that the women spoke Arawak among themselves and Carib to their husbands, while the men and boys conversed in Carib, which functioned as the language of trade and warfare. Meanwhile the old males spoke yet another distinct language—perhaps an archaic dialect related to Arawak, or an earlier variety of Carib.

It is also possible that a distinction between Island Carib language and Island Carib pidgin needs to be made, as Raymond Breton suggests in this statement: "They have several languages. The men have theirs and the women have another, and there is yet another for other sorts of important speech which the young people do not understand" (Breton 1665). It is possible that Breton, who was not a trained linguist, could have used the term *langage* sometimes to indicate an independent language and at other times to indicate a language register or style of speaking. So the women's language would constitute a modified version of Island Arawak, while the men's language would be divided into three registers of Island Carib: the conservative speech register of the old men, perhaps cherished as a symbol of Kalinago identification with their ancient past; the regular speech of the adult and younger males, also used by the women as a second dialect when speaking to the men; and the speech register used by males when speaking of trade and warfare.

Both Taylor and Rouse, who collaborated during the 1940s, refer to a pidginized Carib (men's) language. However, the following statement by Breton is at least ambiguous on this question: referring to the Arawak-speaking women taken as wives by the Caribs, he reports that "les femmes ont toujours gardé quelque chose de leur langue" (1665, 229). One possible reading of this statement is that the women had retained only a residue of their Arawak language—for the implication is that the women had also learned the men's language, Island Carib. (But there is also evidence that during the seventeenth century the women as well as the men spoke a French creole on St. Christophe [St. Kitts], Guadeloupe, Martinique, and Dominica.) Since according to Taylor and Rouse, Island Carib was at least remotely related to the Taino language, or Arawak, one may assume that the pidgin that emerged from the contact would have evolved into a creole or community language shared by all, had it not been for the practice of gender distinction in Island Carib society. Indeed the fact that the women lived together in separate houses makes it likely that their language would be every bit as resistant to extinction as the men's language—assuming that the women spoke only one language, Island Arawak, among themselves.

Based on actual examination of these languages, Taylor declares the identity of the language the women spoke among themselves to be Arawak. One presumes the reason for the survival of Island Carib after generations of Taino-Kalinago contact and intermarriage was the maintenance of separate roles for males and females and the increasingly high prestige placed on the male activities of trade and war. Jay Haviser (1992, 120) suggests that the men attempted to maintain an identity with their mainland traditions, while the women tried to hold on to their Taino traditions. The role of male-created social taboos such as those requiring women to address the males only in Island Carib (never in Island Arawak) ensured for this so-called pidgin not just survival but prestige.

To explore this line of reasoning further, I refer to Bickerton (1981), who defines a pidgin language as a trade jargon used by nonnative speakers (usually adults) who borrow their restrictive trade (or in the case of the Caribs, trade and war) vocabulary from one of the two languages involved in a contact situation. Hence, for example, the contact between Spanish and Portuguese would result in a bilingual situation. A pidgin would normally occur only if three or more languages were involved in the contact situation, with the particular circumstances of the contact situation dictating which language would be pidginized. The language of the dominant or more prestigious group usually provides the vocabulary or lexicon for the pidgin. In cases where a pidgin expands its range of communicative functions, it develops into a native language or mother tongue; it becomes a creole.

Here I hasten to point out that the essential difference between a creole and a standard language is official recognition and, in the case of scribal societies, the cultivation of a tradition of writing, which helps to standardize the language. Since the Kalinago were the dominant group in this extended contact situation, it seems evident that the so-called pidgin that emerged was a variety of Island Carib sharing lexical correspondences with Island Arawak. The two languages were evidently not mutually intelligible, however, even though they might have been as close to each other as French is to Portuguese.

Taylor (1977) provides copious examples of lexical similarities between the St. Vincent–derived Central American variety of Island Carib and Arawak. For example, note the similarity between St. Vincent–derived Central American Carib *li'duma*, "his moustache," and Arawak *lit'ima*, "his moustache" (here it is not assumed that the Arawak example is the same as the Island Arawak expression). Similar examples of Island Carib expressions are *rita*, "calabash, cup," *íari*, "necklace, jewlery." Arawak-derived words include *barbeque, iguana, cacique, canoe, cassava, guava, hammock, hurricane, maize, papaya, tobacco,* and *tomali.*

Examples like the word for moustache are crucial because they constitute what linguists and anthropologists refer to as core vocabulary—body parts, kinship terms, and so forth, considered to be the only part of a language's vocabulary that provides reliable evidence of relationship between languages. Some words from the peripheral vocabulary often represent nothing more than recent borrowings from another language. Peripheral vocabulary items are therefore not considered reliable sources for adjudging the common ancestry of two languages. The systematic correspondences between Island Carib and Arawak sentences and between Karina and Island Carib core vocabularies indicate close relationships between the two languages.

Another related question bears on the nature of the secret language (register) spoken by the older Carib males. As suggested earlier, this was perhaps an older variety of Carib ritualistically preserved as a symbol of the Island Caribs' ancestral South American language. Since no one from that speech community survives to give a native informant's insight or intuition on the relationship of the old men's speech to the other registers of Island Carib language, we probably will never know if the two varieties were viewed as separate languages by the Island Caribs themselves.

Gender Issues

In order to establish a context for my discussion on gender in Kalinago society, I will compare aspects of a typical Kalinago community with aspects of a typical Taino community. Taino homes were built around a central plaza, where both men and women took part in ceremonies, dances, and ball games (*batey*). Island Carib homes (*caney* and *bohio*) were grouped around a house where the men lived. This society featured a gender-determined variety of activities. The men moved into the villages where their wives lived, but some of the polygamous caciques sometimes kept wives on other islands. The women's activities involved cultivating crops and accompanying the men on expeditions to paint their bodies for war and to prepare their meals. The men performed the prestigious roles of trading with allied villages on or off island and of raiding nonallied villages and islands. The Tainos had hereditary chiefs; the Kalinago, who were more egalitarian, elected their war chiefs for specific expeditions (Kerns 1983). The Tainos did service or made payments to obtain their brides; the Island Caribs obtained theirs as the reward for success in warfare. According to seventeenth- and eighteenth-century reports by European observers, the Kalinago males lived in houses separate from the women and young children. The Tainos had a homogeneous society; the Kalinagos, a dual system in which women, according to Nancie Gonzalez (pers. comm., 1993) and Virginia Kerns (1983), played a subservient role.

My discussion of language and gender in Island Carib society in the fifteenth through the seventeenth centuries is based on the assumption that Island Carib was not a homogeneous language or pidgin but a dynamic communication system that reflected the sociocultural flexibility needed for adaptation to maritime travel, trade, warfare, and natural disaster, especially after the encounter with Europeans. For example, it is conceivable that the Kalinago brought with them a language derived from a South American variety of Carib language, which was related to the Island Arawak spoken on Puerto Rico and Hispaniola. As time elapsed, the variety of Carib spoken on the Islands grew apart from the South American parent variety, and the languages became mutually unintelligible. However, during the five hundred years (A.D. 1000–1500) or so of repeated trade between the Kalinago and their increasingly distant South American relatives, the Kalinago used a contact language, a communication system reserved for trade and warfare. This trade jargon, however, must have included a number of pan-Arawakan linguistic features such as words, prefixes, and suffixes (morphemes) common to the various dialects of Arawak spoken in Puerto Rico, Hispaniola, and South America.

Starr Farr notes that by 1618 the indigenous people of Martinique, Dominica, St. Vincent, and Guadeloupe identified themselves as Kalinago. They lived according to the segregation of gendered roles and labors—and with male and female languages, political connections to mainland Carib groups, a male prestige system based on performance in raids, and an origin myth of mainland invasion that associated their living enemies with their conquered past. She also hypothesizes that before the Europeans came, the Island Caribs lacked a common Carib identity and that the women and men both took part in trade and spoke Island Carib as a trading jargon (Farr 1993). But genocidal aggression, first from the Spanish and later from

the British and French, made Kalinago communities increasingly milita-
rized (Beckles 1990, 3) and led to the transformation of trading and warfare into male-dominated activities. This shift was reflected in the increased
distinction between women's language and men's language. Before the Europeans came, Farr asserts (1993), the Island Carib language was not restricted to men.

It is possible that Farr has exaggerated the Europeans' contribution to
gender-based discrimination among the Island Kalinago, for in at least one
South American Carib community, the women were forbidden to touch
the canoes just before a trading or raiding expedition for fear this would
bring bad luck (Keegan, pers. comm.). Farr's position is also refuted by
Kegan and Gonzalez (pers. comm., 1993) who, based on their observation
of twentieth-century Carib communities in Guyana and Central America,
assert that the Carib women in all cases resigned themselves to their increasingly subservient roles.

Douglas Taylor and Berend Hoff (1980) describe the Kalinago men's language as a trade jargon similar to that spoken between Carib and Arawak
speaking groups in South America. Christopher Goodwin (1990) hypothesizes that the Island Carib trade language was derived from the contacts
between the Kalinago and Carib-speaking Amerindians who lived on the
South American mainland. R. P. Labat (1931), who first arrived in the Caribbean at the end of the seventeenth century, reports that women were
required to speak men's language when they conversed with men during
trading activities.

Haviser cites two theories to account for the subservient role of Arawak-
speaking women in Kalinago communities. The first theory, advanced by
Nancy Chodorov, attributes such subservience to sociocultural factors that
direct females into subordinate roles in society. As Haviser notes, the
Chodorov theory asserts that

> when women raise children, the early involvement with a female fig-
> ure provides girl children with an immediate connection to all gen-
> erations of female kin, allowing an easy and rapid transition to wom-
> anhood roles through vertical integration into the adult world of . . .
> responsibilities. . . . However, early involvement with a female figure
> and the general absence of males during this period directs boy chil-
> dren to cross-cut domestic units, creating a form of "pubic" ties. This
> eventually results in dramatic separation from the female figure to
> gain acceptance into manhood. The net result is that females learn

their roles through passive yet rapid vertical lines among other females, while males must dislocate themselves from females to find
their roles among other males, who reinforce a superior perspective
to justify separation. Thus a superior/inferior relationship is created
between the sexes as a result of this dislocation by males and continuity of female's roles. A combination of factors contribute to female
subservience: the practice of polygyny (where males can have more
than one wife), the male's absence from the household activity, the
female control over the domestic activity, all contribute to female sub-
ordination in Kalinago society. (Haviser 1992, 15–16)

The other theory, put forward by Sherry Ortner, describes universal social
structural conditions that associate women with nature (which in modern
Western society is assigned an inferior status) and associate men with culture (universally assigned a superior status). Haviser believes that Chodorov
and Ortner's theories taken together offer at least a partial explanation for
the fact that men have assumed superior roles and women subordinate
roles in Kalinago societies. Indeed Kalinago society, like other societies
throughout history, was male-dominated and segregated along gender-lines.
However, the decimation—and in some cases, the outright extinction—of
Taino and Kalinago populations after the Europeans arrived in 1492 clearly
illustrates the tragedy of catastrophic culture contact and the archetypal
phenomenon of gender politics.

Part 6: Indigenous Resistance and Survival

As has been seen in the discussions in the previous section, the Island Caribs have been the subjects of many myths, some of which persist to the present. One of the most damaging is the idea that the native peoples of the Caribbean did not survive the conquest. As in many places in the Americas, the passing of five hundred years since the arrival of Columbus has been a time to acknowledge that the indigenous people have indeed survived. Moreover—as the essays by Nancie Gonzalez, Samuel Wilson, and Garnette Joseph in this part of the volume demonstrate—the indigenous people have played an important part in the emergence of distinctively Caribbean cultures.

A second damaging myth, also similar to those confronted by many indigenous people in the Americas, is that modern Island Caribs somehow are not "real" Caribs. For anthropologists this is a peculiar way of looking at things, and one that does not make sense: human cultures are constantly changing, and if Island Caribs today do not live as their ancestors did five hundred years ago, neither do people who came from Africa or Europe. The islands of the Caribbean have seen enormous cultural change on the part of all of the immigrants, and the rich and diverse West Indian cultures of our times are the products of that change.

In this part we look at a few aspects of Carib identity and continuity in the modern world. Gonzalez offers a rich and personal exploration of issues of ethnicity and identity among the Garifuna or "Black Caribs" of Central America. Wilson discusses the more general, and pervasive, legacy of indigenous people in the modern Caribbean, and Joseph comments on Island Carib life and issues on Dominica.

20

The Garifuna of Central America

Nancie L. Gonzalez

IN SEARCH OF AN ANTHROPOLOGICAL FIELD SITE

As a young graduate student I spent the summer of 1955 in Guatemala, trying my hand at ethnographic research. After two months of living in a highland village among the descendants of the ancient Maya, I had my fill of cold, dampness, flea bites, and stony-faced natives so shy that they hid their faces when they saw me coming. Therefore, although the summer had been a true anthropological initiation and I felt fulfilled professionally, I looked forward to a few days of basking in the sun and sea breezes of Barrios, the principal Caribbean port of Guatemala, where I would board a banana boat for my return to the States. When a friend suggested that while I waited for the bananas to be loaded I might enjoy a visit to the nearby town of Livingston, I seized upon the idea and started off on what was to become the biggest adventure of my life—one that shaped both my professional career and my personal views of sex, gender, family relations, and the hereafter. I have discussed some of these matters in other publications (see Gonzalez 1984, 1992).

To my great surprise I found Livingston to be largely inhabited not by Indians or Hispanics but by a dark-skinned people who were called (in Spanish) either *morenos* or *caribes*. To the undiscriminating eye (such as mine at the time), they looked like what in the United States were still being called "colored people." But it was other things that struck me much more than their color. First, they spoke a non-European language. Second, there was neither fear nor excessive shyness in their attitude toward me, a white-skinned foreigner: they asked as many questions of me as I of them, and they were apparently delighted when I accepted their invitations to visit their homes and share their food. And finally, it seemed clear from what I saw even on that first visit that women enjoyed a superior status among them.

I decided on the spot that this was a village and culture that I wanted to know better, and I informed them that I would be back in ten months, to stay for more than a year. When I really did come back as I had promised, I was greeted with smiles and offers of hospitality, and soon I felt quite at home in Livingston. That began a study that over the next thirty years was to take me up and down the coast of Central America, from Belize to Trujillo, Honduras, which they said was their "main town," to the Bay Islands off the Honduran coast and eventually to St. Vincent in the Lesser Antilles, which some of the older people told me was their "original homeland." No one mentioned Africa. In fact they made a point of saying that they were in no way related to other colored peoples that I might know. Their ancestors had been light-skinned "like you," they would say, smoothing my arm.

IN SEARCH OF THE "BLACK CARIBS"

My original ethnographic research revealed a culture in which South American Indian traits seemed particularly important. Their language was basically Arawakan, with loan words from Cariban, French, English, and Spanish. It was not, however, related to African languages. Their music, which I taped, was identified as Amerindian and not African by Alan Merriam, then one of the world's foremost musicologists. And the technology they used in growing, harvesting, and processing cassava into large rounds of unleavened flat bread was identical to that pictured and described in the early years of this century for Arawak-speaking natives of South America.

I was puzzled, however, by the fact that much of what I saw recalled descriptions of culture elsewhere in the West Indies, which at that time I did not know firsthand. One of my first publications detailed my thoughts about these similarities (see Gonzalez 1959). I also was perplexed by the Garifunas' denial of what seemed clearly a strong African inheritance, and I decided this dilemma could only be resolved by an examination of their blood-type frequencies. My first finding was that (like other African-derived populations) the Garifuna had a relatively high sickle-cell frequency, which fortuitously protected them from the malaria that was endemic on the Central America coastline through the 1950s (Gonzalez et al. 1965).

A later collaborative study with a physical anthropologist, Michael Crawford, showed that indeed their blood profiles indicated about a 75% African heritage, the remaining 25% derived from South American, not Central American, native peoples (Crawford et al. 1981). Thus it seemed that their own self-identification as non-black could not be substantiated scientifically.

Still drawn to what had become for me a lifetime effort to solve the mystery of Black Carib or Garifuna origins, I went to St. Vincent, which my Central American friends had said I must do if I wanted to learn about the "old ways." After arriving in the capital, Kingstown, I rented a car and drove to the northernmost point on the island, which people told me was where the "Caribs" still lived. Upon my arrival, I was devastated to find that not only did the inhabitants not respond when I greeted them in the Garifuna language, but they had no knowledge of the culture I had been studying in Livingston. After some urging, the village did produce an elderly woman who, they said, knew about the old ways. In her house she proudly brought out a cassava strainer and other basketry items identical to those I had encountered in my research. But when I asked her where she had gotten them, she replied "Belize." And she added, "You must go to Central America if you wish to learn about our old culture."

Increasingly perplexed, I realized that I had come two thousand miles to the St. Vincent "homeland" to discover that the culture traits I was searching for were locally understood to have come from the Central American mainland—from the very area, in fact, that I had just left. How could a people in their so-called homeland have forgotten so much of their past, while their faraway Guatemalan cousins still preserved a distinctive "Black Carib" identity? It was almost as if the Garifuna culture of the Antilles had been mysteriously transported west without leaving a trace.

As it turned out, that notion is close to what did happen. Following my Livingston adventure with several summers of archival and library research, I slowly gathered data that helped me uncover the Garifuna past, starting with the arrival of Columbus and continuing to the present. I also enlisted the help of an archaeologist, Charles Cheek, to help me better understand Garifuna culture history (see Cheek and Gonzalez 1988). The pivotal event in that history was a mass deportation from St. Vincent that occurred under British authority in 1796. But let me start with the events that led up to that exile from the homeland.

THE HOMELAND: "AFRICANIZATION" ON ST. VINCENT

Before 1763 the island of St. Vincent, like three of its neighbors in the Lesser Antilles, had been free of European colonization except for a few French clerics and small farmers who clandestinely settled there despite agreements among the European nations that these islands were to remain refuge sites for Caribs. Over time many Africans also arrived there, either on their own or because they had been captured by Caribs in raids upon other islands where sugar was being grown with slave labor. The nature of Carib slavery was such that if their captives survived being eaten ceremonially, they were given wives and considered members of the community. There is evidence that these blacks, assimilated in this fashion, adopted the Indians' language, technology, and patterns of personal adornment. For example, they bound the children's heads and the girls' calves, and the men painted themselves with red achiote, which led to the mention of "Red Caribs" in European accounts. (Red is still an important ritual color among some Central American Garifuna.)

Married to Carib women, the Africans also produced "Black Carib" offspring. In time, after repeated miscegenation, the gene pool on St. Vincent would have contained more than a sprinkling of African genes, and to the extent that these gave their bearers some biological advantage, blacks would have been more successful and had more children than their lighter-skinned relatives. Thus the population would have become gradually "Africanized."

In 1763 the British formally occupied St. Vincent, an event that brought the French settlers and the Caribs together in opposition. This alliance persisted for over thirty years, during which more or less constant guerrilla warfare delayed, but did not stop, British incursions upon Carib lands. Supplies and ammunition, as well as helping hands, came from both the French and the Caribs on other nearby islands, especially Martinique, Guadeloupe, and Dominica.

THE MASS DEPORTATION OF "BLACK CARIBS"

On June 10, 1796, the French forces surrendered formally to the British. The Caribs held out briefly, despite the fact that their forces and morale were weakened by the spread of a debilitating and often fatal "malignant fever" that was probably smallpox, yellow fever, or typhus. Eventually the British managed to capture most of them and ship them off to temporary rough quarters on Balliceaux, where they continued to die in large numbers (see Gonzalez 1988, 21–22).

Throughout the grisly business, the British continued to separate and imprison those with the darkest skins, often releasing the lighter-skinned individuals who they felt were either innocent or unwilling accomplices of the blacks. There was a strong racist component to this separation. My studies indicate that by the middle of the eighteenth century the "Black Caribs" of St. Vincent were culturally and biologically indistinguishable from the so-called Yellow Caribs. Yet European observers, burdened by a racist imagination and ignorant of Mendelian genetics, insisted on distinguishing between darker, more combative Caribs and lighter, more tractable ones—and in imposing policies that preserved the distinction. In carrying out the deportation policy, of course, they were also reflecting the fear of the possible influence that the continued presence of free blacks might have on their own slaves. In fact, many of these had already escaped over the years to join the Caribs.

Thus the British sent their white French captives back to Europe and then, defining the remaining enemy as black, deported the darker-skinned Caribs, as well as some non-Carib "French" blacks. In doing so, they frequently separated members of the same family who happened to have different skin colors. So convinced were they of the "innocence" of the Yellow Caribs that even years later they expressed surprise when they found some of these in former "Black" Carib settlements and also when these lighter-skinned natives resisted British takeovers.

Between July 1796 and February 1797 more than four thousand Black Caribs, mostly women and children, were sent to Balliceaux. The fever killed about half of them, leaving only about two thousand to be shipped on farther west to Honduras. They landed there during the second week of April 1797, after a lengthy stop in Jamaica for making repairs and replenishing supplies. After a nearly disastrous short residence on the island of Roatan—where they had insufficient food to maintain themselves and where the soils and climate were not favorable for their traditional agriculture—they petitioned the Spanish authorities who had come to observe this apparently British settlement to convey them to the mainland. In May, most of them went to Trujillo and shortly thereafter began to spread up and down the Central American coastline. Thus ended their long journey from their Lesser Antilles homeland.

In Central America, the Garifuna men were immediately employed as soldiers by the Spanish, an occupation that left them time to fish; and the women, whose traditional work had been to grow cassava and other crops, soon had thriving gardens. Because most of the nursing infants had not survived the fever, it is probably safe to say that nearly all of the 806 women who landed in Honduras became pregnant very quickly, and the population apparently grew rapidly, according to Honduran archival notes.

But it is important to note that these Carib pioneers found numerous other free blacks already settled in both Roatan and Trujillo, and the evidence indicates that they quickly joined forces with them. What is especially interesting is that the blacks, originally from Haiti, Guadeloupe, and perhaps elsewhere, seem to have folded themselves into the Carib tradition; that is, like the Africans originally assimilated into the St. Vincent culture, they too identified as Caribs. At the same time they introduced into the Central American Garifuna communities a variety of "West Indian" culture traits (see Gonzalez 1959). The *punta* dance, now thought to be symbolic of the Garifuna "nation," is a primary example.

The Garifuna: Adaptability and Survival

The original Carib population and its culture patterns were largely exterminated by disease, warfare, and slavery during the earliest years of European contact. Later the surviving Carib communities, especially those in St. Vincent and Dominica, began to bring or accept black persons, mostly male, into their midst, and this rapidly brought both biological and cultural changes. Members of the resulting new "race" would have found it advantageous to adopt the Carib cultural patterns, in part because these patterns were suited to the local situation. This included the technology and skills needed for canoe making, "island hopping" to raid or trade, fishing, hunting, basketry, and horticulture.

In addition, if they had continued to identify themselves as black, former slaves and their mixed-blood offspring would have been in danger of being recaptured and sent back into slavery. Therefore they chose to identify as Caribs and to deny their African roots. At the same time, they contributed new genes into the Carib pool, some of which may have conferred a biological advantage in St. Vincent, and which certainly did so in coastal Central America, where malaria was endemic by the beginning of the nineteenth century. Those who survived the unknown epidemic of "malignant fever" on Balliceaux in 1796–97 may also have had a genetic or acquired immunity to the deadly disease.

Culture patterns that worked to their advantage in Central America included not only the technology and skills noted above but also several social and psychological patterns, some of which persist to the present time. Although the Garifuna were never united under a paramount leader in St. Vincent, there was a local organization under headmen termed "chiefs" by the British on St. Vincent and "captains" by the Spanish in Central America. These leaders seem to have dispersed, each with his followers, along the shore, where they established small settlements engaged in fishing and horticulture. The sites seem to have been selected neither at random nor for their agricultural or fishing potential. Rather, the island homesteaders clustered near European settlements where they would find markets for their produce and work for the men. In the beginning, the Caribs were noted primarily for their military skills, but in time they became the preferred workers in various capacities along the coast, known for their relative immunity to tropical diseases that had wiped out indigenous populations as well as for their honesty, hard work, and intelligence.

At the same time that they sought European wages and consumer goods, the Caribs savored their independence and their distinctive culture patterns. They did not particularly welcome outsiders into their villages, but at the same time they were comfortable visiting and working in the white world. Having arrived from St. Vincent with some members already speaking French or English or both, they were quick to pick up Spanish, as well as some dialects of local indigenous groups, although Garifuna remained their principal language, as it still does today. And finally, the men adapted their behavior to whatever the job required, whether it was as soldiers, as woodcutters in the lumber industry, as waiters or cooks, or as long-distance coastal transporters of people and goods. They were willing to travel to work and to remain away from home for weeks, months, or years.

As has been shown elsewhere (Kerns 1983; Gonzalez 1988), because the men traveled extensively, just as they had in the Antilles, it was the women who preserved and nurtured the ancient religious ceremonies and rituals, most of which were based on a belief in souls and in the power of the spirits of deceased ancestors. Ironically it is in just this area that we see today some evidence of African influence, which must have been originally contributed by men. It is very likely, however, that these rituals were modified through contact with other African Americans, both in the Caribbean and later in New York.

Thus the culture of the Garifuna today is, like the people, a hybrid. For centuries they have accepted new ideas, goods, and habits, molding them all to their own purposes and, in so doing, preserving their distinctive identity. Similarly those with whom they have intermarried have tended to identify with their spouses. It is to this ability to acquire and then transform the new into the "traditional," making it peculiarly their own, that I attribute their remarkable success. Starting out in 1797 with a population of fewer than two thousand, they today number perhaps two hundred thousand, counting communities in the United States as well as in Central America.

The modern global emphasis on multiculturalism and the preservation of ethnic identity is nothing new for the Central American Garifuna. It remains to be seen how these currents will be balanced against the inevitable push toward conformity that participation in the modern world so often involves. The rise of a new musical style in Los Angeles, "punta rock," suggests that the Garifuna are continuing to adopt and adapt new cultural patterns to their own, regardless of where they live.

21

The Legacy of the Indigenous People of the Caribbean

Samuel M. Wilson

This chapter explores the important roles the indigenous people of the Caribbean still play in the region today. On many islands some people trace part or all of their ancestry back to those who lived here before Columbus's voyages. On nearly every island, the modern inhabitants relate to the environment in ways they learned from the Indians: they grow some of the same plants for food and other uses, fish the same reefs in the same ways, and follow the same seasonal patterns. Also, on nearly every island—even those where none of the indigenous people have survived—the Indians are powerful symbols of Caribbean identity, national identity, and resistance to colonialism. This chapter examines these themes, assesses the status of the indigenous people in the modern Caribbean, and discusses the history of indigenous survival in the Caribbean.

Although it is the painful truth that the native peoples of the Caribbean were almost completely destroyed by the processes of conquest initiated by Columbus's voyages, it is also true that these peoples still play a significant role in the region. I must say at the outset that the dimensions and nature of indigenous cultural continuity are complex and multilayered: any search for groups that have retained precontact ways of life, untouched by the historical processes of the last five hundred years, would be a futile one. It would also be incorrect, however, to conclude that indigenous people ceased to exist in the tragic years of conquest or that they play no part in the modern Caribbean. Rather, the indigenous people of the Caribbean have played a crucial part in the historical processes that produced the modern Caribbean. Had the archipelago been uninhabited in 1492, the modern

Caribbean would be radically different in language, economy, political organization, and social consciousness.

In looking at the "legacy" of indigenous people in the modern Caribbean, I am attempting to avoid the approach that merely attempts to find persistent traits, words, practices, genetic characteristics, and so forth. I particularly want to avoid what might be called the "contributions" mode of analysis, which identifies modern cultural elements as holdovers from centuries past as "Carib" or "Arawak" contributions. Such an approach makes it seem to me as if the European conquerors had said, "We've come to wipe out you and your people and take your land, but before we do, would you care to make a contribution?" The modern presence of indigenous Caribbean cultures goes far beyond such contributions, but in more subtle and less obvious ways.

In the following, I examine several areas in which indigenous influence can be seen—in economic patterns, language, myth, and even in the genetic makeup of modern Caribbean people. In approaching this I deal first with the "overlap factor"—the time, longer or shorter from place to place, in which indigenous people lived and interacted with the people of African and European descent who were to replace them. I then turn to the main point I hope to make, concerning the role that the conquered Indian people play in modern constructions of Caribbean identity.

THE "OVERLAP FACTOR"

One of the most critical issues in discussions of the indigenous presence in the modern Caribbean is the extent to which indigenous people interacted with people from Africa and Europe. In some areas this period of time—sometimes centuries—allowed for substantial transfer of what cultural geographers call the system of "human-land" interactions. Such a system involves a group's complete way of living in the ecosystem—how they obtain food, shelter, medicines, and tools, and generally fit into the larger rhythms of the environment. In many places throughout the islands one can see the effects of this interaction in fishing techniques, house construction, horticultural practices and crops, social and political structures, and many other ways. But not everywhere. And this fact points to an interesting feature of the overlap issue: the Caribbean archipelago is geographically diverse, and the indigenous groups who lived here in 1491 were also different from one another. Historical change took place in different ways on different islands, and so this "transfer" of indigenous ways of living in Caribbean landscapes took place in different ways, with different results, nearly everywhere. Ironically this complexity seems to stimulate an essentializing impulse among scholars, who are inclined to talk about pan-Caribbean processes and patterns. These pan-Caribbean processes are problematic, however, because obviously what happened on St. Croix is very different from what happened on Cuba or Trinidad or Dominica.

Nevertheless I would add one generalization: I am persuaded that the significance and impact of this "overlap" period is underappreciated in the Caribbean. To give an example, the subsistence economy that developed in the sixteenth century, based on the sea's resources and heavily intercropped kitchen gardens, clearly comes in large part from preconquest, aboriginal economic practices. But documentary historical detail on the patterns of interaction that took place during this period is almost nonexistent because the adoption of indigenous Caribbean practices was going on outside of the contexts with which the people writing about the Caribbean were familiar. The interaction was largely between African people, both free and enslaved, and indigenous people.

In the Lesser Antilles especially, there was considerable interaction between native people and newcomers in the period between 1493 and the beginning of intensive European colonization attempts in the 1620s. From ethnohistorical records made in the seventeenth century, it is clear that the indigenous people of the Lesser Antilles expanded their population through the active incorporation of captives (Hulme and Whitehead 1992). By one estimate made in 1612, there were two thousand Africans living as captives among the Caribs in the Lesser Antilles (Alquiza 1612, in Boromé 1966, 37). The taking of European captives also clearly went on in this period, yet that process remains largely beyond the gaze of contemporary historians.

AGRICULTURAL OVERLAP

Compared with other areas of colonialist conquest and population replacement, North America for example, the degree to which indigenous economic practices were adopted in the Caribbean is remarkable. The modern Caribbean subsistence economy certainly contains more elements of the aboriginal one than is the case anywhere in North America. The long list of crops used in both systems helps to establish this: the most obvious adopted food plants are manioc (*Manihot esculenta*), sweet potatoes (*Ipomoea batatas*), and yams (*Diascorea* sp.), but several kinds of beans (*Phasolus vulgaris* and *P. lunatus*) were used as well. Peanuts (*Arachis hypogaea*) and peppers (*Capsicum annuum*) were also grown in both aboriginal and historic gardens. Sweetsop (*Annona squamosa*) and soursop (*Annona muricata*), guava (*Psidium guajava*), and mamey apples (*Mammea americana*) are other crops that survived large-scale population replacement as important parts of the Caribbean diet (Reynoso 1881; Sauer 1966; Sturtevant 1961; Watts 1987). During this period the newcomers also learned about hundreds of other plants used as medicines, fish poisons, and raw materials for tools.

The new Caribbean people adopted more than just the plants; they used the indigenous plants within a relationship between people and the environment that had been developed over thousands of years by the indigenous peoples. More significant than the individual plants, the human-land relationship survived as one of the most important continuities of the conquest.

LINGUISTIC CONNECTIONS

The indigenous component of postconquest West Indian diets also suggests linguistic connections because many of the words for indigenous foods come from indigenous languages. For example, the mamey fruit kept its indigenous name (*mamey*) in several modern Caribbean languages, from the Spanish-speaking Greater Antilles to the Anglophone and Francophone Lesser Antilles. The names of some ways of preparing foods also come from indigenous languages: in Puerto Rico dishes like *mofongos, casabe, mazamorra,* and *guanimes* are examples (Navarro 1948).

Linguistic continuity is quite variable from island to island, of course, depending on the history of conquest and the duration and nature of the period of overlap. On Hispaniola (Dominican Republic and Haiti) the indigenous population was decimated quickly by the intensity of European exploitation (Wilson 1990). On Puerto Rico, on the other hand, there was a longer period of Indian-European-African interaction, and the indigenous influence can thus be seen more clearly in Puerto Rican culture. A population census from as late as 1787 records the presence of 2,302 Indians, although some might have been brought from outside Puerto Rico (Anderson-Córdova 1990; Brau 1966). And on Puerto Rico there are many Taino place-names, such as *Bayamón, Jayuya, Guánica,* and *Manatí* (see Dick 1977 and Jesse 1966 for other examples of indigenous place-names). Also, more Taino words persist in modern Puerto Rican (and Cuban) language use than in Hispaniola (see Hernández Aquino 1977; Navarro 1948, Tejera 1977). Similarly, more indigenous words have been carried over into modern usage in Dominica and St. Vincent, where the Island Caribs have survived and flourished, than on islands where they were quickly killed or driven out.

Despite these connections, it must be noted that in comparison with other parts of the Americas where indigenous people still make up a large percentage of the population, like the Mexican Highlands or the Andes, the impact of the indigenous Caribbean languages on modern usage is not great. Only around a hundred Taino words are known to modern scholars (Taylor 1977). Caribbean languages are predominantly combinations of diverse European and African languages, mixed together in complex ways (Le Page and Tabouret-Keller 1985).

MYTHOLOGY

Native myths also provide connections between the pre- and postconquest Caribbean peoples. Given the overlap that occurred on many islands, it seems reasonable that some of the rich mythology of the aboriginal people would survive into modern mythology. To a small extent at least, this seems to have happened. The most notable story of clearly preconquest origins is that of the "Carib migration" from the mainland. In the accounts of this, when the Europeans arrived, warlike (and allegedly cannibalistic) Carib Indians were in the process of conquering the Lesser Antilles, killing or capturing the peaceful Arawaks or driving them before the invaders into the Greater Antilles. Whether or not such a Carib migration or "invasion" actually happened is a matter of considerable debate among ethnohistorians and archaeologists (see Allaire, this volume; Davis and Goodwin 1990; Wilson 1993). Nonetheless, as Father Raymond Breton noted in the mid–seventeenth century (see Hulme and Whitehead 1992, 107–16), it did happen in Caribbean mythology when the hero Kalinago, tired of living on the mainland, moved with his family to Dominica. In Dominica, one of his many descendants, the nephew of his nephew in Breton's telling, killed him with poison. But instead of dying, he turned himself into a monstrous fish called *Akaiouman*. This powerful man/fish, called *Atraioman* in contemporary stories, is still recognized in parts the Lesser Antilles. Many other myths in the islands come down from preconquest times, and other stories are of African or European origin but are spiced with twists and turns that come from native Caribbean peoples (Corzani 1994; see also Relouzat 1989 for contemporary myths of Carib origin; and Alegría 1969a for Puerto Rican stories that combine indigenous, African, and European mythological traditions).

POPULATION CONTINUITY

Despite the catastrophic population declines in the conquest period, individuals and groups of Indians managed to survive. Their descendants live in the Caribbean today and carry a genetic legacy of the indigenous people of the Caribbean. On many islands, especially in the Greater Antilles, it is widely said that people who have indigenous traits live in particular regions. The Sierra Maestra and the mountainous area of Baracoa in eastern Cuba are known for this, as are areas in Jamaica, Hispaniola, and Puerto Rico (Omos Cordones 1980). Indigenous genetic traits are of course found among the Caribs of Dominica, but also in other Lesser Antillean populations (Shillingford et al. 1966; Harvey et al. 1969). This attention that scholars have paid to individuals and isolated groups of people who are considered phenotypically "Indian" may mask the fact that a great many Caribbean people have indigenous ancestry. Intermarriage between Europeans, Africans, and indigenous peoples took place very early on after first contact and occurred equally on islands controlled by Spain, France, England, Holland, and other European countries. For example, about one-fifth of the recorded marriages in 1530 in San Juan, Puerto Rico, were between Spaniards and Tainos (Brau 1966). The same practices, probably in even greater numbers, went on throughout the Indies. The result of this in much of the Caribbean is that most peoples' ancestry includes a rich combination of African, European, and indigenous forebears. This is important for understanding what I would argue is another important legacy of the indigenous people in the modern Caribbean.

THE INDIGENOUS PEOPLE AS SYMBOLS IN THE MODERN CARIBBEAN

We looked at some of the tangible ways that the first peoples of the Caribbean were responsible for important parts of Caribbean culture. These individual continuities or "survivals" may seem anachronistic and relatively insignificant when taken by themselves. However, I would argue that the importance of the indigenous people is far greater than the sum of these identifiable "contributions." Its importance comes from the way that Caribbean people understand their own identities, particularly in the sense that many Caribbean people feel they are in part descended from indigenous ancestors. I would argue that the indigenous presence in the modern Caribbean is vitally important in three ways: as a link between people and the land, as a symbol of a shared identity, and as a symbol of resistance to external domination.

When postconquest people adopted the Indians' foods and subsistence practices, they also inherited, at least in part, the relationship that had existed between the indigenous people and the Caribbean environments. This human-land relationship was virtually destroyed by exploitative sugar-cultivation practices. But as sugar became unprofitable, or as the fertility of the land was diminished by overcultivation, the older human-land relationship reasserted itself in Caribbean subsistence practices. The complexly intermixed West Indian gardens, with tree crops, root crops, spices and peppers growing all together, are not unlike those that would have been growing on the same ground a millennium earlier. But what may be more important to modern Caribbean people than the Indians' plants and ways of growing them, however, is that in a real sense these modern people inherited the land itself from their indigenous forefathers. That is, many modern people view themselves as rightful heirs to the land by virtue of their indigenous ancestry rather than because of their relationship to conquering ancestors.

It should perhaps be noted that Caribbean people of predominantly African or European ancestry find it very reasonable to identify and feel kinship with the indigenous people of the Caribbean. Caribbean people of color have expressed the view that the oppression suffered by the Indians was similar to treatment accorded to Africans who were brought to the islands as slaves and that, being descended from both Africans and Indians, they have been twice exploited in history. Africans and indigenous peoples were united in being tyrannized by Europeans and saw the benefits of collaboration, as the emergence of groups such as the "Black Caribs" suggests. In the Greater Antilles, very few people would deny a possible Indian ancestry; most would claim it. Indeed it could even be argued that the essential part of being a Caribbean person is having a multicultural background. For example, María Teresa Babin discusses the Puerto Rican people as a fusion of different backgrounds, but her sentiments might be shared in other parts of the Latino Caribbean and beyond:

> In seeking the points which sustain the cultural homogeneity of the Puerto Rican people, a review of all the attributes contributing to its formation by the Indian, the Black, and the Spaniard is needed, without forgetting the fruitful contributions of the minority groups of foreigners who have been assimilated into our country. With the cultural and racial amalgamation of all these diverse beings, a national reality has been able to coalesce, which persists and is projected toward the future with growing impetus, centered on the impregnable fortress of the Spanish mother tongue and in all that derives from it and the

traditional inheritance accumulated during almost five hundred years of existence in the Hispano-American world. (Babin 1971, 28)

Indigenous people also play a second important symbolic role as representations of unity for diverse people. The history of the Caribbean includes ruthless interethnic conflict, genocidal conquest, and brutal slavery. Yet cooperation within and among ethnic groups is essential. Calling upon a shared indigenous ancestry is a way of bypassing stratigraphic differences that are based on racial, historical, and socioeconomic conditions. Groups that are divided by the historical specter of slavery might find the basis for unity in an older shared history.

An example of the importance of finding something that unites the diverse people of an island may be seen in electoral politics, where invoking a common indigenous heritage is a way of building coalitions. Political parties in the Greater Antilles use indigenous symbols subtly or conspicuously as ways of establishing this common ground. In the same way, calling upon a shared heritage is a way of reinforcing national unity—all Puerto Ricans or Dominicanos, for instance, can share a sense of being related to their countrymen.

A third related way in which indigenous people are important in the modern Caribbean is as symbols of resistance to external domination. In a region that is acutely sensitive to colonialist domination, the Indians stand as symbols of resistance because they were the first to fight against colonialism and the first to fall victim to it. Thus the indigenous people are one of the most powerful symbols of defiance against colonialist oppression. In the modern Caribbean, this sentiment is also shared by the majority and strengthens the sense of national cohesion.

CONCLUSIONS

The numerous and diverse indigenous people who lived in the Caribbean at the time of European conquest play a more important role in contemporary Caribbean society than might be suggested by any listing of the "contributions" they have made to Caribbean culture. Beyond the sum of all of the surviving traits, words, myths, plants, and practices, the importance of the first people of the Caribbean is more far-reaching than is widely recognized. The descendants of the Indians of the Caribbean still live in the islands and play an important political and social role. In economic spheres, where indigenous patterns of human-land relations are part of people's daily lives, and also in the arena of political discourse and nation building, where indigenous people are central symbols, Caribbean cultures carry an indigenous legacy.

22

Five Hundred Years of Indigenous Resistance

Garnette Joseph

Five hundred years after the Europeans came, saw, and plundered the Americas, there still exists a group of indigenous peoples who were one of the first encountered by Columbus on his mission of pillage and destruction. According to Raymond Breton, in Columbus's time they called themselves *Kalinago* and described themselves as "descendants of the people of the mainland closest to the islands" (Breton 1665). Later called the *Karifuna* and now known as the *Caribs,* they reside in a small community in the northeastern part of the island of Dominica. Their struggle to survive European genocide began the moment Columbus arrived. During the centuries that this struggle continued, the Caribs were exterminated in island after island until the only refuges left were St. Vincent and Dominica.

On Dominica, even though the invaders were able to drastically reduce the Carib population, they failed in their attempt to completely eliminate the indigenous people. To survive, the Caribs were forced, except on rare occasions, to abandon the offensive and to avoid all contact with their murderers. This strategy of retreat led them to their present location in Carib Territory, a jurisdiction that was established after a 1901 colonial report indicated that the conditions of the Caribs were deplorable and that there was a need to provide them with some land that they could call their own. Bearing in mind that almost all of their land had been stolen from them by the European invaders, the establishment of the preserve was a minor gesture (Honychurch 1975).

On the arrival of the European invaders, the native people possessed a rich and vibrant culture. They knew how to utilize the things of nature for their survival. They had a natural remedy for any illness. They also had an organized religion (thoroughly misunderstood by the Europeans); rituals of birth, death, initiation into adulthood, and marriage; and a store of myths and legends, some of which are still recounted today. Most of this traditional culture has been lost, and understandably so, for the invaders neither encouraged nor tried to preserve anything that vaguely resembled Carib life. As far as the Europeans were concerned, anything that the Caribs did was either "cannibalistic," "devilish," or "uncivilized."

Today the Carib Territory contains a string of eight hamlets on less than four thousand acres of land—a miserly allotment that recalls the original European objective of eliminating the indigenous people. Any civilized people who were genuinely concerned about the plight of a people whose lands had been stolen and who had been hunted down like wild animals would find it humane to present a reasonable offer to the victims in compensation. What in fact occurred was that out of the more than 185,000 acres of land that native people had occupied before the conquest, their descendants were allotted 3,700 acres. This mere 2 percent of the land was considered by the Europeans to be an equitable remuneration.

Carib Society Today

Although the campaign to eliminate the Caribs succeeded in reducing their numbers in Dominica to fewer than four hundred by 1791, their resilience has resulted in a steady population growth over the centuries. Today population within the Territory stands at approximately 2,700. It is a very youthful population with a birthrate slightly above the national average and an average household size of five members. Survivors as they are, the Caribs have been able to rebuild their society but not without difficulty and significant cultural transformation. Their existence today is due largely to their ability to fight against the odds and to develop effective survival strategies (Hulme 1986).

Economic Patterns

Prior to the arrival of the Europeans, the Caribs had developed a trading network that included native peoples throughout the islands and extended as far as the South American mainland. Father Breton, in describing their commerce, stated that "they trade with everyone with whom they are at peace," offering items such as pigs, parrots, pineapples, and hammocks in exchange for axes, hooks, sailcloth, and other trade goods. By the time they were chased to the northeastern part of Dominica, the Caribs had also

established a vibrant trade with the neighboring French colonies of Guadeloupe and Marie Gallants, to whom they sent craft items, boats, and agricultural products in exchange for soap, sugar, flour, and alcoholic beverages. This link to the French colonies was forcefully severed in 1930, when
the police embarked on a search-and-seizure mission in the Carib Territory. The fatal outcome of this incident seriously dampened the trade relationship, and it was never able to effectively get back on stream (Trouillot
1988).

Today, while very little direct trade exists between themselves and the
neighboring islands, the Caribs continue to produce traditional craft items
as well as several cash crops. Both men and women do craft work, the
women predominating. With more than sixty varieties of traditional Carib
items being produced, there are over fifteen craft shops that cater to visitors to the Territory. Craft items are also sold to shops in the capital, Roseau,
and hucksters do an active business with the neighboring islands. In addition to souvenir items, boats are still constructed today by some Carib
craftsmen, although the volume has decreased considerably and all of them
are sold locally.

The most significant crops produced in the Territory are bananas, copra,
passion fruit, and soya beans. Carib women, like most Dominican women,
are participants in the agricultural effort. Many of them assist their partners in the production and harvesting of crops. Others have their own plots
of land and are assisted by family members, particularly during the harvesting period. Women are involved in planting banana trees, applying fer-
tilizer, caring for the crop during its development stages, and harvesting
and transporting the fruit from the field to the point of sale.

The bulk of the crops are sold to single buyers. Bananas, the most dominant and time-consuming of the four main crops, are sold to the Dominica
Banana Marketing Corporation. The copra goes to Dominica Coconut Products, the passion fruit to Corona Development Limited, and the soya beans—
the least important of the four—to Nature Island Foods. As the future of
the banana industry becomes more uncertain and production procedures
become more frustrating, the smaller farmers are becoming increasingly
discouraged and will inevitably abandon this sector as a cash crop.

HOUSING

Housing conditions in the community can be described as transitional. Approximately 70 percent of the houses are wooden, many of them built of local lumber, while roughly 16 percent utilize a combination of wood and concrete. Many of the dwellings under construction today are of concrete. They are usually smaller than the national average. About 65 percent of the houses in the Territory were constructed during the period from 1970 to 1990, when older structures had to be replaced and when the income of the Carib community was increasing. Over 60 percent of the households in the Territory are headed by men. While the women may be responsible for the purchase of food and other items required on a monthly basis, most of them are dependent on the head of the household to provide the finances for such undertakings.

SOCIAL LIFE

Recreational activities in the Territory are no different from what obtains in most rural communities of Dominica. The usual domino, card, and draft games are played mainly by the men under the shade tree or at the grocery shop. Outdoor games such as cricket, rounders, football, and basketball are also played, but of these only cricket and rounders are organized into teams and played on a regular basis. Cricket is the dominant sport in the community, with at least three teams participating in a league. The Jolly John Memorial Field, named in honor of a former Carib chief, is the one major playing field available to the residents of the Territory. Located in the hamlet of Crayfish River, it is used for cricket, rounders, football, and community rallies. This makes it a hub of activities, particularly on the weekends, when teams from other Dominica villages visit.

The Caribs of today also participate in national activities such as carnival and national day celebrations, and they observe the European holidays brought in by their conquerors. In the midst of ongoing cultural genocide, the Caribs have in recent times tried to reestablish a greater degree of cultural identity. They have established a group called *Karifuna*, which performs traditional Carib dances and songs in an effort to raise popular consciousness. Its performances in Europe and North America are aimed in part at sensitizing the outside world to indigenous peoples' problems. The Carib people have also designated a week in September as Carib Week, during which the focus is on raising consciousness, remembering the Carib War of 1930, and engaging in other activities that will increase solidarity.

They also recognize the need to establish a calendar of activities to mark significant dates in Carib history.

HEALTH CONCERNS

The health conditions in the Carib Territory today resemble those in most Dominica communities. Although the closest hospital is approximately eight miles from the Territory, the population is served by three health centers located in the villages of Atkinson, Saiybia, and Mahaut River.

Access to potable water is a development priority across the entire Territory. While three hamlets are served by freestanding systems constructed in the 1980s by the people with material support from Save the Children Federation, the general consensus among the Carib people is that there is a need for a water system that can adequately serve the entire Territory. Many people question the government's logic in making roads, telephones, and electricity available to the community before such a basic necessity as water. While this issue is being pondered, many of the residents continue to walk to rivers and small underground sources for this vital commodity. Most of the water carriers are women and children, who recognize the fact that much time could be saved if water were more readily available in their communities.

POLITICS

The arrival of the European invaders also brought a brand of politics that was different from what the Karifuna people had been used to. In the past, chiefs were chosen by the people, and while this tradition survived even during the period of intensified terrorism and genocide, the colonial establishment constantly imposed schemes and strategies designed to divide and conquer these proud people. Today the influence of these forces of destruction can still be felt, particularly in the reduction of the authority of chiefs.

Even before the Carib War of 1930, the colonial government imposed on the people the concept of a Carib council run by a chief, rather than the traditional chief without a council. During the Carib war, the colonial bandits further humiliated the Carib chief by stripping him of power altogether and replacing him with a governing council. The treatment of the Caribs in 1930 was designed to intimidate and break the spirit of the people. The shooting of the people, the summoning of a British warship and soldiers to the area, the stripping of the chief of his rights as leader, and the overall arrogant and high-handed manner in which the problem was handled—all were indicative of the lack of respect that the European colonizers had for the Carib people.

But the headless system of government that the colonizers imposed, so alien to the Caribs, led to petitions and requests for the chief's reinstatement. In 1950 the colonial establishment agreed to a "compromise" by introducing the British concept of an elected chiefdom. At the same time, the authorities divided the people by introducing a British-style party system. Tragically but predictably, this divisive system has pitted Caribs against each other, so that politics sometimes take precedence over the welfare of the community. Today party affiliation, a colonial "solution," actually hinders rather than helps Carib development.

RELIGION

Attempts by the early colonizers at converting the Caribs to Christianity failed. But a people who were tired of being harassed and terrorized by an enemy determined to eliminate them soon lost their traditional religious beliefs and adopted those of the European invaders. Today the indigenous people belong to the Christian faith, the vast majority of them Roman Catholics. Four Christian denominations have built churches in the Territory.

EDUCATION

There are four schools serving the five hundred or so primary-school children of the Carib Territory. Two of these schools are located within the community, while the others are in the bordering villages of Atkinson and Concord. Education is compulsory only at the primary level. Due to space limitations, only about 26 percent of Dominica primary-school children ever get an opportunity to attend a secondary school. For the schools serving the indigenous people, the chances are even smaller. Carib students' performance on the common entrance exams has resulted in less than a 25-percent acceptance rate into secondary programs. Moreover the lone secondary school that Carib students attend is located approximately thirteen miles from the Territory, making transportation costs a financial burden that many Carib parents cannot shoulder. At present, there are only seventy-five Carib students at this secondary school.

Many Caribs are of the opinion that the illiteracy rate among the people is too high. The consensus is that the problem must be confronted at the early stages of education rather than at the postprimary and secondary stages. One can understand the implications of illiteracy for the development of the Carib Territory as its people begin the next five hundred years of struggle for survival and recognition.

THE STRUGGLE CONTINUES

As they approach the future, the Caribs must engage in some deep reflection on the past. There must be some focus on how to survive in a rapidly changing environment. The thought of "celebrating" Columbus and his dreadful journey brings pain and sorrow to the indigenous people as they reflect on the suffering endured by their forefathers. There is a feeling of having been cheated at every turn and of needing to put the conquest in proper perspective. The indigenous people believe that it is time the history books were rewritten to give an accurate depiction of their society. And they are prepared to continue the struggle against European domination.

They are very much aware of the fact that the assimilation process continues even as they struggle to maintain the few remaining cultural traits that still exist. For many, survival is the most immediate concern. In a world where financial security is a necessity for economic survival, the Caribs have adopted strategies that allow them to utilize their craft production skills to earn a small income for their families. They have also managed to integrate agriculture and craft production, thus enhancing their chances of success in an increasingly hostile environment. Having discussed their concerns on several occasions, they have been able to highlight some of the most critical ones to be addressed as they approach another five hundred years of struggle.

They see the need to develop a greater sense of identity through increased dialogue and education. In this regard, community meetings and discussions of issues affecting the Territory are vital to increasing understanding and solidarity among the people. The development of craft industry as well as of important historical sites within and outside of the community is essential to the preservation of social memory, and the establishment of a model Carib village is seen as an important component of this process.

They are also concerned about the absence of recognition of Carib history, specifically the fact that there are no established Karifuna national holidays. They feel that Chief Jolly John should be recognized as a national hero for his stance against the colonial forces during the disturbances of 1930. Given the level of activity that related to the Quincentenary in 1992, some say that an attempt should be made to introduce a series of stamps depicting notable aspects of Carib history. In addition, key sites and incidents should be recognized in the form of murals and plaques that would allow the public to develop a better understanding of the historical role of indigenous peoples of the Caribbean.

The people continue to struggle with the question of land ownership, especially as it relates to access to credit. Because Carib land is communally owned, it is not available to the individual as a form of collateral. It is necessary therefore to put some mechanism in place that will permit individuals to secure credit from lending institutions in spite of the fact that the land is held in common. This would positively impact on the quality of housing in the Territory.

The survival of the Territory lies in the adoption of a more integrated economy. Existing economic sectors must be enhanced and new sectors introduced in a manner that improves the quality of life for the family while taking into consideration concerns for the environment. Although Heskieth Bell once described the area as unsuitable for agricultural production, the indigenous people have found a way to make it productive. As the future of bananas and coconuts becomes more uncertain, one can envisage a return to traditional agricultural practices. This would allow the family unit to be more self-sufficient while changing the people's dietary habits for the better.

An increase in agricultural output is another way of meeting the economic challenges of the future. Although two feeder roads were constructed under the Canadian International Development Agency–sponsored coconut rehabilitation project, there is a need for more roads to access the uncultivated lands. This need will become more critical given the fact that the population will keep rising each year without a comparable increase in the size of the Territory.

As the population continues to increase, more attention will have to focus on the carrying capacity of the 3,700 acres. Once again the question of private ownership will arise, along with that of the possibility of territorial expansion. These issues require critical reflection, especially since the long-term consequences of either privatization or expansion could include the further erosion of the Karifuna way of life. Would it signal the beginning of the final stages of the total destruction of the remnants of the Karifuna people?

Since the Carib War of 1930, many Caribs have been of the opinion that the boundaries to the Territory have already been changed. Many have expressed the view, rightly or wrongly, that the original land title was altered by the British at that time and that what they received was a map with "adjusted" boundaries. The Caribs are concerned particularly about their southern boundary, which they believe has been shifting because of encroachment. To this date the issue is outstanding.

After five hundred years of European historical perspective, the indigenous people are demanding further reflection. They recognize the fact that Europe, which has never hesitated to exploit its former colonies even at the expense of human lives, is not interested in their plight. The ceaseless attempt at obliteration should be a convincing reminder of what a military and economic power can do to destroy a people. The lessons from the past are important to the future of the Karifuna people as well as to the rest of the Caribbean region. To allow five hundred years to go by without attempting to better understand the past is to watch the Columbus ship continue its murderous journey and to be satisfied with doing absolutely nothing about it.

Works Cited

Aberle, D. F.
1961 "Matrilineal Descent in Cross-cultural Perspective." In *Matrilineal Kinship,* edited by D. M. Schneider and K. Gough, 655–727. Berkeley and Los Angeles: University of California Press.

Acosta, José de
1950 *Historia natural y moral de las Indias.* Mexico City: Fondo de Cultura Económica.

Adams, Richard Newbold
1975 *Energy and Structure: A Theory of Social Power.* Austin: University of Texas Press.

Alegría, Ricardo E.
1969a *The Three Wishes.* Translated by Elizabeth Culbert. New York: Harcourt, Brace and World.

1969b *Descubrimiento, conquista y colonización de Puerto Rico, 1493–1599.* San Juan: Editorial Edil.

1978a *Apuntes en torno a la mitología de los Indios Taínos de las Antillas Mayores y sus Orígenes Suramericanos.* San Juan: Centro de Estudios Avanzados de Puerto Rico y el Caribe.

1978b *Las primeras representaciones gráficas del Indio Americano, 1493–1523.* San Juan: Centro de Estudios Avanzados de Puerto Rico y el Caribe, Instituto de Cultura Puertorriqueña.

1979 "Apuntes para el estudio de los Caciques de Puerto Rico." *Revista del Instituto de Cultura Puertorriqueña* 85:25–41.

1981 *El Uso de la Terminología Etnohistórica para Designar las Culturas Aborígenes de las Antillas.* Cuadernos Prehispánicos. Valladolid: Seminario de Historia de América, Universidad de Valladolid.

1983 *Ball Courts and Ceremonial Plazas in the West Indies.* Yale University Publications in Anthropology no. 79. New Haven: Yale University.

Alegría, Ricardo E., ed.
1988   *Temas de la Historia de Puerto Rico.* San Juan: Centro de Estudios Avanzados de Puerto Rico y el Caribe.
Allaire, Louis
1977   "Later Prehistory in Martinique and the Island Caribs: Problems in Ethnic Identification." Ph.D. diss., Yale University.
1980   "On the Historicity of Carib Migrations in the Lesser Antilles." *American Antiquity* 45:238–45.
1984   "A Reconstruction of Early Historical Island Carib Pottery." *Southeastern Archaeology* 3(2):121–33.
1987   "Some Comments on the Ethnic Identity of the Taino-Carib Frontier." In *Ethnicity and Culture,* edited by Reginald Auger et al., 127–33. Calgary: Archaeological Association, University of Calgary.
1990   "The Peopling of the Caribbean Islands: A Review of the Latest Evidence." Paper presented at the conference "Non-Imperial Polities in the Lands Visited by Christopher Columbus during His Four Voyages to the New World," Smithsonian Tropical Research Institute, Panama City, Panama.
Alleyne, Mervyn
1980   *Comparative Afro-American.* Ann Arbor, Mich.: Karoma.
Alvarez Nazario, Manuel
1977   *El Influjo Indígena en el Español de Puerto Rico.* Río Piedras: Editorial Universitaria, Universidad de Puerto Rico.
Anderson-Córdova, Karen
1990   "Hispaniola and Puerto Rico: Indian Acculturation and Heterogeneity, 1492–1550." Ph.D. diss., Yale University.
Arrom, José Juan
1970   "Baneque y Borinquen: Apostillas a un Enigma Colombino." *Revista del Instituto de Cultura Puertoriquena* 48 (July–September):45–51.
1975   *Mitología y Artes Prehispánicas de las Antillas.* Mexico City: Siglo XXI.
1980   *Estudios de lexicología antilliana.* Havana: Casa de las Américas.
1988   "La leeches: Motivo recurrente en las artes taínas y el folclor hispanoamericano." In *El Murciélago y la Lechuza en la Cultura Taína,* 15–27. Santo Domingo: Fundación García Arévalo.
1990   "La Lengua de Los Taínos: Aportes Lingüísticos al Conocimiento de su Cosmovisión." In *La cultura Taina,* 53–64. Madrid: Turner.
1992   "La Lengua de Los Taínos: Aportes Lingüísticos al Conocimiento de su Cosmovisíon." In *Las Culturas de América en la Época del Descubrimiento.* Madrid: Turner.
Artiles, Milagros, and Ramon Dacal
1973   *Moluscos Marinos y Terrestres Presentes en el Sitio Arqueológico "Aguas Verdes," Nibujon, Oriente.* Antropología y Prehistoria Serie 9, Centro de Información Científica y Técnica. Havana: Universidad de la Habana.
Babin, María Teresa

1971   *The Puerto Ricans' Spirit: Their History, Life, and Culture.* Translated by
        Barry Luby. New York: Collier.

Bartone, Robert J., and John G. Crock
1991   "Flaked Stone Industries at the Early Saladoid Trants Site, Montserrat,
        West Indies." In *Proceedings of the Fourteenth Congress of the Interna-
        tional Association for Caribbean Archaeology,* edited by Alissandra Cum-
        mins and Philippa King, 124–46. St. Ann's Garrison: Barbados Museum
        and Historical Society.

Beckles, Hilary
1990   "Kalinago (Carib) Resistance to European Colonization of the Caribbean."
        Caribbean Contact 17.

Bennett, John P.
1989   "An Arawak-English Dictionary with an English Word List." *Archaeol-
        ogy and Anthropology* 6(1–2).

Benzoni, Girolamo
1857   *History of the New World.* Translated by W. H. Smith. London: Hakluyt
        Society.

Berchet, Guglielmo, ed.
1893   *Narrazioni sìncrone. Fonti Italiane per la Stòria della Scopèrta del Nuovo
        Mondo.* Rome: Auspice il Ministèrio della Pubblica Instruzione.

Berleant-Schiller, Riva, and Lydia M. Pulsipher
1986   "Subsistence Cultivation in the Caribbean." *New West Indian Guide* 60(1–
        2):1–40.

Bernaldez, Andres
1962   *Memorias del Reinado de los Reyes Católicos.* Madrid: Real Academia de
        la Historia.

Bickerton, Derek
1981   *Roots of Language.* Ann Arbor, Mich.: Karoma.

Boomert, Arie
1985   "The Cayo Complex of St. Vincent and Its Mainland Origin." Eleventh
        International Congress for Caribbean Archaeology, San Juan, July 28–
        July 3, 1985.
1987   "Gifts of the Amazons: 'Greenstone' Pendants and Beads as Items of Cer-
        emonial Exchange in Amazonia and the Caribbean." *Antropológica* 67:33–
        54.

Boromé, Joseph
1966   "Spain and Dominica, 1493–1647." *Caribbean Quarterly* 12(4):30–46.

Boucher, Philip P.
1992   *Cannibal Encounters: Europeans and Island Caribs, 1492–1763.* Balti-
        more: Johns Hopkins University Press.

Bourne, Edward G.
1907   "Columbus, Ramón Pané, and the Beginnings of American Anthropol-
        ogy." *Proceedings of the American Antiquarian Society* 17:310–48.

Brau, Salvador
1966   *La Colonización de Puerto Rico, Desde el Descubrimiento de la Isla hasta la Reversión a la Corona Española de los Privilegios de Colón.* 3rd ed. San Juan: Instituto de Cultura Puertorriqueña.
1972   *Historia de Puerto Rico, 1537–1700.* San Juan: Instituto de Cultura Puertorriqueña.
Breton, Raymond
1665   *Dictionaire Caraïbe-François, Mesle de quantité de Remarques historiques pour l'esclaircissement de la Langue.* Auxerre: Gilles Bouquet.
1892   *Dictionaire Caraïbe-Français.* Réimprimé par Jules Platzman, facsimile édition. Leipzig: B. G. Teubner.
1900   *Dictionaire François-Caraïbe.* 1666. Facsimile édition, Leipzig: B. G. Teubner.
1978   *Relations de L'Ile de La Guadeloupe.* 1647. Rpt., Basse-Terre, Guadeloupe: Société d'Histoire de La Guadeloupe.
Brinton, Daniel G.
1871   "The Arawak Language of Guiana in Its Linguistic and Ethnological Relations." *Transactions of the American Philological Society* 14:427–44.
Bullen, Ripley P.
1962   *Ceramic Periods of St. Thomas and St. Johns Islands, Virgin Islands.* American Studies no. 4. Orlando: William L. Bryant Foundation.
1964   "The Archaeology of Grenada, West Indies." *Contributions of the Florida State Museum, Social Sciences* 11.
Byrne, Bryan T.
1990   "Help the Data Speak: A Formal Procedure for the Retrodiction of an Ancient Kinship Terminology System."
Calderón, Fernando Luna
1985   "Antropología y paleopatología de los pobladores del Soco." In *Proceedings of the Tenth Congress of the International Association for Caribbean Archaeology,* 286–94. Montreal: Centre de Recherches Caraïbes, Université de Montréal.
Cassá, Roberto
1977   *Los Tainos de la Española.* Santo Domingo: Universidad Autónoma de Santo Domingo.
Cassidy, Frederick
1971   "Tracing the Pidgin Element in Jamaican Creole." In *Pidginiation and Creolization of Languages,* edited by Dell H. Hymes. Cambridge: Cambridge University Press.
Castellanos, Juan de
1852   *Elegías de Varones Ilustres de Indias.* Biblioteca de Autores Españoles 4. Madrid: Biblioteca de Autores Españoles.

Chanca, Diego Alvarez
1949   *Navegaciónes Colombinas*. Edited by Edmundo O'Gorman. Mexico City: Secretaria de Educación Pública.

Chanlatte Baik, Luis A.
1986   *Proceso y Desarrollo de los Primeros Pobladores de Puerto Rico y las Antillas*. San Juan.

Chanlatte Baik, Luis A., and Yvonne M. Narganes Storde
1984   *Catálogo Arqueología de Vieques*. 2nd ed. Río Piedras: Centro de Investigaciones Arqueológicas, Universidad de Puerto Rico.
1989   "La Nueva Arqueología de Puerto Rico (su Proyección en las Antillas)." *Museo del Hombre Dominicano Boletín* 22:9–49.

Cody, Annie K.
1991   "Distribution of Exotic Stone Artifacts through the Lesser Antilles: Their Implications for Prehistoric Interaction and Exchange." In *Proceedings of the Fourteenth Congress of the International Association for Caribbean Archaeology*, edited by Alissandra Cummins and Philippa King, 204–26. St. Ann's Garrison: Barbados Museum and Historical Society.

Coll y Toste, Cayetano
1907   *Prehistoria de Puerto Rico*. Bilbao, Spain: Editorial Vasco Americana.

Colombo, Fernando
1571   Historia del S. D. Fernando Colombo Nelle quali s'ha particolare e vera relatione della vita, e de fatti dell'Amiraglio suo padre. Nuovamente di lengua spagnola tradotte nell'italiano dal S. Alfonso Ulloa, Venetia.

Colón, Fernando
1571   *Historie del S.D. Fernando Colombo*. Venice: Apresso Francesco de Franceschi Sanese.
1984   *Historia del Almirante*. Edited by Luis Schneider, translated by Alfonso Ulloa. Madrid: Cronicas de America.

Columbus, Christopher
1988   *Select Documents Illustrating the Four Voyages of Columbus*. Translated and edited by Cecil Jane. New York: Dover.

Cook, Sherburne F., and Woodrow W. Borah
1971   "The Aboriginal Population of Hispaniola." In *Essays in Population History: Mexico and the Caribbean* 1:76–410. Berkeley and Los Angeles: University of California Press.

Corzani, Jack
1994   "West Indian Mythology and Its Literary Illustrations." *Research in African Literatures* 25(2):13–22.

Cosa, Juan de la
1957   *Journal de bord de Jean de la Cosa, second de Christophe Colomb*. Paris: Editions de Paris.

Crawford, Michael, et al.
  1981   "The Black Caribs (Garifuna) of Livingston, Guatemala: Genetic Markers and Admixture Estimates." *Human Biology* 53(1):87–103.
Crock, John G.
  1993   "Saladoid Period Lithic Technology as Seen from the Trants Site, Montserrat, West Indies." Paper presented at the fifty-eighth annual meeting of the Society for American Archaeology, St. Louis, Mo.
Crock, John G., James B. Petersen, and Nik Douglas
  1994   "Preceramic Anguilla: A View from the Whitehead's Bluff Site." In *Proceedings of the Fifteenth Congress of the International Association for Caribbean Archaeology,* edited by Ricardo Alegría and Miguel Rodríguez. San Juan: Centro de Estudios Avanzados de Puerto Rico y el Caribe.
Crosby, A. W.
  1972   *The Columbian Exchange: Biological and Cultural Consequences of 1492.* Westport, Conn.: Greenwood Press.
Cruxent, J. M., and Irving Rouse
  1982   *Arqueología Cronológica de Venezuela.* 2nd ed. Caracas: Ernesto Armitano.
Cúneo, Miguel de
  1927   *De Novitatibus Insularii Occeani Hespeii Repertata a don Xpoforo Columbu, Genuensi.* Barcelona: Ed. R. Cúneo-Vidal.
Cuneo-Vidal, Romulo
  1929   *Cristobal Colón, Genoves.* Barcelona: Maucci.
  1986   *Playita, un Sitio Protoagrícola en las Márgenes del Rio Canímar, Matanzas, Cuba.* Havana: Universidad de la Habana.
Dacal Moure, Ramon
  1986   *Playita, un sitio Protoagrícola en las Margenes del Rio Canímar, Matanzas, Cuba.* Havana: Museo Antropológico Montane, Universidad de la Habana.
Davis, David D.
  1988   Coastal Biogeography and Human Subsistence: Examples from the West Indies. *Archaeology of Eastern North America* 16:177–85.
  1993   "Archaic Blade Production on Antigua, West Indies." *American Antiquity* 58(4):688–98.
Davis, David D., and R. Christopher Goodwin
  1990   "Island Carib Origins: Evidence and Non-evidence." *American Antiquity* 55(1):37–49.
Day, David
  1981   *The Doomsday Book of Animals: A Natural History of Vanished Species.* New York: Viking.
De Booy, Theodoor
  1919   *Archaeology of the Virgin Islands.* Indian Notes and Monographs vol. 1(1): New York: Museum of the American Indian, Heye Foundation.
De Bry, Theodor
  1976   *Discovering the New World.* Edited by Michael Alexander. New York: Harper and Row.

deFrance, Susan D.
  1989   "Saladoid and Ostionoid Subsistence Adaptations: Zooarchaeological Data
          from a Coastal Occupation on Puerto Rico." In *Early Ceramic Popula-
          tion*, edited by Peter E. Siegel, 57–77. Oxford: British Archaeological Re-
          ports International Series no. 56.
Dick, K. C.
  1977   "Aboriginal and Early Spanish Names of Some Caribbean, Circum-Car-
          ibbean Islands and Cays." *Journal of the Virgin Islands Archaeological
          Society* 4:17–41.
Donahue, Jack, David R. Watters, and Sarah Millspaugh
  1990   "Thin Section Petrography of Northern Lesser Antilles Ceramics." *Geo-
          archaeology* 5:229–54.
Drake, Sir Francis
  1963   *The World Encompassed, by Sir Francis Drake, Being His Next Voyage to
          That to Nombre de Dios*. Hakluyt Society Publications no. 16. New York:
          B. Franklin.
Drewett, Peter L.
  1991   *Prehistoric Barbados*. London: Institute of Archaeology.
Dreyfuss, Simone
  1977   "Territoire et résidence chez les Caraïbes insulaires au XVIIème siècle."
          Congress International des Américanistes 42(2):34–46.
Dunn, Oliver, and James E. Kelley Jr.
  1989   *The Diario of Columbus's First Voyage to America*. Norman: University
          of Oklahoma Press.
Dunn, Richard S.
  1972   *Sugar and Slaves: The Rise of the Planter Class in the English West Indies,
          1624–1713*. Chapel Hill: University of North Carolina Press.
Durbin, Marshall
  1986   "A Survey of the Carib Language Family." In *South American Indian Lan-
          guages: Retrospect and Prospect*, edited by Harriet E. Manelis Klein and
          Louisa R. Stark, 325–70. Austin: University of Texas Press.
Du Tertre, J. B.
  1667   *Historie Gènèrale des Antilles*. Vol. 1 of 4. Paris: Th. Jolly.
Ekholm, Gordon
  1961   "Puerto Rican Stone Collars as Ballgame Belts." In *Essays in Pre-Colom-
          bian Art and Archaeology*, edited by S. K. Lothrop, 356–71. Cambridge,
          Mass.: Harvard University Press.
Ember, M.
  1974   "The Conditions That May Favor Avunculocal Residence." *Behavior Sci-
          ence Review* 9:203–9.
Farr, Starr
  1993   "Gender and Ethnogenesis in the Early Colonial Lesser Antilles." Paper
          presented at the fifteenth congress of the International Association for

Caribbean Archaeology, Centro de Estudios Avanzados de Puerto Rico y el Caribe, San Juan.

Fernández de Oviedo y Valdés, Gonzalo

1950 *Sumario de la Natural Historia de las Indias.* Introducción y Notas de José Miranda. Mexico City: Fondo de Cultura Economico.

1959 *Historia General y Natural de las Indias.* 1535. Rpt., 5 vols, edited by Juan Pérez de Tudela Bueso. Madrid: Ediciones Atlas.

Fewkes, Jesse Walter

1907 *The Aborigines of Porto Rico and Neighboring Islands.* Washington, D.C.: Government Printing Office.

Figueredo, Alfredo E.

1978 "Prehistoric Ethnozoology of the Virgin Islands." In *Proceedings of the Seventh International Congress for the Study of Pre-Columbian Cultures of the Lesser Antilles,* edited by Jean Benoist and Francine M. Mayer, 39–46. Montreal: Centre de Recherches Caraïbes, Université de Montréal.

1978 "The Virgin Islands as an Historical Frontier between the Tainos and the Caribs." *Revista/Review Interamericana* 8(3):393–99.

Fox, R.

1967 *Kinship and Marriage.* New York: Cambridge University Press.

Fuson, R., ed.

1987 *The Log of Christopher Columbus.* Camden, Maine: International Marine.

1992 *The Log of Christopher Columbus.* Revised ed. Camden, Maine: International Marine.

García Arévalo, Manuel A.

1977 *El Arte Taíno de la República Dominicana.* Barcelona: Museo del Hombre Dominicano.

1982 *Museo Arqueológico Regional, Altos de Chavón. Regional Museum of Archeology, Altos de Chavón* [English and Spanish]. Translated by Michele Seminatore. La Romana, D.R.: Ediciones Museo Arqueológico Regional de Altos de Chavón.

Gil, Juan, and Consuelo Varela, eds.

1984 *Cartas de Particulares a Colon y Relaciones coetaneas.* Madrid: Alianza Editorial.

Gill, F., ed.

1978 *Zoogeography of the Caribbean.* Philadelphia: Academy of Natural Science.

Goeje, C. H. de

1928 *The Arawak Language of Guiana.* Amsterdam: Koninklijke Akadamie van Wetenschappen.

1939 "Nouvel examen des langues des Antilles." *Journal de la Société des Américanistes* 31:1–120.

Gonzalez, Nancie L.

1959   "West Indian Characteristics of the Black Carib." *Southwestern Journal of Anthropology* 15:300–307.

1984   "The Anthropologist as Female Head of Household." *Feminist Studies* 10(1):97–114. Reprinted in *Self, Sex, and Gender in Cross-Cultural Fieldwork*, edited by Tony Whitehead and Mary Ellen Conaway. Urbana: University of Illinois Press.

1988   *Sojourners of the Caribbean: Ethnogenesis and Ethnohistory of the Garifuna.* Urbana: University of Illinois Press.

In press "Spirits and Spiritism: African-Caribbean Influences in Contemporary North America." Lecture series on Africa in the New World. St. Mary's City: St. Mary's College of Maryland.

Gonzalez, Nancie L., et al.

1965   "El factor Diego y el gene de células falciformes entre los caribes de raza negra de Livingston, Guatemala." *Revista de Colegio Médico de Guatomala* 16:83–86.

Gonzalez, Nancie L., and Charles D. Cheek

1988   "Garifuna Settlement Patterns in Nineteenth-Century Honduras: The Search for a Livelihood." *Third World Studies,* special issue on ethnohistory, edited by Dennis Weidman, 403–29.

Goodenough, W. H.

1955   "Residence Rules." *Southwestern Journal of Anthropology* 12:22–37.

Goodwin, R. Christopher

1979   "The Prehistoric Cultural Ecology of St. Kitts, West Indies: A Case Study in Island Archaeology." Ph.D. diss., Arizona State University.

Greenberg, Joseph H.

1987   *Languages in the Americas.* Stanford: Stanford University Press.

Gregor, Thomas

1977   *Mehinaku: The Drama of Daily Life in a Brazilian Indian Village.* Chicago: University of Chicago Press.

Guarch Delmonte, José M.

1973   *Ensayo de Reconstrucción Etno-histórica del Taíno de Cuba.* Serie Arqueologica 4. Havana: Instituto de Arqueología, Academia de Ciencias de Cuba.

Gudschinsky, Sarah

1964   "The ABC's of Lexicostatistics." In *Language in Culture and Society: A Reader in Linguistics and Anthropology,* edited by Dell Hymes, 612–23. New York: Harper and Row.

Gullick, C. J. M. R.

1976   *Exiled from St. Vincent: The Development of Black Carib Culture in Central America up to 1945.* Malta: Progress Press.

1985   *Myths of a Minority.* Assen, Neth.: Van Gorcum.

Hall, Neville A. T.
  1992   *Slave Society in the Danish West Indies.* Mona: University of West Indies Press.
Harrington, Mark R.
  1924   "A West Indian Gem Center." *Indian Notes* 1:184–89.
Harvey, R. G., et al.
  1969   "Frequency of Genetic Traits in the Caribs of Dominica." *Human Biology* 41(3):342–64.
Hatt, Gudmund
  1924   "Archaeology of the Virgin Islands." *Proceedings of the Twenty-first International Congress of Americanists* 1:29–42.
  1932   "Notes on the Archaeology of Santo Domingo." *Geografisk Tidskrift* 35(1–2).
  1941   "Had West Indian Rock Carvings a Religious Significance?" *Ethnografisk Raekke* (National Museum Skriften) 1:165–202.
Haviser, Jay B.
  1991   "Preliminary Results from Test Excavations at the Hope Estate Site (SM–026), St. Martin." In *Proceedings of the Thirteenth Congress of the International Association for Caribbean Archaeology,* edited by Edwin N. Ayubi and Jay B. Haviser, 647–66. Curaçao: Anthropological Institute of the Netherlands Antilles.
  1992   "Amerindian Women of the Caribbean." In *Mundu Yama Sinta Mira: Womanhood in Curaçao.* Curaçao: Fundashon Publikashon.
Hernández Aquino, Luis
  1977   *Diccionario de voces indígenas de Puerto Rico.* Río Piedras: Editorial Cultural.
  1993   *Diccionario de Voces Indígenas de Puerto Rico.* Tercera edición. Río Piedras: Editorial Cultural.
Highfield, Arnold R.
  1993   "Toward a Language History of the Danish West Indies and the U.S. Virgin Islands." In *The Danish Presence and Legacy in the Virgin Islands,* edited by Svend E. Holsoe and John H. McCollum, 123–39. Frederiksted, St. Croix: St. Croix Landmarks Society.
  1995   *St. Croix 1493: An Encounter of Two Worlds.* St. Thomas: Virgin Islands Humanities Council.
Hofman, Corinne L. and Menno L. P. Hoogland
  1991   "Ceramic Developments on Saba, N.A. (350–1450 A.D.)." In *Proceedings of the Fourteenth Congress of the International Association for Caribbean Archaeology.* Barbados: Barbados Museum and Historical Society.
Honychurch, Lennox
  1975   *The Dominica Story: A History of the Island.* Roseau, Dominica: Honychurch.

Hulme, Peter
  1986   *Colonial Encounters: Europe and the Native Caribbean, 1492–1797.* New York: Methuen.
Hulme, Peter, and Neil L. Whitehead
  1992   *Wild Majesty: Encounters with Caribs from Columbus to the Present Day.* Oxford: Clarendon Press.
Hymes, Dell
  1971   *Pidginization and Creolization of Languages.* Cambridge: Cambridge University Press.
Jane, Cecil, trans. and ed.
  1988   *The Four Voyages of Columbus: A History in Eight Documents, including Five by Christopher Columbus, in the Original Spanish, with English Translations.* New York: Dover.
Jesse, Charles
  1966   "St. Lucia: The Romance of Its Place Names." In *St. Lucia Miscellany*, vol. 1. Castries, St. Lucia: St. Lucia Archaeological and Historical Society.
Johnson, Allen, and Timothy K. Earle
  1987   *The Evolution of Human Societies.* Stanford: Stanford University Press.
Johnson, T.
  1988   *Biodiversity and Conservation in the Caribbean.* ICBP Monograph no. 1. Cambridge, Mass.: International Council for Bird Preservation.
Jones, Alick R.
  1985   "Dietary Change and Human Population at Indian Creek, Antigua." *American Antiquity* 50(3):518–36.
Jones, David J., and Clarence L. Johnson
  1951   *Report on Historic Sites of St. Croix, Virgin Islands of the United States,* part 2: *Salt River Bay Area.* San Juan: San Juan National Historic Site.
Keegan, William F.
  1986   "The Ecology of Lucayan Fishing Practices." *American Antiquity* 51(4): 816–25.
  1987   "Diffusion of Maize from South America: The Antillean Connection Reconstructed." In *Emergent Horticultural Economies of the Eastern Woodlands,* edited by William F. Keegan, 329–44. Center for Archaeological Investigations Occasional Paper no. 7. Carbondale: Southern Illinois University Press.
  1989   "Transition from a Terrestrial to a Maritime Economy: A New View of the Crab/Shell Dichotomy." In *Early Ceramic Population Lifeways,* edited by Peter E. Siegel, 119–28.
  1992   *The People Who Discovered Columbus: The Prehistory of the Bahamas.* Gainesville: University Press of Florida.
  n.d.   "The Caribbean (including Northern South America and Eastern Central America)." In *The Cambridge Historical, Geographical, and Cultural Ency-*

clopedia of Human Nutrition, edited by Kenneth F. Kipple. Cambridge: Cambridge University Press.

Keegan, William F., and Jared M. Diamond
1986   "Colonization of Islands by Humans: A Biogeographical Perspective." *Advances in Archaeological Method and Theory* 10:49–92.

Keegan, William F., and M. D. Maclachlan
1989   "The Evolution of Avunculocal Chiefdoms: A Reconstruction of Taino Kinship and Politics." *American Anthropologist* 91:613–30.

Keesing, R. M.
1975   *Kin Groups and Social Structure.* New York: Holt, Rinehart and Winston.

Kerns, Virginia
1983   *Women and the Ancestors: Black Carib Kinship and Ritual.* Urbana: University of Illinois Press.

Kirby, I. E., and C. I. Martin
1972   *The Rise and Fall of the Black Caribs.* Kingstown, St. Vincent.

Kirch, Patrick V.
1988   "Long-distance Exchange and Island Colonization: The Lapita Case." *Norwegian Archaeological Review* 21:103–17.
1991   "Prehistoric Exchange in Western Melanesia." *Annual Review of Anthropology* 20:141–65.

Krieger, Herbert W.
1938   "Archaeology of the Virgin Islands." In *Explorations and Fieldwork of the Smithsonian Institution in 1937,* 95–102. Washington, D.C.: Smithsonian Institution.

Kurlansky, M.
1988   "Haiti's Environment Teeters on the Edge." *International Wildlife* (March–April):35–38.

Labat, R. P.
1931   *Voyages aux Isles de l'Amerique (Antilles), 1603–1705.* Paris: Editions Duchartre.

Landstrom, Bjorn
1967   *Columbus: The Story of Don Cristobal Colon, Admiral of the Ocean, and His Four Voyages Westward to the Indies, According to Contemporary Sources.* Translated by Michael Phillips and Hugh W. Stubbs. New York: Macmillan.

Las Casas, Bartolomé de
1909   *Apologética Historia de las Indias.* Vol. 1 of *Historiadores de Indias,* edited by Daniel Serrano y Sanz. Madrid: Bailly, Baillière e Hijos.
1951a   *Historia de las Indias.* 3 vols. Edited by Agustín Millares Carlo. Mexico City: Fondo de Cultura Económica.
1951b   *Brevísima Relación de la Destrucción de las Indias.* Mexico City: Prólogo y selección de Agustín Millares Carlo.

1967 *Apologética Historia Sumaria*. 3rd ed., 2 vols. Edited by Edmundo O'Gorman. Mexico City: Universidad Nacional Autonoma de Mexico, Instituto de Investigaciones Historicas.

1971 *Bartolomé de Las Casas: History of the Indies*. Edited and translated by Andree M. Collard. New York: Harper and Row.

Lawaetz, Erik J.
1991 *St. Croix: 500 Years Pre-Columbus to 1990*. Herning, Denmark: Pout Kristensen.

Le Page, R. B., and Andree Tabouret-Keller
1985 *Acts of Identity: Creole-based Approaches to Language and Ethnicity*. New York: Cambridge University Press.

Lery, Jean de
1990 *History of a Voyage to the Land of Brazil, Otherwise called America*. Translated by Janet Whatley. Berkeley and Los Angeles: University of California Press.

Lévi-Strauss, Claude
1958 *Anthropologie Structurale*. Paris: Plon.

Lippold, Lois K.
1991 "Animal Resource Utilization by Saladoid Peoples at Pearls." In *Proceedings of the Thirteenth Congress of the International Association for Caribbean Archaeology*, edited by Edwin N. Ayubi and Jay B. Haviser, 261 68. Curaçao: Anthropological Institute of the Netherlands Antilles.

López de Gómara, Fernando
1954 *Historia General de las Indias*. Barcelona: Ed. Iberia.

López-Baralt, Mercedes
1985 *El Mito Taíno: Lévi-Strauss en las Antillas*. Río Piedras: Ediciones Huracán.

Lovén, Sven
1935 *Origins of the Tainan Culture, West Indies*. Goteborg, Sweden: Elanders Boktryckeri Aktiebolag.

Lundberg, Emily R.
1989 "Preceramic Procurement Patterns at Krum Bay, Virgin Islands." Ph.D. diss., University of Illinois.

1991 "Interrelationships among Preceramic Complexes of Puerto Rico and the Virgin Islands." In *Proceedings of the Thirteenth Congress of the International Association for Caribbean Archaeology*, edited by Edwin N. Ayubi and Jay B. Haviser, 73–85. Curaçao: Anthropological Institute of the Netherlands Antilles.

Major, Richard Henry
1972 *The Bibliography of the First Letter of Christopher Columbus, Describing His Discovery of the New World*. 1872. Rpt., Amsterdam: Meridian.

Martinez-Hidalgo, José Maria
1966 *Columbus' Ships*. Edited by Howard I. Chapelle. Barre, Mass.: Barre Publishers.

Martyr D'Anghera, Peter
  1944   *Décadas del Nuevo Mundo*. Buenos Aires: Editorial Bajel.
  1966a *Opera*. Graz, Austria: Akademische Druck u. Verlagsanstalt.
  1966b *The Decades of the Newe Worlde or West India*. Translated by Richard Eden. 1555. Rpt., Ann Arbor, Mich.: University Microfilms.
  1970   *De Orbe Novo: The Eight Decades of Peter Martyr D'Anghera*. Translated by Francis Augustus MacNutt. 1912. Rpt. New York: Burt Franklin.
Mason, J. Alden
  1941   *A Large Archaeological Site at Capá, Utuado, with Notes on Other Puerto Rican Sites Visited in 1914–15*. Scientific Survey of Puerto Rico and the Virgin Islands, vol. 18(2). New York: New York Academy of Sciences.
Mattioni, Mario
  1980   *L'Archèologie et la Faune du Passé*. Fort-de-France: Musée Departmental de la Martinique.
  1982   *Salvage Excavations at the Fond-Brulé Site, Martinique, Final Report*. University of Manitoba Anthropology Papers no. 27. Winnipeg: University of Manitoba.
McKusick, Marshall
  1960   *Aboriginal Canoes in the West Indies*. Yale University Publications in Anthropology no. 63. New Haven: Department of Anthropology, Yale University.
Meggers, Betty J., and Clifford Evans
  1978   "Lowland South America and the Antilles." In *Ancient Native Americans*, edited by Jesse D. Jennings, 543–91. San Francisco: W. H. Freeman.
Mintz, Sidney W.
  1989   *Caribbean Transformations*. New York: Columbia University Press.
Moreau, Jean-Pierre, ed.
  1990   *Un Filibustier Français dans la Mer des Antilles, 1618–1620: Relation d'un Voyage Infortune fait aux Indes Occidentals par le Capitaine Fleury avec la Description de quelques iles qu'on y Rencontre, Recueille parl'un de ceux de la Companie qui fait le Voyage*. Paris: Editions Seghers.
Moreau, Jean-Pierre
  1992   *Les Petites Antilles de Christophe Colomb à Richelieu (1493–1635)*. Paris: Karthala.
Morgan, Gary S., and Charles A. Woods
  1986   "Extinction and the Zoogeography of West Indian Land Mammals." *Biological Journal of the Linnean Society* 28:167–203.
Morison, Samuel Eliot
  1983   *Admiral of the Ocean Sea: A Life of Christopher Columbus*. Boston: Northeastern University Press.
Morison, Samuel Eliot, trans. and ed.
  1963   *Journals and Other Documents on the Life and Voyages of Christopher Columbus*. New York: Heritage Press.

Morse, Birgit Faber
1989   "Saladoid Remains and Adaptive Strategies in St. Croix, Virgin Islands."
       In *Early Ceramic Population Lifeways,* edited by Peter E. Siegel.
1990   "The Precolumbian Ball and Dance Court at Salt River, St. Croix." *FOLK:
       Journal of the Danish Ethnographical Society* 32:45–60.
Moscoso, Francisco
1981   "The Development of Tribal Society in the Caribbean." Ph.D. diss., State
       University of New York at Binghamton.
Murdock, G. P.
1949   *Social Structure.* New York: Macmillan.
Myers, Robert A.
1984   "Island Carib Cannibalism." *Nieuwe West-Indische Gids* 158:147–84.
Narganes Storde, Yvonne M.
1985   "Restos Faunisticos Vertebrados de Sorce, Vieques, Puerto Rico." In *Pro-
       ceedings of the Tenth International Congress for the Study of the Pre-
       Columbian Cultures of the Lesser Antilles,* edited by Louis Allaire and
       Francine M. Mayer, 251–64. Montreal: Centre de Recherches Caraïbes,
       Université de Montréal.
1991   "Los Restos Faunisticos del Sitio de Puerto Ferro, Vieques, Puerto Rico."
       In *Proceedings of the Fourteenth Congress of the International Associa-
       tion for Caribbean Archaeology,* edited by Alissandra Cummins and Phil-
       ippa King, 94–114. St. Ann's Garrison: Barbados Museum and Historical
       Society.
1993   *Fauna y Cultura Indígena de Puerto Rico.* Museo de Historia, Antropología
       y Arte. Río Piedras: Universidad de Puerto Rico, Centro de Investigaciones
       Arqueológicas.
Nash, Manning
1989   *The Cauldron of Ethnicity in the Modern World.* Chicago: University of
       Chicago Press.
Navarrete, Martín Fernández de
1825   *Colección de los Viages y Descubrimientos que hicieron por Mar los Es-
       pañoles desde Fines del Siglo XV.* 5 vols. Madrid: Imprenta Real.
1828   *Relations des Quatre Voyages Entrepris par Christophe Colomb.* Paris:
       Treuttel et Wurtz.
1954   *Colección de los Viajes y Descubrimientos que hicieron por Mar los
       Españoles desde Fines del Siglo XV.* Madrid: Biblioteca de Autores
       Españoles.
Navarro Tomás, Tomás
1948   *El Español en Puerto Rico: Contribución a la Geografía Lingüística His-
       panoamericana.* Río Piedras: Editorial Universitaria, Universidad de Puerto
       Rico.
Newsom, Lee Ann
1993   "Native West Indian Plant Use." Ph.D. diss., University of Florida.

1994   "Paleoethnobotanical Investigations of the Saladoid Trants Site, Montserrat: Preliminary Results." *Annals of the Carnegie Museum* 63.

Newsom, Lee Ann, and Kathleen A. Deagan
1994   *"Zea mays* in the West Indies: The Archaeological and Early Historic Record." In *Corn and Culture in the Prehistoric New World,* edited by Sissel Johannessen and Christine A. Hastorf. Boulder: Westview Press.

Nietschmann, Bernard
1973   *Between Land and Water: The Subsistence Ecology of the Miskito Indians, Eastern Nicaragua.* New York: Seminar Press.

Nilsson, G.
1983   *The Endangered Species Handbook.* Washington, D.C.: Animal Welfare Institute.

Oliver, José R.
1989   "The Archaeological, Linguistic, and Ethnohistorical Evidence for the Expansion of Arawakan into Northwestern Venezuela and Northeastern Columbia." Ph.D. diss., University of Illinois.
1992a   "The Caguana Ceremonial Center in Puerto Rico: A Cosmic Journey through Taíno Spatial and Iconographic Symbolism." Paper presented at the Tenth International Symposium of Latin American Indian Literatures, San Juan.
1992b   "Chican-Taíno Iconography and Spatial Symbolism." Paper presented at the ninety-first annual meeting of the American Anthropological Association, San Francisco, California.
1993   "El centro ceremonial de Caguana. Un análisis interpretativo del simbolismo iconográfico y de la cosmovisión taína de Borínquen." Unpublished manuscript.

Olsen, Fred
1974   *On the Trail of the Arawak.* Norman: University of Oklahoma Press.

Omos Cordones, Hernán
1980   "Tres Rasgos Géneticos en una Poblactón Dominicana." *Boletín del Museo del Hombre Dominicano* 15:89–102.

Ortiz Aguilú, J. J., et al.
1991   "Intensive Agriculture in Pre-Columbian West Indies: The Case for Terraces." In *Proceedings of the Fourteenth Congress of the International Association for Caribbean Archaeology,* edited by Alissandra Cummins and Philippa King, 278–85. St. Ann's Garrison: Barbados Museum and Historical Society.

Paiewonsky, Michael
1990   *Conquest of Eden, 1493–1515: Other Voyages of Columbus, Guadeloupe, Puerto Rico, Hispaniola, Virgin Islands.* Rome: MAPes MONDe.

Pané, Ramón
1972   *Légendes et Croyances des Indiens des Antilles,* edited by Emile Désormeaux. Martinique: Fort-de-France.

1974 *Relación Acerca de las Antigüedades de los Indios.* New version, with notes, maps, and appendixes by José Juan Arrom. Mexico City: Siglo XXI.

1989 *Relación Acerca de las Antigüedades de los Indios.* 8th ed. Mexico City: Siglo XXI.

Panofsky, Erwin

1962 *Studies in Iconology: Humanistic Themes in the Art of the Renaissance.* New York: Harper and Row.

Pantel, Agamemnon Gus

1988 *Precolumbian Flaked Stone Assemblages in the West Indies.* Ann Arbor, Mich.: University Microfilms.

Paryski, P., C. A. Woods, and Florence Sergile

1989 "Conservation Strategies and the Preservation of Biological Diversity in Haiti." In *Biogeography of the West Indies,* edited by Charles A. Wood, 855–78. Gainesville, Fla.: Sandhill Crane Press.

Pearsall, Deborah M.

1989 "Plant Utilization at the Krum Bay Site, St. Thomas USVI." In Emily R. Lundberg, "Preceramic Procurement Patterns at Krum Bay, Virgin Islands," 290–361. Ph.D. diss., University of Illinois.

Perea, Juan Augusto, and Salvador Perea

1941 *Glosario Etimológico Taíno-Español: Histórico y Etnográfico.* Mayagüez: Tip Mayagüez Printing.

Petersen, G.

1982 "Ponapean Matriliny: Production, Exchange, and the Ties That Bind." *American Ethnologist* 9:129–44.

Petersen, James B., and David R. Watters

1991a "Amerindian Ceramic Remains from Fountain Cavern, Anguilla, West Indies." *Annals of the Carnegie Museum* 60:321–57.

1991b "Archaeological Testing at the Early Saladoid Trants Site, Montserrat, West Indies." In *Proceedings of the Fourteenth Congress of the International Association for Caribbean Archaeology,* edited by Alissandra Cummins and Philippa King, 286–305. St. Ann's Garrison: Barbados Museum and Historical Society.

Petitjean Roget, Henry

1975 "Contribution à l'étude de la Préhistoire des Petites Antilles." Ph.D. diss., École Practique des Hautes, Paris.

1976a "Los Populations Amérindiennes: Aspects de la Préhistoire Antillaise." In *L'Historial Antillais* 1:77–152. Pointe à Pitre, Guadaloupe.

1976b "Note sure le motif de la grenouille dans l'art arawak des Petites Antilles." In *Proceedings of the Sixth International Congress for the Study of Pre-Columbian Cultures of the Lesser Antilles,* 171–81.

1976c "Le theme de la chauvre-souris frugivore dans l'art arawak des Petites Antilles." In *Proceedings of the Sixth International Congress for the Study of Pre-Colombian Cultures of the Lesser Antilles,* 182–86.

1978   "Note sure un vase arawak trouvé à la Martinique." In *Proceedings of the Seventh International Congress for the Study of Pre-Columbian Cultures of the Lesser Antilles*, 99–155.

1980   "Faraguanaol: Zemi du miel chez les Taïnos des Grandes Antilles." In *Proceedings of the Eighth International Congress for the Study of the Pre-Columbian Cultures of the Lesser Antilles*, edited by Suzanne M. Lewenstein, 195–205. Anthropological Research Papers no. 22. Tempe: Arizona State University.

1985   "Mythes et Origines des Maladies Chez les Tainos: les Zemis Bugia et Aiba (Badraima) et Corocote." In *Proceedings of the Tenth Congress of the International Association for Caribbean Archaeology*, 455–77. Montreal: Centre de Recherches Caraïbes, Université de Montréal.

Petitjean Roget, J. and Henry Petitjean Roget

1973a   "Recherche d'une méthode pour l'étude de la décoration des céramiques précolombiennes de la Martinique." In *Proceedings of the Fourth International Congress for the Study of Pre-Colombian Cultures of the Lesser Antilles*, 151–56.

1973b   "Étude comparative des tessons gravés ou incisés." In *Proceedings of the Fourth International Congress for the Study of Pre-Colombian Cultures of the Lesser Antilles*, 57–73.

1973c   "Étude de la décoration des vases précolombiennes de la Martinique." In *Proceedings of the Fourth International Congress for the Study of Pre-Colombian Cultures of the Lesser Antilles*, 151–56.

Pino, Milton

1970a   *La Dieta y el Ajuar Aborigenes en el Sitio Mejias, Mayari, Cuba.* Havana: Academia de Ciencias de Cuba.

1970b   *La Dieta de los Aborígenes de Cueva Funche, Guanahacabibes, Pinar del Rio, Cuba.* Havana: Departmento de Antropología, Academia de Ciencias de Cuba.

Pino, Milton, and Nilecta Castellanos

1985   *Acerca de la Asociación de Perezosos Cubanos Extinguidos con Evidencias Culturales de Aborígenes Cubanos.* Havana: Academia de Ciencias de Cuba.

Prato-Perelli, Antoinette da

1983   "Relations Existantes au début de la colonisation espagnole entre les populations Caribes des Petites Antilles et celles du Venezuela" [Relations existing between the Caribes of the Lesser Antilles and those of Venezuela at the beginning of the Spanish Colonization]. In *Proceedings of the Ninth Congress of the International Association for Caribbean Archaeology*, 459–83. Montreal: Centre de Researches Caraïbes, Université de Montréal.

Pregill, Gregory K., and Storrs L. Olson
1981   "Zoogeography of West Indian Vertebrates in Relation to Pleistocene Climatic Cycles." *Annual Review of Ecological Systematics* 12:75–98.

Pregill, Gregory K., et al.
1988   *Late Holocene Fossil Vertebrates from Burma Quarry, Antigua, Lesser Antilles.* Smithsonian Contributions to Zoology no. 463. Washington, D.C.: Smithsonian Institution Press.

Rainey, Froelich G.
1940   *Porto Rican Archaeology.* Scientific Survey of Porto Rico and the Virgin Islands, vol. 18(1). New York: New York Academy of Sciences.
1952   *Porto Rican Prehistory.* Scientific Survey of Porto Rico and the Virgin Islands no. 18(1). New York: New York Academy of Sciences.

Redmond, Elsa M., and C. S. Spencer
1994   The Cacicazgo: An Indigenous Design. In *Caciques and Their People: A Volume in Honor of Ronald Spores,* edited by J. Marcus and J. F. Zeitlin, 189–225. Anthropological Papers no. 89. Ann Arbor: Museum of Anthropology, University of Michigan.

Reichel-Dolmatoff, Gerardo
1971   *Amazonian Cosmos: The Sexual and Religious Symbolism of the Tukano Indians.* Chicago: University of Chicago Press.
1975   *The Shaman and the Jaguar: A Study of Narcotic Drugs among the Indians of Colombia.* Philadelphia: Temple University Press.
1976   "Cosmology as Ecological Analysis: A View from the Tropical rain Forest." *Man* (Royal Anthropological Institute of Great Britain and Ireland), n.s., 2:307–18.

Reitz, Elizabeth
1982   "Vertebrate Fauna from Krum's Bay, St. Thomas, Virgin Islands." Unpublished manuscript on file at the Division for Archaeology and Historic Preservation, DPNR, Nisky Center, St. Thomas, V.I.
1986   "Vertebrate Fauna from Locus 39, Puerto Real." *Journal of Field Archaeology* 13:317–28.
1989   "Vertebrate Fauna from Krum Bay, Virgin Islands." In Emily R. Lundberg, *Preceramic Procurement Patterns at Krum Bay, Virgin Islands,* 274–89. Ph.D. diss., University of Illinois.
1994   "Vertebrate Fauna from Trants (MS-G1), Montserrat." *Annals of the Carnegie Museum* 63.

Relouzat, Raymond
1989   *Le Référent Ethno-culturel dans le Conte Créole.* Paris: L'Harmattan, Presses Universitaires Creoles.

Rey Betancourt, Estrella E.
1988   "Esbozo Etnohistórico del Siglo XVI Temprano (Cuba: 1511–1553)." *Revista Cubana de Ciencias Sociales* 16:162–85.

Reynoso, Alvaro
1881   *Notas acerca del Cultivo en Camellones; Agricultura de los Indígenas de Cuba y Haiti.* Paris: E. Leroux.

Righter, Elizabeth, and Emily R. Lundberg
1991   "Preliminary Findings at the Tutu Archaeological Village Site, St. Thomas, U.S. Virgin Islands." In *Proceedings of the Fourteenth Congress of the International Association of Caribbean Archaeology,* edited by Allisandra Cummins and Philippa King. St. Ann's Garrison: Barbados Museum and Historical Society.

Rodríguez, Miguel
1989   "Investigaciones arqueológicas en Punta Candelero, Puerto Rico: Un sitio cerámico temprano de caracteristicas únicas en el noreste del Caribe." In *Proceedings of the Thirteenth Congress of the International Association of Caribbean Archaeologists,* edited by Edwin N. Ayubi and Jay B. Haviser. Curaçao: Anthropological Institute of the Netherlands Antilles.
1991   "Early Trade Networks in the Caribbean." In *Proceedings of the Fourteenth Congress of the International Association for Caribbean Archaeology,* edited by Alissandra Cummins and Philippa King, 306–14. St. Ann's Garrison: Barbados Museum and Historical Society.

Rodríquez, Miguel, and Virginia Rivera
1981   "Sitio 'El Destino,' Vieques, Puerto Rico, informe preliminar." In *Proceedings of the Ninth Congress of the International Association for Caribbean Archaeology.* Montreal: Centre de Researches Caraïbes.
1991   "Puerto Rico and the Caribbean Saladoid 'Crosshatch Connection.'" In *Proceedings of the Twelfth Congress of the International Association for Caribbean Archaeology,* edited by L. S. Robinson, 45–52. Cayenne, French Guiana.

Rodríguez Ferrer, Miguel
1876   *Naturaleza y Civilización de la Gradiosa Isla de Cuba.* 2 vols. Madrid: J. Noguera.

Rodríguez Suarez, Roberto, Omar Fernandez Leyva, and Ercilio Vento Canosa
1984   "La Convivencia de la Fauna de Desdentados Extinguidos con el Aborigen de Cuba." *KOBIE* 14:561–66.

Roe, Peter G.
1989   "A Grammatical Analysis of Cedrosan Saladoid Vessel Form Categories and Surface Decoration: Aesthetic and Technical Styles in Early Antillean Ceramics." In *Early Ceramic Population Lifeways,* edited by Peter E. Siegel, 267–382.
1991a   "Cross-Media Isomorphisms in Taíno Ceramics and Petroglyphs from Puerto Rico." Paper presented at the Fourteenth Congress of the Interna-

tional Association for Caribbean Archaeology, Barbados Museum and Historical Society, St. Ann's Garrison, Barbados.

1991b "The Best Enemy Is a Defunct, Drilled and Decorative Enemy: Human Corporeal Art (Frontal Bone Pectorals-Belt Ornaments, Carved Humeri and Pierced Teeth) in Pre-Columbian Puerto Rico." In *Proceedings of the Thirteenth Congress of the International Association for Caribbean Archaeology*, edited by Edwin N. Ayubi and Jay B. Haviser, 858–64. Curaçao: Anthropological Institute of the Netherlands Antilles.

1993 "Cross-Media Isomorphisms in Taíno Ceramics and Petroglyphs from Puerto Rico." In *Proceedings of the Fourteenth Congress of the International Association for Caribbean Archaeology*, edited by Allisandra Cummins and Philippa King.

Roosevelt, Anna C.

1980 *Parmaná: Prehistoric Maize and Manioc Subsistence along the Amazon and Orinoco.* New York: Academic Press.

Rosman, Abraham, and Paula G. Rubel

1986 *Feasting with Mine Enemy: Rank and Exchange among Northwest Coast Societies.* Prospect Heights, Ill.: Waveland Press.

Rouse, Irving

1948a "The West Indies." In *The Circum-Caribbean Tribes,* vol. 4 of *Handbook of South American Indians*, edited by Julian H. Steward, 497–565.

1948b "The Arawak." In *The Circum-Caribbean Tribes,* vol. 4 of *Handbook of South American Indians,* edited by Julian H. Steward, 507–46.

1948c "The Carib." In *The Circum-Caribbean Tribes,* vol. 4 of *Handbook of South American Indians,* edited by Julian H. Steward, 547–65.

1960 "The Entry of Man into the West Indies," In *Papers in Caribbean Anthropology,* compiled by Sidney W. Mintz. Yale University Publications in Anthropology no. 61. New Haven: Department of Anthropology, Yale University.

1982 "Ceramic and Religious Development in the Greater Antilles." *Journal of New World Archaeology* 5(2):45–55.

1986 *Migrations in Prehistory: Inferring Population Movement from Cultural Remains.* New Haven: Yale University Press.

1992 *The Tainos: Rise and Decline of the People Who Greeted Columbus.* New Haven: Yale University Press.

Rouse, Irving, and Louis Allaire

1978 "Caribbean." In *Chronologies in New World Archaeology,* edited by R. E. Taylor and C. W. Meighan, 431–81. New York: Academic Press.

Ruhlen, Merritt

1987 *Classification.* Vol. 1 of *A Guide to the World's Languages.* Stanford: Stanford University Press.

Santa Cruz, Alonso de

1920 *Islario General de Todas las Islas del Mundo, por Alonso de Santa Cruz,*

Cosmografo mayor de Carlos I de España. 2 vols. Madrid: Publicaciones de la Real Sociedad Geografica.

Sauer, Carl O.
1966   *The Early Spanish Main.* Berkeley and Los Angeles: University of California Press.

Scudder, Sylvia
1991   "Early Arawak Subsistence Strategies on the South Coast of Jamaica." In *Proceedings of the Thirteenth Congress of the International Association for Caribbean Archaeology,* edited by Edwin N. Ayubi and Jay B. Haviser, 297–315. Curaçao: Anthropological Institute of the Netherlands Antilles.

Shillingford, D. C., et al.
1966   "Etude hémotypologique de la population indienne de l'île Dominique." *L'Anthropologie* 70(3–4):319–30.

Siegel, Peter E., ed.
1989   *Early Ceramic Population Lifeways and Adaptive Strategies in the Caribbean.* Oxford: British Archaeological Reports, International Series, no. 506.

Siegel, Peter E.
1989   "Political Evolution in the Caribbean." Paper presented at the Thirteenth Congress of the International Association for Caribbean Archaeology, Anthropological Institute of the Netherlands Antilles, Curaçao, Netherlands.
1991   "On the Antilles as a Potential Corridor for Cultigens into Eastern North America." *Current Anthropology* 32(3):332–34.

Sleight, Fredrick
1962   *Archaeological Reconnaissance of the Island of St. John, United States Virgin Islands.* American Studies no. 3. Orlando: William L. Bryant Foundation.

Steadman, David W., et al.
1984   "Vertebrates from Archaeological Sites on Montserrat, West Indies." *Annals of the Carnegie Museum* 53(1):1–29.

Stevens-Arroyo, Antonio M.
1988   *Cave of the Jagua: The Mythological World of the Taínos.* Albuquerque: University of New Mexico Press.

Steward, Julian H., ed.
1946–   *Handbook of South American Indians.* 7 vols. Smithsonian Institution,
59   Bulletin of the Bureau of American Ethnology no. 143. Washington, D.C.: Government Printing Office.

Stewart, W.
1962   "Creole Languages in the Caribbean." In *Study of the Role of Second Languages in Africa,* edited by Frank Rice. Washington, D.C.: Center for Applied Linguistics.

Sturtevant, William C.

1961   "Taino Agriculture." In *The Evolution of Horticultural Systems in Native South America: Causes and Consequences,* edited by Johannes Wilbert. Caracas, Venezuela: Sociedad de Ciencas Naturales.

Sued Badillo, Jalil

1975   *La Mujer Indígena y su Sociedad.* Río Piedras: Editorial el Gazir.

1979   *La Mujer Indígena y su Sociedad.* 2nd ed. Río Piedras: Editorial Antillana.

Tabío, Ernesto E.

1989   *Arqueología: Agricultura Aborigen Antillana.* Havana: Editorial de Ciencias Sociales.

Tabío, Ernesto E., and José M. Guarch

1966   *Excavaciones en Arroyo del Palo, Mayari, Cuba.* Havana: Departamento de Antropología, Academia de Ciencias de Cuba

Tabío, Ernesto E., and Estrella Rey

1966   *Prehistoria de Cuba.* Havana: Academia de Ciencias de Cuba.

Taylor, Douglas M.

1951   *The Black Caribs of British Honduras.* Viking Fund Publications in Anthropology no. 17. New York.

1956   "Languages and Ghost Languages of the West Indies." *International Journal of American Linguistics* 22 (April):180–83.

1957   "Languages and Ghost Languages of the West Indies: A Postscript." *International Journal of American Linguistics* 23(2):114–16.

1977   *Languages of the West Indies.* Baltimore: Johns Hopkins University Press.

Taylor, Douglas M., and Berend J. Hoff

1980   "The Linguistic Repertory of the Island-Carib in the Seventeenth Century: The Men's Language—A Carib Pidgin?" *International Journal of Anthropological Linguistics* 46(4):301–12.

Taylor, Douglas M., and Irving Rouse

1955   "Linguistic and Archeological Time Depth in the West Indies." *International Journal of American Linguistics* 21(2):105–15.

Tejera, Emilio

1977   *Indigenismos.* 2 vols. Santo Domingo: Editora de Santo Domingo.

Thompson, W. A.

1961   "A Note on Some Possible Affinities between the Creole dialects of the Old World and Those of the New." In *Creole Language Studies,* edited by Robert Lepage. London: Macmillan.

Trouillot, Michel-Rolph

1988   *Peasants and Capital: Dominica in the World Economy.* Baltimore: Johns Hopkins University Press.

Varner, J. G., and Jeanette J. Varner

1983   *Dogs of the Conquest.* Norman: University of Oklahoma Press.

Vega, Bernardo

1979   *Los Metales y los Aborígenes de la Hispaniola.* Santo Domingo: Museo del Hombre Dominicano.

Veloz Maggiolo, Marcio
 1972   *Arqueología Prehistórica de Santo Domingo*. Singapore: McGraw-Hill Far
        Eastern Publishers.
 1976   *Medioámbiente y Adaptación Humana en la Prehistoria de Santo Domingo*.
        Colección Historia y Sociedad 24. Santo Domingo: Universidad Autónoma
        de Santo Domingo.
 1991   *Panorama Histórico del Caribe Precolumbino*. Santo Domingo: Banco
        Central del la República Dominicana.
 1992   "Notas Sobre La Zamia en la Prehistoria del Caribe." *Revista de Ar-
        queología Americana* 6:125–38.
Veloz Maggiolo, Marcio, and Elpidio Ortega
 1976   "The Preceramic of the Dominican Republic: Some New Finds and Their
        Possible Relationships." In *Proceedings of the First Puerto Rican Sympo-
        sium on Archaeology*, edited by Linda S. Robinson, 147–201. San Juan:
        Fundación Arqueológica, Antropológica e Histórica de Puerto Rico.
Veloz Maggiolo, Marcio, et al.
 1977   *Arqueología de Cueva de Berna*. San Pedro de Macorís: Universidad Cen-
        tral del Este.
Veloz Maggiolo, Marcio, and Bernardo Vega
 1982   "The Antillean Preceramic: A New Approximation." *Journal of New World
        Archaeology* 5(1):33–44.
Versteeg, Aad H.
 1990   "Investigations of the Golden Rock Site GR–1, St. Eustatius." In *Proceed-
        ings of the Eleventh Congress of the International Association for Carib-
        bean Archaeology*, edited by Pantel Tekakis et al., 370–75. San Juan:
        Fundación Arqueológica, Antropológica e Histórica de Puerto Rico.
Versteeg, Aad H., and Kees Schinkel
 1992   *The Archaeology of St. Eustatius: The Golden Rock Site*. Oranjestat: St.
        Eustatius Historical Foundation Publication no. 2.
Vescelius, Gary S.
 1952   "The Cultural Chronology of St. Croix." Senior thesis, Yale University.
Vescelius, Gary S., and Linda S. Robinson
 1979   "Exotic Items in Archaeological Collections from St. Croix: Prehistoric
        Imports and their Implications." Paper presented at the Eighth Interna-
        tional Congress for the Study of Pre-Columbian Cultures of the Lesser
        Antilles, St. Kitts, West Indies.
Vivanco, Julian
 1946   *El Lenguaje de los Indios de Cuba*. Havana: Editorial Ilustración Pan-
        americana.
Wagner, Erika, and Carlos Schubert
 1972   "Pre-Hispanic Workshop of Serpentine Artifacts, Venezuelan Andes, and
        Possible Raw Material Sources." *Science* 175:888–90.

Walker, Jeffery Bruce
1980   "Analysis and Replication of the Lithic Artifacts from the Sugar Factory Pier Site, St. Kitts, West Indies." Master's thesis, Washington State University.

Watters, David R., et al.
1984   "Vertebrates from Archeological Sites on Barbuda, West Indies." *Annals of the Carnegie Museum* 3(13):383–412.

Watters, David R., and Irving Rouse
1989   "Environmental Diversity and Maritime Adaptations in the Caribbean Area." In *Early Ceramic Population Lifeways,* edited by Peter E. Siegel, 129–44.

Watters, David R., and Richard Scaglion
1994   "Beads and Pendants from Trants, Montserrat: Implications for the Prehistoric Lapidary Industry of the Caribbean." *Annals of the Carnegie Museum* 63:215–37.

Watts, D.
1987   *The West Indies: Patterns of Development, Culture and Environmental Change since 1492.* Cambridge: Cambridge University Press.

Weinreich, U.
1953   *Languages in Contact.* New York: Linguistic Circle of New York.

Whinnom, Keith.
1962   "Creole Languages in the Caribbean." In *Pidginization and Creolization of Languages,* edited by Dell H. Hymes. Cambridge: Cambridge University Press.
1971   "Linguistic Hybridization and the Special Case of Pidgins and Creoles." In *Pidginization and Creolization of Languages,* edited by Dell Hymes, 91–115.

Whitehead, Neil L.
1984   "Carib Canbibalism: The Historical Evidence." *Journal Societe des Americanistes* 70:69–87.

Wilson, Samuel M.
1989   "The Prehistoric Settlement Pattern of Nevis, West Indies." *Journal of Field Archaeology* 16(4):427–50.
1990   *Hispaniola: Caribbean Chiefdoms in the Age of Columbus.* Tuscaloosa: University of Alabama Press.
1993   "The Cultural Mosaic of the Prehistoric Caribbean." *Proceedings of the British Academy* 81:37–66.
1996   "The Rise of Complex Societies in the Caribbean." In *Preprints of the Thirteenth International Congress of Prehistoric and Protohistoric Sciences.* Forlí, Italy.

Wing, Elizabeth S.
1969   "Vertebrate Remains Excavated from San Salvador Island, Bahamas." *Caribbean Journal of Science* 9(1–2):25–29.

1973   "Notes on the Faunal Remains Excavated on St. Kitts, West Indies." *Caribbean Journal of Science* 13(3–4):253–55.

1989   "Human Exploitation of Animal Resources in the Caribbean." In *Biogeography of the West Indies, Past, Present and Future,* edited by Charles Woods, 137–52. Gainesville, Fla.: Sandhill Crane Press.

1991   "Animal Exploitation in Prehistoric Barbados." In *Proceedings of the Fourteenth Congress of the International Association for Caribbean Archaeology,* edited by Alissandra Cummins and Philippa King, 360–67. St. Ann's Garrison: Barbados Museum and Historical Society.

Wing, Elizabeth S., Charles A. Hoffman, and Clayton E. Ray

1968   "Vertebrate Remains from Indian Sites on Antigua, West Indies." *Caribbean Journal of Science* 8(3–4):123–39.

Wing, Elizabeth S., and Elizabeth J. Reitz

1982   "Prehistoric Fishing Economies of the Caribbean." *Journal of New World Archaeology* 5(2):13–32.

Wing, Elizabeth S., and Sylvia Scudder

1980   "Use of Animals by Prehistoric Inhabitants on St. Kitts, West Indies." In *Proceedings of the Eighth International Congress for the Study of the Pre-Columbian Cultures of the Lesser Antilles,* edited by Suzanne M. Lewenstein, 237–45. Arizona State University Anthropological Research Papers no. 22. Tempe: Arizona State University.

Woods, Charles A., ed.

1989   *Biogeography of the West Indies: Past, Present and Future.* Gainesville, Fla.: Sandhill Crane Press.

Contributors

Ricardo Alegría is director of the Centro de Estudios Avanzados de Puerto Rico y el Caribe, San Juan.

Louis Allaire is professor of anthropology at the University of Manitoba, Winnipeg.

Vincent O. Cooper is professor of English and Linguistics at the University of the Virgin Islands, St. Croix.

Alissandra Cummins is director of the Barbados Museum and Historical Society, St. Ann's Garrison, Barbados.

Richard L. Cunningham was regional chief of interpretation for the National Park Service in San Francisco.

Nancie L. Gonzalez is professor emerita at the University of Maryland.

Jay B. Haviser is senior archaeologist at the Institute of Archaeology and Anthropology of the Netherlands Antilles, Curaçao.

Arnold R. Highfield is professor of social sciences and linguistics at the University of the Virgin Islands, St. Croix.

Garnette Joseph is affiliated with the Karifuna Cultural Group in Dominica.

William F. Keegan is professor of anthropology at the University of Florida and curator at the Florida Museum of Natural History, Gainesville.

Birgit Faber Morse is a curatorial affiliate in the Division of Anthropology, Yale University.

Ignacio Olazagasti is the director of Ignacio Olazagasti and Asociados, Inc., San Juan, Puerto Rico.

José R. Oliver is lecturer in Latin American archaeology at the Institute of Archaeology, University College, London.

James B. Petersen is professor of anthropology at the University of Vermont.

Elizabeth Righter is senior archaeologist at the State Historic Preservation Office, St. Thomas, Virgin Islands.

Miguel Rodríguez is professor of anthropology at the Universidad de Turabo, Puerto Rico.

Henry Petitjean Roget is conservateur en chef at Museé Schoelcher, Pointe-à-Pitre, Guadeloupe.

David R. Watters is curator of anthropology at the Carnegie Museum of Natural History in Pittsburgh.

Samuel M. Wilson is professor of anthropology at the University of Texas at Austin.

Index

Florida Museum of Natural History
Ripley P. Bullen Series
Edited by Jerald T. Milanich

Tacachale: Essays on the Indians of Florida and Southeastern Georgia during the Historic Period, edited by Jerald T. Milanich and Samuel Proctor (1978); first paperback edition, 1994

Aboriginal Subsistence Technology on the Southeastern Coastal Plain during the Late Prehistoric Period, by Lewis H. Larson (1980)

Cemochechobee: Archaeology of a Mississippian Ceremonial Center on the Chattahoochee River, by Frank T. Schnell, Vernon J. Knight, Jr., and Gail S. Schnell (1981)

Fort Center: An Archaeological Site in the Lake Okeechobee Basin, by William H. Sears, with contributions by Elsie O'R. Sears and Karl T. Steinen (1982); first paperback edition, 1994

Perspectives on Gulf Coast Prehistory, edited by Dave D. Davis (1984)

Archaeology of Aboriginal Culture Change in the Interior Southeast: Depopulation during the Early Historic Period, by Marvin T. Smith (1987)

Apalachee: The Land between the Rivers, by John H. Hann (1988)

Key Marco's Buried Treasure: Archaeology and Adventure in the Nineteenth Century, by Marion Spjut Gilliland (1989)

First Encounters: Spanish Explorations in the Caribbean and the United States, 1492-1570, edited by Jerald T. Milanich and Susan Milbrath (1989)

Missions to the Calusa, edited and translated by John H. Hann, with an Introduction by William H. Marquardt (1991)

Excavations on the Franciscan Frontier: Archaeology at the Fig Springs Mission, by Brent Richards Weisman (1992)

The People Who Discovered Columbus: The Prehistory of the Bahamas, by William F. Keegan (1992)

Hernando de Soto and the Indians of Florida, by Jerald T. Milanich and Charles Hudson (1993)

Foraging and Farming in the Eastern Woodlands, edited by C. Margaret Scarry (1993)

Puerto Real: The Archaeology of a Sixteenth-Century Spanish Town in Hispaniola, edited by Kathleen Deagan (1995)

A History of the Timucua Indians and Missions, by John H. Hann (1996)

Archaeology of the Mid-Holocene Southeast, edited by Kenneth E. Sassaman and David G. Anderson (1996)

Bioarchaeology of Native American Adaptation in the Spanish Borderlands, edited by Brenda J. Baker and Lisa Kealhofer (1996)

The Indigenous People of the Caribbean, edited by Samuel M. Wilson (1997); first paperback edition, 1999

Hernando de Soto Among the Apalachee: The Archaeology of the First Winter Encampment, by Charles R. Ewen and John H. Hann (1998)

The Timucuan Chiefdoms of Spanish Florida (vol. 1: *Assimilation;* vol. 2: *Resistance and Destruction*), by John Worth (1998)

Ancient Earthen Enclosures of the Eastern Woodlands, edited by Robert J. Mainfort and Lynne P. Sullivan (1998)

An Environmental History of Northeast Florida, by James J. Miller (1998)

Precolumbian Architecture in Eastern North America, second edition, by William Morgan (1999)

Archaeology of Colonial Pensacola, edited by Judith A. Bense (1999)

Grit-Tempered: Early Women Archaeologists in the Southeastern United States, edited by Nancy Marie White, Lynne P. Sullivan, and Rochelle A. Marrinan (1999)